BETTER THINKING, BETTER RESULTS

*Using the Power of Lean
as a Total Business Solution*

Bob Emiliani

with David Stec, Lawrence Grasso, and James Stodder

The **Center for Lean
Business Management,** LLC

Kensington, Connecticut

The Center for Lean Business Management, LLC
266 Newton Street
Kensington, CT 06037
Tel: 860.558.7367   Fax: 860.529.9381
www.theclbm.com

The Center for Lean Business Management® is a registered trademark of The Center for Lean Business Management, LLC.

Cover design and page layout by Tracy Cole, Horizon Designs, LLC.
Copyediting and proofreading by Michael J. London & Associates, Inc.

10 9 8 7 6 5 4 3 2 1

Printed on acid-free paper.

Library of Congress Control Number: 2002113686

Emiliani, M.L., 1958-
        Better thinking, better results: using the power of lean as a total
        business solution / M.L. Emiliani, with David Stec, Lawrence Grasso,
        and James Stodder; foreword by Bill Moffitt

Includes bibliographical references and index
ISBN 0-9722591-0-4

1. Leadership   2. Management   3. Stakeholders   4. Lean management
system   5. Teamwork   6. Lean enterprise   7. Kaizen   8. Organizational
effectiveness   9. Business ethics   I. Title

First Edition   January 2003

ORDERING INFORMATION
www.theclbm.com

Made in the U.S.A. using digital print-on-demand technology.

Contents

To

Cesare & Rosita
Lucinda
Michael & Julia

the value stream of life

It is like people going into the ocean. Some have just gone in, some have gone all the way to the depths. Although there is a difference between the shallow and the deep, they are both said to have entered.

Thomas Cleary
Zen and the Art of Insight

Foreword

The opportunity to write the Foreword to a book that describes both one of my very best friends and my very best client has evoked many emotions. The strongest is pride. Having even a minor role in helping to document the great success of The Wiremold Company's transformation to Lean is indeed an honor for this old factory rat. My sixteen-year association with Art Byrne, dating back to our days at Danaher Corporation, has been symbiotic, very rewarding, and above all great fun.

Our early friendship, professional relationship, and Lean training naturally continued as Art took the reins at Wiremold. I recall with considerable pride that I was one of the first people that he asked to visit the West Hartford headquarters during his first week in office. Wiremold was to become just the third client for my nascent consulting practice. Together we also struggled through some of the early kaizens[1] in 1991 before we could get additional help from our Shingijutsu teachers. Over the ensuing years, we watched the diligent application of Lean principles, embodied in the Toyota Production System, yield impressive and ever-improving results. As one of Art's coaches, helpmates, and good friends, I have had the privilege of watching this star performer deliver exceptional results year-in and year-out.

This book presents the enterprise-wide nature of the Lean transformation process. Only two chapters, 3 and 4, relate directly to operations. Properly, the other important areas of the business that require Lean transformation and changed behavior are addressed in the remaining chapters. It is a fundamental precept of Lean that you can tell much about a company by the way it produces its products. Most companies address only operational aspects — defining value streams and establishing product flow, reducing lot sizes, etc. — without bringing all other elements of the business into the effort to become Lean.

A Lean transformation that does not extend beyond the operations or manufacturing areas will succumb from lack of understanding and critical support. Although there is abundant literature explaining the operations aspects of Lean, especially from the early Japanese writings, there is little that adequately describes the integrated relationships necessary for a true enterprise-wide success. This book fulfills that need. The "Key Points for Senior Managers" in the boxes at the end of each chapter are worthy of special attention. They send important messages and underscore the importance of an educated and committed senior leadership to the Lean transformation effort.

Exhortations, management buzzwords, mission statements, and pledges of support will not propel a company on its journey to Lean. Nothing generates the energy for transformation better than the changed behavior of associates at all levels in all functions, from the batch-and-queue authoritarian model to the Lean management system, based on teamwork, trust, openness and "respect for people." Art Byrne and those of us close to him had this epiphany earlier in our careers, so evangelizing the Wiremold team was never a major issue. It happened because the top leadership set such an outstanding example of recognizing all forms of waste.

The growth provided from new product development is a key requirement that does not get sufficient attention in the Lean literature. This book does a commendable job of exploring the early efforts with Quality Function Deployment and the product mapping techniques used at Wiremold to expand market coverage without allowing product proliferation to take place.

Similarly, the book's treatment of acquisition strategy and the strong emphasis on an immediate start to the Lean transformation at acquired firms is very instructive. There has never been any question in a new Wiremold company that change was going to happen, and that there was no acceptable alternative to Lean. Both the future change agents and the "concrete-heads" received an early wake-up call before the ink was dry on the acquisition documents. Of course having the senior leadership of the company doing the first kaizens with Art as the principle facilitator underscored the message in the strongest terms. Orry Fiume's quotations provide a short course in how to quickly leverage the Lean strategy to rapidly improve the acquired firm's financial performance.

The Wiremold story and record of accomplishment has provided my associates and I with numerous case histories, anecdotal examples, and best practices to challenge many other clients. Nowhere are the lessons more pronounced than in the area of leadership. Art is fond of saying: "It's all about people," to which I would add: "It's all about leadership." From the early training of staff and shop associates, all performed by Art, to the visionary decisions to knock down walls, rebuild rolling mills, rework countless dies for quick changeover, and invest significantly in quick change modifications to molding equipment, the message has been consistent over time. The Wiremold leadership was willing from the outset to invest itself in the Lean management system and make the necessary day-to-day commitments to support the strategy of becoming a top time-based competitor. Later, major initiatives to establish load-leveling pull techniques, and the new information systems to support them, secured the desired gains and made reversion to batch-and-queue management an impossibility.

Subsidiaries were given clear direction and then allowed to pursue their own growth and performance improvements within the corporate strategy guidelines and the boundaries of the application of Lean principles and practices in the crusade against waste. This posture was clearly demonstrated in the case of the Brooks Electronics Division, a truly outstanding Wiremold subsidiary. Here growth and operational improvement has been almost completely centered on the dramatic development of a disadvantaged inner-city workforce into a vibrant, productive, and committed industrial team. Brooks outgrew its old "combat zone" factory in the inner city through the sheer determination of leadership. The constant and intense education of all elements of the workforce changed the organization into a family of strong Lean performers, achieving new levels of performance. A bright new plant in a new industrial park was the reward for greatly improved performance, previously undreamed of levels of inventory turns, profit sharing, productivity, and equipment development. The improvements continue.

The Brooks story was repeated in other Wiremold facilities where clear-minded corporate leadership entrusted talented people and committed local leadership with the Lean transformation, responsibility and authority to implement the necessary changes in practices and behavior. We Lean consultants preach rapid implementation, rather than endless justification, due to the powerful leverage generated by time-based operational techniques. The traditional requirement for elaborate justification of rational Lean management actions is perhaps the greatest waste of conventional leadership practice. The Wiremold story demonstrates that a handful of dedicated corporate leaders with a clear strategy can leverage the organization's strengths through true delegation to carefully chosen change agents who, in turn, can produce dramatic results.

The different labor relations environments at the various facilities did not really affect the rate of transformation. Union plants may have required slightly more attention due to contractual issues. However, once people realized that leadership really meant what it said and would stick to the "Code of Conduct" and truly show respect and concern for people, the workforce responded constructively. The profit sharing plan showed that there was a clear recognition that everyone's efforts were needed and would be rewarded. When all associates are on a first name basis with the CEO and the corporate staff, and understand that the company's financial success will return corresponding rewards to them, then a comfort level rarely achieved in traditional hierarchal organizations develops.

The profit sharing plan started by D. Hayes Murphy more than eighty years ago is simple. It is unencumbered by the complex formulae and calculations of so-called gain-sharing plans. There are no exotic systems for identifying who or what brought about the success. The underlying assumption is simple: a "we are all in this together" team mentality governs. Interestingly, there was never a problem with sharing financial information with the entire team, including associates. This is quite contrary to the almost paranoid aversion to disclosure of profitability exhibited by many privately held firms, which in turn has led them to adopt the aforementioned cumbersome gain-sharing plans.

The employment security issue associated with dramatic gains in productivity needs to be addressed by all who plan to lead a Lean transformation of their company. Wiremold successfully fended off workforce reductions after efforts at resizing the workforce took place through early retirement, attrition, and some involuntary reductions in parts of the organization that were just plain fat. After that, growth from acquisitions, new product development, and market share improvement was sustained by productivity improvement that freed-up[2] the necessary resources — people, space, and working capital. Only in the recent severe market recession has the company been forced to make involuntary reductions in force. The original qualified job guarantee referred to in Chapter 5 has always been maintained.

Leadership in other companies will no doubt craft different language for making the employment security commitment, but the essence of the qualified job guarantee is to treat associates at all levels as fixed assets rather than variable costs, both in good times and in bad. Only when events and conditions are sufficiently threatening to warrant consideration of reducing traditionally defined fixed assets should reduction of the human fixed assets be considered. Most associates and their representatives can understand and rationalize this policy. When properly administered and communicated, this should prevent fear of job loss from impacting the progress of the Lean transformation.

The underlying principle of the qualified job guarantee is the promise that people will not be used as pawns in the short-term profitability game. The common practice of using layoffs to meet monthly or quarterly financial objectives or cost reduction goals must be abandoned. If circumstances threaten the future financial viability of the firm, then the leadership has a responsibility to act. However, such action should involve all levels of the organization and all functional units. The classic tactic of slicing off the "bottom-most" layer of the organization is not an option in a "Real Lean" company. The damage inflicted to the value-adding capability of the company by this outmoded behavior flies in the face of modern Lean thinking.

Any committed Lean leader will find insight, encouragement, and energy from the Wiremold story. In my own Lean consulting practice, we "fire" clients who succumb to the easy road of "Imitation Lean," since we know that contradictory behaviors by the CEO will make them "also-rans." Unless we can transform the CEO and other key leaders, we do not want to be counted as advisors to such firms. This has never been an issue in our relationship with Art and the Wiremold leadership team. They provide excellent role models for those embarking on this exciting journey.

A fine example of coordinated top leadership is discussed in the Chapter 8, which deals with production leveling and the removal of "mura" (unevenness), and "muri" (unreasonableness). This topic is discussed under the title "Delivering the Benefits of Lean to Customers," and highlights a departure from conventional wisdom regarding production scheduling. The assignment of significant responsibility for leveling sales, and thus production, to the Marketing and Sales organizations is a rarity but right on target. Leveling can only be effective with the cooperation of the markets, and those with the broadest interface with the customer are best positioned to make a major contribution to the leveling task.

Another thought-provoking and innovative chapter deals with a new way to look at the change process. By using the machine set-up reduction model to suggest ways by which senior leadership can achieve the required behavioral changes, Bob Emiliani sheds new light on the most critical aspect of the Lean transformation — the effectiveness of change management across the entire organization. It should give the executive reader much to ponder and act upon.

The reader should take time to look carefully at the numerous quotations from the authors' interviews. These are the words of the people who made Lean work so effectively, yet one will notice a sense that each speaker is still learning and growing.

I have just begun what will be my fiftieth year as a manufacturing executive and business consultant. Nothing has been so rewarding for me during this time than to be associated with the Wiremold team, and to be able to fully endorse this account of their accomplishments. Each of these quotes evokes special memories and reminds me of special friendships. In particular:

> Tom Fairbank — One of the first kaizen team leaders and who
> now manages the entire West Hartford production facility.

Steve Maynard — An engineering executive who tackled unplugging the materials requirement planning system from his new and strange role as chief information officer, and also one of the early kaizen team leaders.

Tom Goetter — An engineering vice president currently getting "training" as a plant manager. Imagine that!

Judy Seyler — The human resources vice president who volunteered to serve on several of the early kaizen teams, now enjoying a well-earned retirement.

Gary Brooks — A family-style entrepreneur whose dedication to Lean principles and practices will make him a key leadership force in the future of Wiremold.

Orry Fiume — The bean counter who kept the beans from getting in the way of executing the strategy.

And, of course, Art, whose near fatal ski accident five years ago proved that the leadership team he built was strong enough to carry on in noteworthy style during his lengthy recuperation. A valued friendship I shall always cherish.

The people stories are endless.

The transformation of The Wiremold Company clearly demonstrates the principle that productivity yields wealth,[3] and it is a tribute to the Murphy family and the Wiremold board of directors for their support of Art and his team.

On that September day in 1991 when Art first showed me the West Hartford facility, I was surprised that he had chosen an old "brownfield" company for his next career move. I was also skeptical that the ownership would entrust the future of their company to this certifiable revolutionary. Thank goodness my early skepticism was proven wrong, for the Wiremold story clearly proves once again that "It's all about people" and, of course, "It's all about leadership."

Bill Moffitt

November 2002
Hilton Head Island, South Carolina

Notes

1. Kaizen is the Japanese word for "continuous improvement."
2. The term "freed-up" (or "free-up") is commonly used by Lean practitioners to describe the creation of new resources from existing means. While the grammar is poor, it successfully conveys one of the principal benefits of the Lean management system.
3. Art Byrne is fond of saying: "Productivity = Wealth." If that is not compelling enough, then consider the converse: "Waste = Poverty" (Note added by Emiliani).

Preface

We live in a world dominated by modes of thinking that often do not yield effective results and therefore do not serve us very well. This is particularly true in the practice of management. The leaders of companies typically follow well-worn paths for improvement that seem sensible enough, at least when viewed superficially. Deeper thought, however, reveals that many of the things that we believe in actually drive us toward behaviors that result in competencies that lead to sub-optimal performance, both personally and in business. CEO's play to win, but quite often lose instead, along with other key stakeholders such as employees, suppliers, customers, investors, and communities.

For example, the relentless focus on maximizing shareholder value over the last twenty years or so has led to unintended consequences, not the least of which is the destruction of shareholder value — the very outcome management is so focused on avoiding! Think too hard about your golf swing and you will surely hit the ball wrong. Likewise, an obsessive focus on maximizing shareholder value invariably results in great distress to a business and its key stakeholders. Witness the recent calamities at companies such as WorldCom, Enron, Adelphia, Qwest, Xerox, Ford Motor Company, Merrill Lynch, Lucent Technologies, Global Crossing, Arthur Andersen, Computer Associates, Warnaco, Sunbeam, and Rite-Aid. Unfortunately, the list goes on and on. Stable long-term growth simply has had little or no appeal among many investors in recent times.

With all the unfortunate outcomes that have befallen marquee companies in the last few years, it would seem the time is right for business leaders to accept a new challenge: to significantly improve the practice of management. However, they will do so only if they can accept the fact that many of their deeply held beliefs about business must change. Ordinary solutions such as new policies and procedures, additional audits, a new code of ethics, or greater regulatory oversight won't be much help because none of these solutions address the root cause of the problem. So how then, can managers expect to truly improve the practice of management to realize the results people rightly expect?

In general, the value that management places on human resources has steadily declined over the last 20 years. Although managers often say that people are their most important resource, they do not behave in ways that concretely demonstrate this belief. Not surprisingly, there is a pervasive angst among managers and associates; angst about their jobs, the future, their self-esteem, and the ability of the company to satisfy its customers. They know in their hearts and minds that something is very wrong, but they are not quite sure what it is or how to go about fixing it.

Paradoxically, while the value of human resources steadily erodes, billions of dollars continue to be spent on training programs for managers and associates. However, little benefit seems to have come of it, particularly on the macro-scale of the enterprise. Managers willingly adopt the latest management fad in the hope that it will quickly solve the problem at hand. Before long, however, it becomes yet another "flavor of the month," providing a clear indication that the root cause of the problem was not understood. So there is something else at play here, something that the training programs, as well as business schools, have not yet addressed successfully.

This book aims to show a better way of managing a business to achieve outcomes that benefit all stakeholders, and on a time-scale that can be acceptable even to many of today's impatient investors. The Wiremold Company, headquartered in West Hartford, Connecticut, is a mid-sized, privately owned, company that underwent a remarkable change in management practice starting in September 1991. The results the people of Wiremold achieved are noteworthy not just because they achieved success by another means, but because they did it in a way that avoided making destructive tradeoffs between key stakeholders. This management practice, called the "Lean management system," is available to any CEO who is willing to think and learn new ways of doing things, regardless of whether the company is publicly or privately owned, small or large, or in manufacturing or service.

Importantly, this book is not about management theory. Rather, it is about the actual practice of business, and a story of the great things that can be achieved when the CEO has the desire to challenge his or her beliefs and begin looking at things from a different perspective — indeed, *the correct perspective.* It is a detailed account of how a business was successfully managed as an enterprise, rather than a collection of functions to be individually optimized, using an entirely different set of management principles and practices. These same management principles and practices also apply to non-profit and government organizations.

It is our sincere hope that you will find this a valuable resource for both strategic and day-to-day management of a business — *any business.* To be sure, you will become uncomfortable at times. It is challenging from both an intellectual and a practical management perspective. For a brief period in my former life as a manager at a Fortune 60 company, I lived the kind of experience represented in this book. I know firsthand that Wiremold's story is neither fluff nor an anomaly that can be easily dismissed.

This book may be interpreted as sharp in tone or highly critical in the way it depicts conventional management practices. The intent is simply to drive home key points, overcome important areas of ambiguity or misunderstanding, and show the tremendous opportunities that exist for greatly improving the practice of management. If communication were indirect, it would invite much wasted time and effort in interpretation. So instead, we thought it would be better to communicate directly and aggressively challenge conventional management thinking and practice.

We do not present philosophical arguments when we challenge conventional management thinking and practice. Many other authors have covered that ground. Instead, we present new facts and data, with the aim of *proving* that the benefits of the Lean management system are beyond question. We hope this will be sufficient to convince many CEO's of the merits of the Lean management system, and that they will act upon this new information and embark on the journey to "Real Lean."

An important component of this book is the information contained in the endnotes. They are an integral part of this book and contain valuable information that will greatly enrich your understanding of the Lean management system. We urge you to read them carefully. Finally, your feedback is important. We invite you to contact us via e-mail at wmbook@theclbm.com and share your thoughts.

Bob Emiliani[1]
with David Stec, Lawrence Grasso, and James Stodder

November 2002
Wethersfield, Connecticut

Note

1. Conflict of Interest Statement: There were no direct or indirect financial interests between The Wiremold Company, its officers, employees, or agents and the authors or The Center for Lean Business Management, LLC in the preparation and publication of this book, nor any explicit or implicit promises to establish direct or indirect financial interests between said parties. This work is a free and independent study by the authors.

Acknowledgments

This book is made possible by the enthusiastic efforts of many people. The authors would like to express their sincere thanks to Arthur Byrne, Orest Fiume, and the rest of the Wiremold senior management team for agreeing to participate in this project, for the long hours they spent in interviews, and for their help in clarifying many key points. It was a great pleasure working with them and to be able to tell the story of a company that successfully practiced "Real Lean."

Thanks also to Jo-Anne Mazzeo and Mary Ann Reliford. Importantly, this great story is made possible by the dedicated efforts of thousands of Wiremold associates over the last eleven years. Their many contributions are recognized.

We also would like to acknowledge David Rainey, Chair of the Lally School of Management and Technology (Hartford, CT department), Rensselaer Polytechnic Institute, for supporting the data gathering activities. Other interview team members whose various contributions must be acknowledged include Martha Fransson, Robin Chase, Frank Jenkins, and Guido Slangen, all members of the faculty of Rensselaer Polytechnic Institute, Lally School of Management and Technology, in Hartford, Connecticut. Martha's contributions to Chapters 1 and 2, and related discussions on corporate strategy, are much appreciated. The important work of the transcribers, Irene Cooper, Eileen Hoyt, and Pamela Harrison, is gratefully acknowledged.

We are grateful for the copyediting performed by Allison B. Spitzer and Michael J. London of Michael J. London & Associates, and thank Ed Arnheiter for the final proof reading of the manuscript. We also thank Michael J. London for his insights and many helpful suggestions, and Tracy Cole of Horizon Designs Inc. for her fine work in creating the cover design and page layout, as well as her diligent attention to detail.

The principal author (Emiliani) would like to express his sincere thanks to Lloyd Tirey, who provided him with the opportunity to learn about kaizen[1] many years ago, and to Mr. Doi Yoshihisa, his first sensei, the master of "kaizen heart and mind" and human-centric management practice. Finally, and most importantly, thank you, Lucinda, for everything.

Note

1. Kaizen is the Japanese word for "continuous improvement."

Introduction

In today's business world, we see many companies worldwide trying to replace batch-and-queue,[1] or conventional management practices, with Lean[2] management practices. Most companies struggle with their Lean transformation, and the majority are ultimately unsuccessful. The purpose of this book is to chronicle, in detail, the actions taken by The Wiremold Company[3] between 1991 and 1999 to achieve a successful Lean transformation.[4]

First, it is important to provide some background on the term "Lean." Where did it come from? At its core, the term "Lean" refers to the Toyota Production System developed by the Toyota Motor Corporation, under the leadership of its long-time Executive Vice President of Operations, Mr. Taiichi Ohno. Over the years, there have been many excellent books written on the Toyota Production System. The term "Just-In-Time" (JIT) was perhaps the most common description of the Toyota Production System when it first became known in the United States. Unfortunately, few people understood that the Toyota Production System was really a total management system. It was, and still is, Toyota's management practice and day-to-day culture. They may have called it the Toyota *Production* System, but it means much more than simply the way in which automobiles are produced.

Early books on this subject did not go far enough towards helping people understand the totality of Toyota's management practice, how it is embedded in their corporate culture, and how it enables them to successfully achieve their strategies despite the existence of large and formidable competitors. What stood out was Toyota's ability to produce "Just-In-Time," and therefore operate with low inventories. The term "Just-In-Time" caught on quickly, and companies began their pursuit of this approach. However, most managers thought of the Toyota Production System in a very narrow sense, JIT, and looked at it as simply a way to better manage inventory. People thought "Just-In-Time" meant "Just-In-Time *Inventory*," which was also translated into aggressive efforts by buyers to "beat up" suppliers in order to improve their own inventory turns. Thus, JIT was seen as only one element of a company's manufacturing practice – another tool for the manager's toolbox. It sounded like a good thing to do, and it did not really disrupt the rest of the business and other functional areas such as engineering, finance, marketing, sales, etc. JIT was perceived as low risk, not too disruptive, and would deliver good results if successful.

The first book to show that the Toyota Production System was a much broader approach to management was *The Machine That Changed the World*, by J. Womack, D. Jones, and D. Roos in 1990.[5] In its study of the worldwide automotive industry, the book showed that Toyota's management system was far superior to all other automobile companies. It showed comparative results for not only inventory, but also for productivity, quality, supply chain management, and the speed of new product development as well. People who read this book with an open mind could see how the same principles and practices could be applied to non-automotive manufacturing businesses. Some even were able to see how these findings could be applied to service businesses.

While *The Machine* generated a lot of interest, it also raised some important questions among business practitioners:

- "But how do you do this?"
- "Show us examples of companies that have been successful outside of Japan."
- "We don't make cars; show us some companies that are more like us."

Jim Womack and Dan Jones set out to answer such questions. But how would they get across to people the idea that Toyota's approach was a total management system and not just a "manufacturing thing?" They, of course, knew it was much more than that. They wanted to describe the larger picture of how Lean companies create value across the value stream. They wanted to get people, particularly senior managers, to start thinking that way.

As a result of their next book, *Lean Thinking*,[6] the word "Lean" has successfully replaced "Just-In-Time" as the new terminology and has become the new thing for companies to do. Unfortunately, just as people did with "Just-In-Time" when they added the word *inventory,* and thus defined it as a narrow functional tool, people have added another word to Lean – *manufacturing* – to narrow its meaning. Today when people hear the word "Lean," they think of "Lean manufacturing." This is a step up from the sub-set of manufacturing methods that JIT connoted, but it is still functional in its interpretation. It remains as just one element of a company's overall approach to management – just another tool in management's tool kit.

Success consistent with the use of Lean as a complete management system requires a company to adopt Lean for *everything* it does and commit the entire senior management team to achieving the transformation. Doing so has strategic implications. Managers have to start out with the idea that what they are ultimately trying to do is:

- Create value for their end-use customers to distinguish themselves as the supplier of choice
- Change the very nature of the conversation they have with customers
- Improve relationships with all key stakeholders

This, of course, is a very big change – one that most senior managers are unwilling to make. Or, if they are willing to make such a change, they delegate it to people down in the organization and do it incrementally – and thus far less effectively.

Womack and Jones tried to answer the question, "How do you do it?" by presenting five examples of companies they felt were implementing Lean correctly and getting good results, including The Wiremold Company for the period 1991–1995.[7] However, there is much more to Wiremold's story than was reported there. While *Lean Thinking* is one of the better resources to help guide the Lean transformation, the basic question, "How do you do it?" still lingers in the minds of many. What has been lacking is a detailed presentation and analysis of the Lean transformation that touches all aspects of the changes needed to be successful. The purpose of this book is to provide that detailed analysis by showing how The Wiremold Company went about its Lean transformation, with the intent of helping other companies achieve similar success.

Senior managers continue to have great difficulty applying Lean principles and practices in a coherent and systematic fashion in operations, not to mention expanding it across the enterprise. Part of the challenge is the general failure to understand the role of people in the Lean transformation, as well as how to measure Lean business performance. While interest in Lean remains high, success for most companies has been elusive because they continue to use behaviors, tools, and measures that are inconsistent with Lean principles and practices. In addition, senior managers typically favor a "local incremental" approach in which pieces of the business are transformed sequentially over long periods of time. Wiremold's Lean transformation is strikingly different and very rare. Their Lean transformation was "widespread fast," meaning that the senior management team drove the transformation across the enterprise concurrently and quickly. This unique feature is part of what makes Wiremold's Lean transformation worth a much closer look.

The Center for Lean Business Management, LLC (The CLBM)[8] developed a working relationship with Orest "Orry" Fiume, Wiremold's Vice President of Finance and Administration, starting in early 2000. Emiliani approached Fiume to see if he was interested in teaching a workshop on how to align financial measurement and reporting with Lean operating practices. The resultant workshop, "Management Accounting for Lean Businesses," was first offered in May 2000. At a dinner meeting in December 2000, Emiliani asked Fiume if The CLBM could produce a case study on Wiremold's Lean transformation. The request was followed up with a detailed proposal, which Orry took to the senior management team for review and discussion. The senior management team agreed, and a series of interviews was scheduled with thirteen of Wiremold's top managers. The managers interviewed were:

- Scott Bartosch, Vice President of Sales
- Don Beaver, General Manager, Walker Systems
- Gary Brooks, President, Brooks Electronics
- Art Byrne, Chairman, President and CEO
- Kevin Fahey, Vice President of Human Resources
- Tom Fairbank, General Manager, West Hartford Plant

- Orest "Orry" Fiume, Vice President of Finance and Administration
- Frank Giannattasio, Vice President of Operations
- Tom Goetter, Vice President of Engineering
- Rich Levesque, Vice President of Engineering and Marketing, Walker Systems
- Steve Maynard, Chief Information Officer
- Ed Miller, Vice President of Marketing
- Judy Seyler, retired Vice President of Human Resources

Don't let the functional titles fool you. Each member of the senior management team possesses remarkable cross-functional experience, broad management capabilities, and detailed knowledge of Lean principles and practices.

The interviews took place in July and August of 2001 at Wiremold's West Hartford, Connecticut facility.[9] Profiles of the senior managers interviewed are contained in the section entitled "Wiremold Management Team." Approximately 60 hours of taped interviews were collected, resulting in nearly 900 pages of transcripts. What started out as a case study quickly turned into a book. The amount of material gathered was overwhelming in the level of detail and insights related to Lean business management. There was a much bigger story to tell than could have possibly been conveyed in a single case study, or even a series of case studies. Such a story might even help answer the question often asked by senior managers: "How do you do it?"

The purpose of this book is to provide a very detailed account of a Lean transformation; specifically, Wiremold's "widespread fast" Lean transformation, compared to both conventional (batch-and-queue) management practices and "local incremental" Lean transformations. The focus is on management practices in general, not manufacturing management. A key lesson from Wiremold's Lean transformation is the broad applicability of Lean principles and practices to any business and every business process. Lean principles and practices have to be part of how all senior managers think about everything all the time, not just how a few senior managers think about operations.

This book was written principally for the CEO and other senior managers, and thus was designed to address the important issues they face every day. **It is not theory.**[10] Certainly, many others will find it very useful as well, including mid-level managers, supervisors, and individual contributors. Other audiences that will benefit from reading this book include investors, suppliers, customers, community leaders, elected or appointed government officials, teachers, students, and consultants. This book contains dozens of extended quotes from senior managers.[11] Their purpose is to provide a means for direct communication between Wiremold senior managers and the senior management audience. This is important because the quotes more effectively convey the thinking, language, logic, passion, and intent of their efforts.

The Foreword contains commentary by Bill Moffitt, a long-term colleague of Art Byrne's at Danaher Corporation and a consultant for The Wiremold Company's Lean transformation. Chapter 1, "The Need for Change," presents Wiremold's condition prior to Art Byrne's arrival as CEO in September 1991. It describes the changes made to the business in response to increasing competition, its deteriorating financial condition, and the search for a new CEO. Chapter 2, "Wiremold's New Strategy," discusses the long-term strategy Art Byrne installed shortly after his arrival, how that strategy quickly evolved to become more specific, and its congruence with Wiremold's long-standing corporate purpose. Chapter 3, "The First Priority: Kaizen," describes Wiremold's early shop and office kaizen[12] activities, and the important shift from a results focus to process focus.

Chapter 4, "Transforming the Factory," provides a detailed description of how Wiremold changed all aspects of their operations from batch-and-queue to Lean. It describes processes and tools such as one-piece flow, kanban, production leveling, and visual controls, and the manner in which these practices were implemented. Chapter 5, "Lean is a People System," presents the fundamental differences in how managers view people in batch-and-queue and Lean management systems. It describes how Wiremold senior management gained widespread acceptance of the Lean management system and discusses important changes to human resource policy and practices. Chapter 6, "Growth Through New Products," discusses Wiremold's efforts to grow the business through new product development and take advantage of the additional productive capacity created by the Lean transformation, as well as the methodology for reducing new product development cycle times and filling gaps in their product line. Chapter 7, "Growth Through Acquisitions," describes the domestic and international acquisitions that Wiremold made to fill additional gaps in their product lines and increase market share, sales, and earnings. Their unique acquisition and integration processes are also discussed.

Chapter 8, "Delivering the Benefits of Lean to Customers," provides rare insight into the important practices developed to ensure that both intermediate and end-use customers benefited from Wiremold's Lean transformation. It contains important lessons in value stream management. Chapter 9, "Performance Measurement," discusses how business performance is measured in both conventional and Lean businesses, as well as the reasons why Wiremold abandoned traditional cost accounting. Chapter 10, "Wiremold's Results," summarizes the impressive financial and non-financial results that Wiremold achieved between 1990 (base year) and 1999.

Chapter 11, "Real Lean vs. Imitation Lean," presents the profound differences in conventional business practices compared to the Lean management system. It includes a new model for the Lean transformation and the development of new leadership skills based upon the machine change-over method used by Lean businesses to reduce set-up times. This chapter also discusses the difference in the level of discipline between conventional batch-and queue business practices and the Lean management system, and concludes with commentary by Wiremold senior managers on their important accomplishments. The end of each chapter contains a table summarizing the key points for senior managers.

The Postscript, "Solving the Liquidity Problem," discusses the sale of The Wiremold Company to Legrand S.A., a French manufacturer of low voltage electrical equipment, in July 2000. It presents the rationale for the sale, and includes an analysis of the value that Legrand saw in Wiremold. The Afterword discusses a few key challenges for CEO's that wish to achieve the type of results that Wiremold achieved, and answers some important questions that readers will likely have. The book concludes with a list of in-print and out-of-print books for those interested in learning more about the Lean management system.

Wiremold's Lean transformation is striking in many different aspects and contains dozens of valuable lessons for CEO's that wish to realize similar exceptional results. The way in which Wiremold carried out the Lean transformation was impressive. For example:

- Wiremold did not follow a precisely defined formula to achieve its Lean transformation, as none existed. The senior management team internalized the general principles and practices and applied them to business processes that span all functions. They used Lean as a total business solution, rather than simply as a group of tools to solve some problems in operations.

- Nearly every company that embarks on the Lean transformation has great difficulty with four key aspects: 1) understanding Lean as a management system, 2) CEO commitment and participation, 3) recognizing that Lean requires a completely different set of leadership behaviors, and 4) performance measurements, especially in management accounting. Most managers can't or won't abandon conventional leadership behaviors and business performance measures. The latter are ineffective and drive poor decision-making in a Lean business. They struggle to understand what the new leadership behaviors and measures should be. Wiremold did not suffer from these common problems, which are the primary modes of failure in Lean transformations.

- Art Byrne knew Lean was not just a "manufacturing thing." He realized that Lean principles represented the means to achieve a time-based competition business strategy, and that Lean practices must be applied to all business process. His prior experience with Just-In-Time at General Electric in the early 1980's and the Lean management system at Danaher Corporation starting in the late 1980's provided very important preparation for the Lean transformation at Wiremold. This helped accelerate the pace of the transformation and to avoid major errors.

- Art Byrne cultivated talent from within. He kept nearly the entire senior management team when he arrived and brought in only two new people. Senior managers participated in kaizen and learned about Lean first-hand, which helped overcome the common bias that conventional business practices are the best way to solve a problem or perform an activity. He transformed existing managers into highly effective Lean leaders.

- There was a tremendous amount of activity going on in parallel throughout the enterprise, versus the more common sequential, function-based type of Lean transformation. Wiremold's "widespread fast" Lean implementation is unique.

- The senior management team created a culture that asked "Why?" which helped avoid debilitating organizational politics that block the flow of information between key internal and external stakeholders. Kaizen and Wiremold's "Code of Conduct" helped make this happen.

- All senior managers interviewed possessed detailed knowledge of Lean principles and practices, regardless of functional responsibility. All have led or participated in numerous two-, three-, or five-day kaizens. This is rare.

- Wiremold senior management did not optimize individual business functions or processes. Instead, they improved the entire business system consistent with value stream management principles. This is extremely rare.

- The senior management team was committed to process and developed the discipline to sustain Lean practices, enabling them to achieve remarkable results.

- Wiremold achieved considerable success, financial and otherwise, with a stakeholder-centered management system. The company did not make destructive tradeoffs among key stakeholders to optimize their own position.[13] The focus was on the end-use customer, not share price. Eliminating waste created value for end-use customers, benefiting all stakeholders. This stands in contrast to the conventional management system constructed around the "maximize shareholder value" principle, which typically leads to inconsistent financial performance as well as employee, supplier, customer, and investor dissatisfaction.

- The senior management team understood that Lean is *not* just a bunch of tools for the manager's toolbox. "Real Lean" is a comprehensive management system that embodies two key principles: "continuous improvement" and "respect for people."[14] In contrast, "Imitation Lean" embodies only one of the two key principles: "continuous improvement."

Readers will quickly discover that the CEO, Art Byrne, played a vital role in Wiremold's Lean transformation. His hand, or more correctly, his heart and mind were seemingly everywhere. However, one person cannot make the transformation to "Real Lean." It takes the dedicated efforts of every manager and every associate. Art is quick to point out that it was the people of Wiremold who made the change to Lean. He isn't being modest when he says that. It's the truth.

While their accomplishments are many and varied, the Wiremold senior management team understands that their success, and the success of all Wiremold associates, is yesterday's news. They believe that they have just "scratched the surface." There is much more to do. Lean is a never-ending journey.

Notes

1. Throughout this book, the terms "batch-and-queue" (B&Q) and "conventional business practices" are used interchangeably to connote common business thinking and practice, in contrast to Lean principles and practices. Batch-and-queue is a method of producing goods in which materials are processed in large batches, which results in long queue times between operations. While this term originated in manufacturing, the conventional method for delivering services is also batch-and-queue (i.e. processing information in large batches). Batch-and-queue business practices result in lower quality and higher cost products or services.

2. Throughout this book, the terms "Lean," "Lean management system," and "Lean principles and practices" are used interchangeably. These terms are synonymous with the management system developed and practiced by the Toyota Motor Corporation, called "The Toyota Production System," and as more generally characterized by "The Toyota Way" ("Toyotawei," in Japanese), including Total Quality Control (see *Toyota Management System*, Y. Monden, Productivity Press, Portland, OR, 1993, and *Total Quality Control for Management*, M. Nemoto, translated by D. Lu, Prentice Hall, Inc. Englewood Cliffs, NJ, 1987). It does not refer to the idiomatic usage of the term "lean," which to most people has negative connotations such as: doing more with less, cutting the fat, or layoffs. A name that perhaps better captures the essence of the challenge and also describes a key desired human practice is "Thinking" ("Kangae" in Japanese) – thus, Thinking (or Kangae) management system.

3. The Wiremold Company, based in West Hartford, CT, produces wire and cable management solutions that integrate power, data, voice, video, and communications. Year 2000 sales were approximately $460 million. See http://www.wiremold.com.

4. The period covered begins when Art Byrne was hired as CEO in September 1991 and extends to when Legrand S.A. announced the acquisition of The Wiremold Company in July 2000, thus covering the final nine years of private ownership.

5. *The Machine That Changed the World*, J. Womack, D. Jones, and D. Roos, Rawson Associates, New York, NY, 1990.

6. *Lean Thinking*, J. Womack and D. Jones, Simon & Schuster, New York, NY, 1996.

7. *Lean Thinking*, J. Womack and D. Jones, Simon & Schuster, New York, NY, 1996, pp. 125–150.

8. The Center for Lean Business Management, LLC provides management consulting and executive education services to help organizations achieve "Real Lean." See http://www.theclbm.com.

9. The interview team consisted of: Bob Emiliani (lead), Martha Fransson (co-lead), Larry Grasso, James Stodder, David Stec, Robin Chase, Frank Jenkins, and Guido Slangen. All are either faculty or adjunct faculty of Rensselaer Polytechnic Institute's Hartford, Connecticut, department of the Lally School of Management and Technology. See http://www.rh.edu/lsmt.

10. In general, people unfamiliar with a concept, principle, or practice will immediately label it as "theory." This book is not about theory or abstract business practices. It is about business activities and results achieved in the "real world."

11. Quotes were edited by Emiliani to ensure clarity, ease of comprehension, and concise meaning.

12. Throughout this book, the term "kaizen" (Japanese for "continuous improvement") is used in preference to the term "kaizen event" which is commonly used in the West. The reason is twofold: 1) the original use of the term by the Japanese is "kaizen," not "kaizen event," and 2) the term "kaizen event" implies that continuous improvement is an infrequent, event-driven activity, when, in fact, kaizen is a daily activity. The word "event" is a Western interpretation of the structured (typically) five-day kaizen format facilitated by an internal or external consultant, culminating in a semi-formal presentation of the team's accomplishments to senior management. The term "kaizen event" may have been coined by Bill Moffitt or Bob Pentland c.1988. The term "kaizen blitz," a more recent Western derivative, also is not used for similar reasons.

13. In business, this type of selfish behavior is called "corporate unilateralism." See "Beyond Selfishness," H. Mintzberg, R. Simons, and K. Basu, *Sloan Management Review*, Vol. 44, No. 1, Fall 2002, pp. 67–74.

14. "Toyota Way 2001," Toyota Motor Corporation, internal document, April 2001.

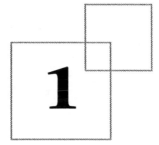

THE NEED FOR CHANGE

Historical Perspective

The Wiremold Company traces its history back to 1900,[1] when Daniel Murphy purchased Richmondt Electric Wire Conduit Company of Milwaukee, Wisconsin, for $10,000, and named his son, Daniel Hayes (hereafter D. Hayes) Murphy (Figure 1-1) as secretary. The company moved to a larger factory in Waukegan, Illinois, and in 1901[2] was renamed The American Interior Conduit Company. In 1902, The American Interior Conduit Company merged with the then-largest conduit manufacturer, Safety Armorite Company of Pittsburgh, Pennsylvania, becoming a subsidiary. The Garland family, principal owners of Safety Armorite, ran into financial difficulties in 1911, giving D. Hayes Murphy the opportunity to purchase The American Conduit Manufacturing Company. The company then moved to Woodbine Street in Hartford, Connecticut, in 1919, and was renamed The American Wiremold Company in 1920. The word "American" was dropped from the name in 1926, and the company moved to a new facility at 60 Woodlawn Street, West Hartford, Connecticut, in 1929.

Figure 1-1 D. Hayes Murphy

Source: The Wiremold Company

The Wiremold Company prospered in the post-depression era as cities grew and demand for electrical conduit increased. D. Hayes Murphy's sons, John Davis Murphy and Robert H. Murphy (Figure 1-2), joined the business in the early 1930's as part-time sales persons while completing their college degrees. They joined the company full-time in the mid-1930's. D. Hayes Murphy continued to serve as President until 1955, when John Davis Murphy was named President. At the same time, Robert H. Murphy was named Executive Vice President. The company grew steadily throughout the 1960's and 1970's, introducing many successful products and expanding facilities.

Figure 1-2 John Davis and Robert H. Murphy

Source: The Wiremold Company

Warren Packard, who joined the company in 1973, was appointed Corporate Secretary in 1974. He was named Executive Vice President and Director in 1977, while John Davis Murphy was named Chairman and CEO and Robert became President and COO. In 1979, Warren Packard became the first President and CEO of The Wiremold Company who was not a member of the Murphy family. The Wiremold Company continued to prosper under his leadership with sales of over $50 million in 1981. Sales grew dramatically over the next four years, reaching $75 million, and Wiremold had 2,500 distributors and employed 900 people in seven North American locations.

Wiremold's diverse product line, some of which was obtained through acquisitions, was turning into a liability as the traditional batch-and-queue[3] production system relied on large quantities of finished goods inventory. As product lines and sales expanded, inventories grew and customer service declined. Business practices that served Wiremold well in the past were now keeping it from responding to changes in the marketplace led by more flexible competitors.

In response, Wiremold hired a consultant to analyze its strengths and weaknesses and recommend ways to improve performance. Actions taken to improve Wiremold's position in the marketplace included the sale of the Flexible Duct Division in 1986, which served the increasingly volatile automotive market, and acquisition of Brooks Electronics and Nepco in 1988, and Shape Electronics in 1990. However, the acquisition of companies whose products had future growth potential did nothing to improve the underlying business performance problems.

The Next Step: Total Quality Management

In 1987, NBC News re-broadcasted its 1980 documentary "If Japan Can... Why Can't We?" which presented the highly efficient management system that enabled Japan to compete against America in the rapidly emerging global market. One viewer was Orry Fiume. He was impressed by what he saw and obtained a copy of the program and showed the company's executive group. They, in turn, decided to show it to the entire workforce. This sudden introduction to Japanese manufacturing practices was the beginning of the company's realization that it could no longer rely on past success.

The Total Quality Management (TQM)[4] philosophy espoused by W. Edwards Deming[5] shared many similarities with Japanese industrial management practices. Gary Brooks, president of the newly acquired Brooks Electronics, had studied Deming's management model in the early 1980's and shared his extensive knowledge of TQM with Wiremold's managers. For a while it looked as if TQM might be the "silver bullet" the company needed. Deming's 14 principles fit well with the company's values, but there was no accompanying operating manual or guidebook to follow to make the principles actionable. So while Wiremold managers espoused the principles, they, like most managers, did not understand how to implement TQM.

Despite this, Wiremold management started on the Total Quality journey by attending Dr. Deming's seminar, and later attempting to adopt the Just-In-Time (JIT)[6] production method shown in the NBC documentary. The experiment with Just-In-Time failed because nobody at Wiremold knew how to implement the system and the specific related methods that enable it to work. Plus, management did not have an accurate understanding of what JIT was; they viewed it simply as an inventory management system. By the time they realized there was more to JIT than just inventory, the company was falling behind on order fulfillment and getting into deep trouble. According to Orry Fiume:

> "It was very bad. The changes we tried to implement almost sank the company."

Management did not give up. In fact, the mistakes led to the creation of Wiremold's "Total Quality Process" (TQP). In January 1990, Wiremold published a small booklet called "Vision and Principles" which outlined TQP. The booklet started with a message from the president, Warren Packard:

> The Wiremold Company is truly special. For over 90 years, this company has been guided by D. Hayes Murphy's vision which embodies the best of our American System. An uncompromising commitment to customer service has made The Wiremold Company an industry leader. Unshakeable beliefs in job security and sharing the profits with employees have combined to make Wiremold a preferred employer. To survive as an independent and profitable company we need to focus all of our attention on continuously improving the quality of everything we do — not just the products we make but also every service we provide, both to our internal and external customers. Until

now, you may have had little to say about the quality of materials you received and perhaps less opportunity to be sure what your customer required of you. Now that will change because we have adopted the Total Quality Process — TQP — a process which gives you the means to get exactly what you need from your supplier and the ability to find out precisely what your customer requires from you. While there is no question that TQP calls for a big commitment from everyone, The Wiremold Company already has all the right ingredients to make it work: hard working dedicated people, a strong business, and a management team firmly committed to the Total Quality Process. As you read through this booklet think about how these principles relate to you. Write down ways you can improve service to your customer.

The booklet contained the following vision:

Vision
People and products are the fundamentals of our business. Our vision is to provide continuing growth opportunities and a good place to work for employees, and attractive returns to shareholders by providing our customers with quality wire management and line conditioning products and service. We aim to continuously and systematically improve upon Wiremold's tradition of excellence by the application of our operating principles.

The operating principles are:

Quality
Our number one priority is quality. We will not compromise the quality of product or service to our customers. Quality is defined as meeting or exceeding the needs of internal and external customers.

Customer
Customers, internal and external, are the focus of all we do. By keeping customers in mind we will provide more value than our competitors.

Employment
Our philosophy is one of continued employment for all Wiremold people without discrimination.

Continuous Improvement
By continuously improving all areas of the Company, we will be rewarded with growth, satisfied customers and happy employees.

Employee Involvement
We are a team. Through teamwork, mutual trust and respect, education and training we will grow together.

Leadership
The primary job of management is to provide leadership to help people do a better job.

Partnership
Success depends upon our continued, mutually beneficial relationship with customers and suppliers.

Community and Business Citizens
We will conduct business in a professional and ethical manner and support worthwhile causes.

Taken together, the vision and operating principles represent, in large part, a complete definition of Wiremold's long-standing stakeholder-centered management practices.

One month after the "Vision and Principles" booklet was distributed, management gave an overview for all employees and trained all leaders in TQP.[7] The first project teams were deployed in March 1990. In June 1990, 40 company and union[8] managers attended Dr. Deming's seminar and by August 1991 there were 47 project teams working in all areas of the company.

A Change in Leadership

Shortly after the "Vision and Principles" booklet was distributed, Warren Packard announced his retirement from active management. He remained a director of the company until 1999. The search for a new President and Chief Executive Officer was initiated in February 1991.

The search committee was composed of three members of the Board of Directors: an inside director, Orry Fiume, Vice President of Finance and Administration; an outside director, Millard Pryor, who headed the committee; and a family director, Robert H. Murphy, Jr. The search, supported by an executive recruiting agency, was national in scope. A key criterion for the candidate was to have demonstrated successful implementation of the Just-In-Time production method.

Numerous candidates were considered between March and July of 1991. All of the candidates shared a common problem: they knew the words "Just-In-Time," but did not have any substance behind the words. That is, they had not actually implemented a JIT system. The search took longer than expected because no candidate met this key criterion. It was not until late summer of 1991 that a strong candidate emerged.

Art Byrne heard that The Wiremold Company was looking for a new President and CEO. He sent his resume to John Davis Murphy, the Chairman, who in turn forwarded it to Orry Fiume. The resume ended up with the executive recruiter who initiated the formal interview process. Art first met individually with Orry, Millard, and Robert H. Murphy, Jr. They were impressed with Art's background,[9] which included six years at General Electric Company. Subsequently, Art became one of two Group Executives of the Danaher Corporation. He was responsible for day-to-day operations of eight business units, including Jacobs Vehicle Equipment Company, of Bloomfield, Connecticut.

The search committee learned that Art's first exposure to JIT was in 1982 when he was general manager at General Electric Company's High Intensity and Quartz Lamp division.[10] He began studying the overall management system that included JIT, called the Toyota Production System (TPS),[11] later known as "Lean Production" (hereafter referred to as "Lean").[12] They were very impressed with the work he had done in the preceding six years at Danaher Corporation, where Art helped lead the systematic conversion of all 13 of Danaher's traditional batch-and-queue businesses to ones using Lean manufacturing techniques.[13] Importantly, Art came to realize over time that Lean principles and practices *could be applied to any business* and *any business process*; it is not just limited to manufacturing operations. The same principles and tools also could be used to improve processes in service and support functions.

The search committee recommended to the principal owners and directors, John Davis Murphy and Robert H. Murphy,[14] that they meet with him. The meeting went well and the terms of the offer were constructed. The management team at Wiremold saw Art Byrne as a perfect fit. They were looking for an executive who had successfully implemented the Japanese management systems highlighted in the NBC News documentary four years earlier and could lead the company's transformation. They had found a person who had successfully implemented those concepts in America nine years earlier. According to Judy Seyler, then Vice President for Human Resources,

> "He walked in, and you just had the sense that he knew what to do."

Art knew that if he accepted the job offer he would have to move quickly to address Wiremold's deteriorating financial condition (Tables 1-1 and 1-2). Although Wiremold remained marginally profitable even in 1990, they had been in a financial tailspin since 1988. Sales in Wiremold's core business declined from 1988 through 1990. The corporate sales gains in 1989 and 1990 were primarily the result of the acquisition of Brooks Electronics, Nepco Canada, and Shape Electronics. While overall corporate sales increased 7.3% and 9.7% in 1989 and 1990, overall assets increased by 16% and 7.3% due to the acquisitions.

Inventory turnover and working capital turnover improved in 1988 and 1989, but declined in 1990 as Wiremold aborted its first attempt at JIT in the face of declining customer service. Although there was a slight rebound in 1990, sales per employee generally declined, and in 1990 was below its 1987 level.

A slight rebound in 1990 stopped what had been a steady decline in gross profit and operating profit. Some of the reported gross profit improvement may have resulted from pushing 1990 manufacturing costs onto the balance sheet in the form of higher inventories as Wiremold's JIT efforts were abandoned. Greater selling, administrative, and non-operating expenses offset the improvement in gross profit. Net profit declined consistently from 1987 through 1990 for both the overall corporation and the core business.

Table 1-1 Wiremold Corporate Results: 1987–1990*

	1987	1988	1989	1990
Net Sales Index	90	85	91	100
Gross Profit Index	110	94	88	100
Operating Profit Index	400	217	91	100
Net Profit Index	668	533	184	100
Inventory Turnover**	3.5	3.7	4.2	3.8
Working Capital Turnover***	4.5	4.6	5.0	4.5
Sales per Employee (000's)	101	99	94	97

  *All sales and profit values are indexed to 1990 = 100.
 **Sales divided by the average of beginning and end of year inventory values on a first-in, first-out basis to approximate the average inventory held during the year. Wiremold uses a 12-month rolling average in its internal reporting.
***Sales divided by the average of beginning and end of year working capital as defined by Wiremold. To focus on the working capital demanded to support production and sales, Wiremold defines working capital as accounts receivable plus FIFO inventory less trade payables.

Wiremold had bought sales, but the acquisitions had not resulted in any improvements in overall productivity. While Wiremold was using greater resources to generate higher sales, profits were vanishing.

Table 1-2 Wiremold Core Business Results: 1987–1990*

	1987	1988	1989	1990
Net Sales Index	109	103	102	100
Gross Profit Index	128	110	98	100
Operating Profit Index	608	329	110	100
Net Profit Index	607	484	146	100

*All values are indexed to 1990 = 100.

Art evaluated the job offer he had received to become president and CEO of Wiremold. As part of his decision-making process, he identified the problems and opportunities at Wiremold's West Hartford plant (Table 1-3). He decided that Wiremold's core business in West Hartford represented a significant opportunity for improvement through the implementation of Lean principles and practices. Based on prior experiences at Danaher, he knew this was the right solution and that it could be done. Although there were many problems to solve, he would be given free rein to put the company back on track. Art accepted the offer, and his first day on the job was September 23, 1991.

Table 1-3 The West Hartford Plant in September, 1991

Item	Art Byrne's Observations	Art Byrne's Goals
Market share	Wiremold had up to 70% of the markets it served	Find new and growing markets; increase market share
Sales growth	Stagnant	Improve quality and on-time delivery performance; introduce new products
New products under development	About 35 new products in development	Focus on fewer projects and those most important to customers
New product development cycle time	3–4 years	Reduce cycle time using Quality Function Deployment.[15] Target 6–9 months.
Inventory	3 turns per year	20 turns per year
Warehouse	Negotiations underway for additional 100,000 ft^2	Close the existing warehouse. Stop negotiations for new warehouse
Control system	Mainframe computer (MRP)	Use visual controls wherever possible
Equipment	Old equipment; organized in functional departments	Reconfigure equipment layout for one-piece flow
Quality	Total Quality Management had been attempted; little or no sustained improvement achieved	Year-over-year reduction in defects
Employee values	Typical of family-owned business; basic value set similar to his	Build upon existing value set to achieve goals
Profitability	Low and falling	Reduce inventory and warehouse space to free-up cash, restore profit sharing, and finance growth with higher productivity
Operations	No changes in methods for the last 40–50 years	Teach people to see the system totally differently; use kaizen to change their thinking and improve productivity

Summary

The Wiremold Company had a long history of success and had become a leader in the markets it served. However, competition was intensifying. The business strategies and management practices that had served Wiremold well for 70 years, since D. Hayes Murphy became President, were no longer effective. The management team realized the company had to change the way it did business or it would cease to exist. Their experiments with JIT would be the first step on the path to transforming the business. While unsuccessful, they led to the second step, adoption of TQM, and then the creation of the Total Quality Process.

The description of TQP in the "Vision and Principles" booklet began the process of defining the key characteristics of The Wiremold Company. The TQP booklet also can be viewed as a summary expression of the family values approach to management that the Murphy family championed for nearly a century. This would serve as a foundation for the upcoming change in leadership and the subsequent implementation of the Toyota Production System.

In accepting the job at Wiremold, Art Byrne made what some would perceive to be a high-risk commitment to a turn-around situation. Based on his prior experience with the Toyota Production System, Art knew that it was the only way Wiremold would regain profitability and growth. More importantly, Art understood the Toyota Production System as a management system for the entire business, not just a method for managing operations. He overcame such common misconceptions[16] as: TPS is just for manufacturing, it only works in Japan, it applies only to the automotive industry, and that Lean only works in high volume environments.[17] This later proved to be one of a handful of critical factors that enabled Wiremold to achieve great success.

Key Points for Senior Managers

- The terms "Toyota Production System" and "Lean Production" are synonymous, though Toyota considers TPS as a management system that is applicable to its entire business, not solely production.[18]
- The Wiremold Company's management team understood that Japanese management practices would be the key to their future success and that few individuals were capable of implementing a successful transformation.
- The principles and practices of TPS apply to all businesses: manufacturing and service; profit and non-profit; private and public, and government.
- The principles and practices of TPS apply to all processes, including those in Engineering, MIS, Human Resources, Sales, Marketing, Finance, etc.

Notes

1. For the complete history of The Wiremold Company, see *The Wiremold Company, A Century of Solutions*, J. Smith, published by The Wiremold Company, West Hartford, CT, 2000.

2. The Wiremold Company and the Toyota Motor Corporation share an interesting bit of history with regards to looms. Up until about 1950, one of Wiremold's principal products was a woven tubular electrical conduit product called "loom" (cotton thread and twisted paper impregnated with resin). The Toyota Motor Corporation was created in 1937 from the parent company, Toyoda Automatic Loom Works, Ltd., a manufacturer of automatic looms founded in 1929 by Sakichi Toyoda, one of Japan's greatest inventors. Mr. Toyoda perfected the Toyoda power-driven wooden loom in 1897 (for making flat cloth), three years before Daniel Murphy (father of D. Hayes) purchased Richmondt Electric Wire Conduit Company of Milwaukee, WI.

3. Batch-and-queue (B&Q) is a method of producing goods in which materials are processed in large batches, which results in long queue times between operations. While this term originated in manufacturing, the conventional method for delivering services is also batch-and-queue (e.g. processing information in large batches). Batch-and-queue business practices result in lower quality and higher cost products or services.

4. TQM is a management philosophy that places the customer first and provides all employees with the responsibility and tools to assure than quality goals are met throughout the organization. Derived from the Deming philosophy of management, TQM places emphasis on the understanding and control of the processes that generate a company's product or service, rather than reliance on inspections to control quality. Typical methodologies include root cause analysis, statistical process control, and the "seven tools" of quality. TQM is now generally recognized as a subset of the Lean management system.

5. For more information on W. Edwards Deming, see http://www.deming.org.

6. "Just-In-Time" is a fundamental component of the overall management system known as the Toyota Production System (see Note 11) whereby parts are withdrawn from the preceding operation just-in-time by the subsequent operation. The JIT system provides what is needed, when it is needed, in the quantity needed. Kanban is the tool used to manage JIT production (see *Toyota Production System*, T. Ohno, Productivity Press, Portland, OR, 1988, pp. 33 and 123–124).

7. Wiremold had about 960 associates (660 in Connecticut) in 1991, and about 3600 associates in 1999, 600 of whom were located in West Hartford and Rocky Hill, Connecticut.

8. Wiremold hourly associates in the West Hartford, CT and Rocky Hill, CT plants are members of the International Brotherhood of Electrical Workers Union (IBEW), Local 1040. The circumstances by which the workforce became members of the IBEW in 1939 are unusual. Wiremold's employees never asked for union representation. Rather, Wiremold management encouraged unionization as a means to access major markets, such as in New York City, where trade unions resisted the use of its non-union made products. Once the hourly associates gained union representation, Wiremold's sales force enjoyed unrestricted market access and thus higher sales.

9. Art Byrne earned a B.A. in Economics from Boston College and an M.B.A. from Babson College. Art had this to say regarding his M.B.A. degree: "The MBA has proven more valuable to me in my career [compared to the BA degree]. The MBA has been very useful in the Lean transformation as it helped me to see the big picture of how a business operates, and thus I was able to recognize very quickly how significant Lean could be if it was implemented in all areas of a business."

10. Art's first exposure to the Toyota Production System came in early 1982 when he was General Manager of GE's High Intensity and Quartz Lamp division, part of GE's Lighting Business Group. His manufacturing manager had attended a GE course in Japan and needed to demonstrate a Just-In-Time example. They decided on a simple supplier kanban example with another unit of the Lighting Business Group that supplied Art's plant. When they first started, all of the other general managers thought that what Art and Gary Carlson, the general manager of the supplier business, were trying to do was crazy. According to Art Byrne, they said: "All that will happen is that Gary's inventory will go up if Art's goes down and you'll probably endanger customer service as well". What actually happened was probably the first successful implementation of Just-In Time at General Electric. Art's inventory of quartz arc tubes went from 40 days down to three days. Customer service actually improved, space was freed-up, the shop floor was neater and cleaner than before, and both quality and productivity improved. Six months later, Gary Carlson invited Art to his plant about 30 minutes away and took him into a large empty room. When Art asked why, Gary explained that before the kanban system was started, the room was full of quartz arc tubes waiting for Art's business to order them. The inventory had truly come out of both businesses to the benefit of the Lighting Business Group in total. From that point forward, Art was hooked on Lean.

11. The Toyota Production System (TPS) was initially developed by Kiichiro Toyoda of the Toyota Motor Corporation starting in the late 1930's. Mr. Taiichi Ohno, former Executive Vice President of Toyota Motor Corporation, is credited with having developed the Toyota Production System as it is known today. (Note

that Shigeo Shingo made many important contributions, particularly with regards to set-up reduction). TPS is a management system that embodies the philosophy and practice of eliminating waste and creating value for end-use customers. It is a make-to-order (i.e. "pull") production system, as compared to less effective make-to-forecast (i.e. "push") batch-and-queue production system. The two pillars of the Toyota Production System are "Just-In-Time" (JIT) and "Autonomation" (automation with a human touch, also called "jidoka" in Japanese). The Toyota Production System is also known as "Lean Production" or "Lean."

12. John Krafcik coined the term "Lean Production," in recognition of the fact that the Lean production method consumes less resources compared to conventional mass production methods. See "Triumph of the Lean Production System," J. Krafcik, *Sloan Management Review*, Fall 1988, Vol. 30, No. 1, pp. 41–51, and *The Machine that Changed the World*, J. Womack, D. Jones, and D. Roos, Rawson Associates, New York, NY, 1990, p. 13.

13. Several managers from Danaher Corporation would later be recognized as responsible for helping to bring the Toyota Production System to the United States (separate from Toyota's joint venture with General Motors, NUMMI, in Fremont, CA, which started in 1984). This included: Art Byrne, John Cosentino, George Koenigsaecker, Bob Pentland, Mark DeLuzio, Bill Moffitt, and Jim Cutler. Art Byrne left General Electric's Battery Business division in 1985 and joined Danaher Corporation as a Group Executive responsible for Jacobs Brake, Jacobs Chuck, Veeder Root, Holokrome, and four smaller instrument companies. The other Group Executive was John Cosentino, who joined Danaher in late 1987. John Cosentino's prior experience was with Otis Elevator and UT Automotive, both units of United Technologies Corporation. He left Danaher in late 1990 and returned to UTC as President of Otis North America. George Koenigsaecker left Rockwell International Automotive Operations and was hired as Vice President of Sales and Marketing for The Jacobs Manufacturing Company in 1986 and later became President of Jacobs Vehicle Equipment Company in 1987. Bob Pentland left Rockwell International Automotive Operations and was hired by George Koenigsaecker in 1988 as Vice President of Operations. Mark DeLuzio joined Jacobs Vehicle Equipment Company in 1988 as the Cost Systems Manager, charged with establishing a JIT accounting system. Mark held various positions including Vice President of Finance and Operations Manager for the Asian Business Sector at Jake Brake. In 1993 he joined the Danaher Corporate Office as a Corporate Vice President where he built and improved the Lean promotion office (developing training materials, internal training workshops, and kaizen consulting) and developed and deployed the Danaher Business System across all Danaher companies (about 65 companies ranging in size from $10M–$600M in about 250 locations worldwide). Bill Moffitt was a long-time manager at Jacobs Chuck and Chicago Pneumatic. His last position was Vice President and Technical Director for The Jacobs Chuck Manufacturing Company from August of 1988 until his retirement in 1991. At the same time, he worked for Art Byrne as head of Danaher's initial Just-In-Time promotion office. He left Danaher in 1991 to form Moffitt Associates (where later Bob Pentland and Jim Cutler would become partner and managing partner, respectively), and consulted with Wiremold in its conversion to Lean from the very beginning. Jim Cutler, a NUMMI veteran, was hired by Art Byrne in the early days of the Danaher transformation as Vice President of the Qualitrol Division.

14. The principal owners in 1991 were the four surviving children of D. Hayes Murphy: his sons John Davis Murphy and Robert H. Murphy, and his daughters Rosalie Murphy Massey and Marjorie Murphy Morrisey.

15. Quality Function Deployment is a product (or service) development process in which decisions are driven by the "Voice of the Customer." Cross-functional teams participate in the construction of QFD charts that reflect customer wants and needs with regards to design, manufacturing, and other attributes.

16. Other misconceptions include: Lean is a "flavor-of-the-month;" Lean is an inventory reduction program; Lean results in layoffs; Lean costs a lot of money to implement; process improvement reduces output; Lean yields only long-term results; Lean destroys creativity; layoffs make companies Lean; it requires a big capital investment to create manufacturing cells; standardization is not practical; Lean runs equipment to the breaking point; Lean can not respond quickly to changes in business conditions; Lean can be successful with high management turnover; management can pick and choose Lean tools; 1990's Japanese economy proves that Lean does not work, etc.

17. The Toyota Production System was created in a low volume "job shop" environment as a means to compete against high volume automotive producers (i.e. General Motors-Japan and Ford-Japan). Thus, Lean principles and practices also are applicable to low volume manufacturing (and service) businesses.

18. "Toyota Way 2001" is a Toyota Motor Corporation internal document (April 2001) that describes Toyota's management system in terms of managerial values, business methods, and standards of behavior. This is Toyota's first-ever effort to document The Toyota Way — "the company's fundamental DNA."

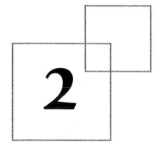

WIREMOLD'S NEW STRATEGY

Identifying a Strategy

In 1991, several leading contemporaneous strategy models had been developed and were available for senior managers to use. The strategy models and a summary of their main thrusts are presented in Table 2-1. Table 2-2 shows the business issues at Wiremold accompanied by an assessment of models that might be relevant to each issue. Each model listed in Table 2-1 suggests policies for managers to improve the organization's competitive performance. The first four strategy models listed are mostly *descriptive*. That is, they describe the strategies and practices of then-current industry leaders, but do not provide specific information on how to implement that advice. The next three models are more *prescriptive*.

Table 2-1 Prominent Strategy Models in 1991

Strategy Model	Key Thrust	Implementation Method
Descriptive		
Logical Incrementalism[a]	Organizations change in series of small experiments as they adopt to changing environments	Legitimize experimentation and delegitimize large scale long range planning typically used in PIMS model
Global Strategy[b]	Develop a strategy to enter all markets	Control at product line level
PIMS/McKinsey[c]	Achieve market dominance or divest	Analyze relative market share and apply to all product lines
Value Chain[d]	Add value at each stage of of production process	Reengineer all processes in firm; discontinue non-value adding activities
Prescriptive		
Core Competence[e]	Develop new core competences	Develop new product and new markets
Time-Based Competition[f]	Just-In-Time (JIT) products and services create value for customers around the world	Adopt JIT and Toyota Production System or similar approach
Product Development[g,h,i]	Growth through new products	Product line mapping; formalize product development process

[a] *Strategies for Change: Logical Incrementalism*, J. Quinn, Richard D. Irwin, Inc., Homewood, Il, 1980.
[b] *Competitive Advantage: Creating and Sustaining Superior Performance*, M. Porter, The Free Press, New York, NY, 1985.
[c] *The PIMS Principles: Linking Strategy to Performance*, R. Buzzell and T. Bradley, The Free Press, New York, NY, 1987.
[d] *Competitive Advantage*, M. Porter, The Free Press, New York, NY, 1985, Ch. 2.
[e] "The Core Competence of the Corporation", C. Prahalad and G. Hamel, *Harvard Business Review*, Vol. 68, No. 3, 1990, pp. 79–91.
[f] *Competing Against Time: How Time-Based Competition is Reshaping Global Markets*, G. Stalk Jr. and T. Hout, The Free Press, New York, NY, 1990.
[g] *Dynamic Manufacturing*, S. Wheelwright, R. Hayes, and K. Clark, The Free Press, New York, 1988.
[h] "The New Product Development Map", S. Wheelwright and W. Sasser, Jr., *Harvard Business Review*, Vol. 67, No. 3, 1989, pp. 112–124.
[i] *Product Development Performance: Strategy, Organization and Management in the World Auto Industry*, K. Clark and T. Fujimoto, Harvard Business School Press, Boston, MA, 1991

The prescriptive models are more specific in describing the means to achieve a strategy. Only three of the seven prominent strategy models, core competence, time-based competition and product development, provide explicit methods for implementation. The means identified to implement a strategy based upon time-based competition was the Toyota Production System, while the prescription provided by product development was to abandon conventional product development processes and instead follow a specific sequence of steps to reduce cycle time.

Art was familiar with the management literature on strategy models, but was not significantly influenced by any of them except the time-based competition strategy advocated by George Stalk, whom Art had met while at Danaher Corporation. Art's greatest influences were three little-known books published prior to 1991[1] that explained various facets of the Toyota Production System.[2]

- *Toyota Production System* by Taiichi Ohno
- *The SMED System* by Shigeo Shingo
- *A Study of the Toyota Production System* by Shigeo Shingo

Table 2-2 Analysis of Strategy Models for Relavancy to Wiremold in 1991

Wiremold Issue	Applicable Strategy Model	Comment
Improve profitability	• Value Chain	• Customers will not pay for non-value added activities
	• Time-Based Competition	• Application of TPS results in lower costs
Achieve sales growth	• Time-Based Competition	• Introduce new products
Full product line	• Product Development	• Mapping to discern gaps between competing product lines
	• Time-Based Competition	• Provide product variety to meet customer needs
Reduce product development cycle time	• Product Development	• New series of steps in the process to reduce cycle time
	• Time-Based Competition	• Fast cycle product development
Acquire new businesses as needed	• Product Development	• Fill gaps in product line through acquisition when more efficient
	• Time-Based Competition	• Convert all acquisitions to Lean management system
Global markets	• Global Strategy	• Control at product line level appropriate
	• Time-Based Competition	• Lower cost / more responsive products gain entry into new markets and reshape competition

Most of the strategy models shown in Table 2-1 were relevant in one form or another to Wiremold's business condition in 1991, as shown in Table 2-2.

However, only the time-based competition and new product development models fit all of Wiremold's needs and had associated with them specific implementation methodologies.

Art Byrne arrived at this conclusion independently, based upon the books by Ohno and Shingo, as well as his prior experience with the Toyota Production System at Danaher Corporation, as taught to him by consultants from Shingijutsu Company, Ltd.[3] Orry Fiume had this to say about the poor understanding that Wiremold's senior management had about Lean prior to Art's arrival:

> "We didn't understand that 'Just-In-Time' is a business strategy. We looked at it as a manufacturing strategy. Actually, we looked at it as an inventory management program."

In April 1992, Art presented the following strategy to associates in all-employee meetings and to shareholders:

- Strengthen existing operations
- Profitably double the business over next five years
- Become one of the premiere time-based competitors in the USA with world class manufacturing and product development skills

The management team recognized the upcoming changes would be dramatic and that family shareholders would need to understand what was happening if they were to support the Lean transformation.[4] Orry Fiume describes the senior management team's efforts to keep shareholders informed:

> "We had about 150 family shareholders. Every year a very small number of shareholders attend the meeting here in Hartford. But we've got shareholders in California, Chicago, etc. I said to Art, 'If we're going to keep the shareholders on board in terms of where we want to take this company, then we've got to get all of the shareholders to understand what's happening.' So starting in January of 1993, and each January thereafter, we started holding informal shareholder information sessions. They weren't the legally required shareholder meetings, but just informational meetings. A team of people, about four or five of us, would go to Los Angeles and we'd put a presentation on in the morning, have lunch with the shareholders in that area, get on a plane and fly to Chicago, give a presentation the next morning, have lunch, get on a plane and come to Hartford, give a presentation and have lunch. The team changed every year so that the shareholders got exposed to the entire management group. So over three days, we touched almost all the shareholders to let them know what we

were doing, why we were doing it, and where we wanted to see the company go. That, to me, was one of the most important things that we did in terms of getting the company to double in size every four years. I think that if we hadn't done that, we would have had a lot of pressures from shareholders outside of Connecticut to sell the company a long time ago."

Evolution of the Strategy

As the challenges at Wiremold became clearer and as the management team worked more closely together, the strategy became better articulated in several important ways. Becoming a leading time-based competitor, however, would remain the foundation of the strategy. In January 1993, the strategy was improved as follows:

Become one of the leading time-based competitors in the United States by:

1. Strengthening our base operations
   * 100% on time customer service
   * 50% reduction in defects per year
   * 20% gain in productivity per year
   * 20× inventory turns
   * Establish visual control and 5C's[5]

2. Profitably double the size of the business
   * Use Quality Function Deployment and similar approaches to introduce new products every quarter
   * Pursue selective acquisitions

There are several important features to notice about this strategy and its sub-components. First, it did not include any explicit financial goals or cost savings targets. Instead, the focus was on positive improvement rather than negative cost cutting. The strategy included specific non-financial measures that, if achieved — even partially — would lead to cost reductions. The non-financial measures were largely, but not exclusively, related to operating performance. Thus, operations was seen as a key element of company performance, working in concert with other functional areas such as finance, marketing, or engineering. To double in size in a slow-growth market, Wiremold needed both operational improvements and rapid new product development. All functions had to work together.

Second, there was no tradeoff between cost, delivery, and quality. Art knew these variables could be improved both rapidly and simultaneously using the principles and practices of the Toyota Production System, rather than making trade-offs between these variables as batch-and-queue businesses are forced to do.

Third, the growth strategy was articulated through new product development and by acquiring selected businesses. Having a growth strategy is an essential component of the Lean transformation because kaizen activities create additional productive capacity from existing internal resources — people, machines, and factory space, for example — that must be used effectively by management rather than simply disposed of to cut costs. Finally, the strategy was simple and transcended company or industry boundaries. This would become very important as businesses were later acquired.

The strategy underwent a third round of improvement and by summer of 1993 it read:

> Become the leading supplier in the electrical products industry and one of the top 10 time-based competitors:
>
> 1. Constantly strengthen our base operations
>   - 100% customer service
>   - 50% reduction in defects — each year
>   - 20% productivity gain — each year
>   - 20× inventory turns
>   - 20% profit sharing
>   - Visual control and the 5C's
>
> 2. Double in size every 3–5 years
>   - Use Quality Function Deployment and similar approaches to introduce new products every quarter
>   - Pursue selective acquisitions

There are three changes from the previous strategy. First, the characterization related to becoming a leading time-based competitor was now more specific: to become one of the top ten time-based competitors. Second, the profit sharing goal was included. This provided an explicit link between the strategy and the near-term financial interests of associates, and recognized the importance of letting everyone share in the gains resulting from kaizen — an essential component of Lean management practice. Third, the growth goal would include a specific time frame: from "Profitably double the size of the business" to "Double in size every 3–5 years."

After a fourth round of improvement in early 1994, the strategy read:

> Be the leading supplier in the industries we serve and one of the top 10 time-based competitors globally:
>
> 1. Constantly strengthening our base operations
>   - 100% on time customer service
>   - 50% reduction in defects per year
>   - 20% productivity gain — each year
>   - 20× inventory turns
>   - 20% profit sharing
>   - Visual control and the 5C's

2. Double in size every 3–5 years
   - Pursue selective acquisitions
   - Use Quality Function Deployment to introduce new producrs every month

There are two more changes compared to the previous strategy. The characterization related to becoming the leading supplier was generalized to "the industries we serve," rather than the more narrowly defined "electrical products industry." In addition, Quality Function Deployment would be used to introduce new products every month, rather than quarterly.

The basic strategy, time-based competition, remained constant while each of the sub-components of the strategy contain within them one or more aspects related to time. The sub-components evolved to include a higher degree of specificity related to non-financial measures and time frames. This reflects the increasing availability of internal resources due to kaizen and capability building by the organization, which after the first year or two could begin to respond to more specific time-based challenges. Art had this to say about Wiremold's strategy:

> "This is not some manufacturing thing. It is 'How do I beat the other guy by serving the customer better?' It is a set of principles and tools that allow you to do that on a pretty consistent basis. The rules are simple and the tools are simple. But doing it is really hard. That is why it is such a competitive weapon — it takes time to do this. You can't do it overnight. You physically have to move things and change things. If you get a head start over somebody else, if you can keep pushing it hard enough, you are going to wind up with a lead that the other guy probably will never catch. Because even if two of your competitors started doing the stuff, first of all they probably wouldn't be successful because it is hard to do. Secondly, even if they were really successful, if you continue to be successful you still have a five, six, or seven-year lead on them and they will never close the gap. I look at Lean has having major strategic implications."

According to Scott Bartosch:

> "Time relates to competitiveness. If you give us an order and we can enter it into our system in two minutes, make the product in 20 minutes, and ship it in two hours, while our competitor takes two days to enter the order, two weeks to make it, and three weeks to ship it, who's going to win? That's the issue. Then you have to learn how to do that reliably and consistently."

Art's initial plan for Wiremold's transformation would include:

- A commitment to continuous improvement through the use of kaizen.
- A 15% reduction in workforce, mostly through early retirements, and a qualified guarantee of employment for all who remained; i.e. nobody would lose their job due to kaizen.
- Leveling production and converting to one-piece flow.
- The introduction of visual controls.
- Discontinuance of the material requirements planning (MRP) system as soon as possible and adoption of a "pull" manufacturing system.
- Discontinuance of many of the products in development.
- A reorganization along product family lines so that the company was in a position to receive kaizen and take ownership of results.
- Creating a budget for kaizen consulting services paid for by the CEO's office.[6]

Corporate Purpose

Having a strategy that is responsive to the marketplace is obviously a critical component of business practice. However, many businesses experience conflict between strategy-based objectives and other high-level objectives that are typically contained in vision, mission, or value statements.[7] People, especially employees, suppliers, and customers, can easily become confused by inconsistent messages from senior management. Some of the messages are explicit, while others can be inferred from management's actions. A simple example is a mission statement that says customer satisfaction is the top priority, while management's daily actions focus instead on achieving a quarterly earnings target for investors to increase the stock price. Most employees view these objectives as contradictory and will have great difficulty reconciling them. The resulting confusion and conflict is wasteful and will result in a loss of customer focus.

An essential part of being a Lean business is having a purpose — the reason for existence or ultimate end-objective.[8] The Lean leader understands that a corporation's purpose must transcend narrow-minded, single-valued functions such as maximizing shareholder value.[9] Without doubt, the leaders of Lean businesses are certainly interested in creating shareholder value, but they recognize that this cannot be the sole purpose. Instead, they see companies as socio-economic entities that serve both social and economic interests.[10]

Social interests, however, are not considered welfare or charity. It is simply good business conduct that leads to reduced conflict between stakeholders, lower costs, and greater customer satisfaction. Toyota Motor Corporation's corporate purpose, rooted in stakeholder-centered management principles, has not reduced its competitiveness. Rather, it has greatly strengthened its competitiveness over decades and helped deliver consistent financial performance.

Ever since D. Hayes Murphy obtained control of the American Conduit Manufacturing Company from the Garland family in 1911, he set out to make sure that the company was managed ethically and in a way that balanced the interests of key stakeholders. He said:

- "That's why they [the Garland family] went broke. They were fighting among themselves instead of fighting to protect the business."
- "[We] make an honest product and give good service to our customers. [I never] paid a nickel to anybody for graft. It just isn't done in *this* business."
- "I also believe that any man or any woman who really takes an interest in the business of this company, and to help make profits for the company, should receive a share of those profits."
- "[1900–1950] was a period of great progress in the world — progress in all the sciences except social science, the one that teaches us to get along with each other."
- "Our management is dedicated to the philosophy that if you have a share in our enterprise, you will want to do your full part in making it successful."[11]

D. Hayes Murphy's business meant more to him than simply maximizing profits to serve his own interests. He operated his business with a purpose: "people and products," which could clearly be inferred from D. Hayes Murphy's frequent communications with employees and customers, as well as his actions (see Exhibit 2-1 at the end of Chapter 2). Wiremold's corporate purpose was not explicitly stated in writing until the Total Quality Process booklet was published in January 1990. Clearly, Wiremold has a long history of purposeful management practice embedded in the words "people and products," which is a dual-objective function. "People" includes associates, customers, suppliers, investors, community, etc., while "products" are the goods and services created by Wiremold that provide value to customers. By hiring Art Byrne, the Board of Directors would reinforce and perpetuate this long-standing corporate purpose.

The significance of corporate purpose, whether stated or inferred, cannot be overemphasized. In a Lean business, corporate purpose serves as a unifying and coordinating mechanism among senior managers. This helps assure that both strategy-based and daily business decisions are made in a consistent manner over decades. The corporate purpose provides direction, alignment, and motivation. It serves as a moral compass, gives meaning to work, and is transferable across geographic boundaries. Importantly, it also helps eliminate conflict between people:[12] internal stakeholders (e.g. managers) and external stakeholders. Thus, businesses without purpose, or with purpose that is singular in focus — such as maximizing shareholder value — will have great difficulty realizing the full potential of the Lean management system.

Mr. Ohno, the creator of the Toyota Production System said: "The basis of the Toyota production system is the absolute elimination of waste."[13] That, of course, would include conflict between stakeholders. Note that "absolute elimination" is a goal, not a discrete or necessarily achievable endpoint. Conventional corporate philosophies and operating practices create a great deal of waste between stakeholders.[14] This waste can be eliminated if the corporation has a purpose, stated or inferred, that achieves balance between the interests of key stakeholders. Conflict, however, can lead to improved outcomes, but usually only when it is goal-oriented.[15]

Summary

Art mitigated the risks associated with a turn-around situation by adopting a strategy based upon time-based competition[16] and using the Toyota Production System as the prescriptive implementation methodology to achieve the strategy. While the initial strategy was modified slightly over the next few years, the basic theme remained consistent and was aligned with Wiremold's long-standing corporate purpose. The strategy evolved and became more specific and actionable as Wiremold's capabilities expanded. The principal focus was on customers, operating performance, and growth. Importantly, the strategy fit on just one page, thus making it easier for people to remember.

The non-financial measures contained in the strategy are an interesting mix of fixed (i.e. 100% customer service) and continuous (i.e. 50% reduction in defects each year) metrics. The emphasis on improving non-financial measures is the key to achieving improved financial results in the Lean business system. Art Byrne and his management team would use the Toyota Production System to manage the business "box score," instead of the "scoreboard" as batch-and-queue business do. They were committed to the idea that improved processes would generate better results. This is the exact opposite of most batch-and-queue businesses, which instead focus on results without understanding the fundamental business processes.[17]

Art understood something about the Toyota Production System that few others understood in the early 1990's and still don't to this day: that TPS is a complete management system, not simply a set of tools for improving manufacturing performance.[18] This understanding would be critical for achieving a rapid change-over from Wiremold's historical batch-and-queue practices to the Lean management system.

In addition, the time-based competition strategy would place a special demand on the senior management team: they would all have to behave in a manner consistent with the strategy and not waste people's time. Their decisions and communications would have to be both precise and consistent over many years. The 20% annual productivity goal combined with a qualified job guarantee put tremendous pressure on senior management to grow sales. It would be essential for Art and his team to grow sales and carry forward D. Hayes Murphy's commitment to protect the jobs of all associates.[19]

Key Points for Senior Managers

- Wiremold's strategy was to become a leading time-based competitor.
- The strategy was simple and transcends company or industry boundaries.
- The measures associated with the strategy were specific and would stretch organizational capabilities, and require associates and managers to learn new ways to do work.
- The Wiremold Company had a corporate purpose that balanced the interests of key stakeholders.
- The Toyota Production System was the means used to achieve the strategy and thus capture the opportunities shown in Table 1-3 and Table 2-2.
- The Toyota Production System was deployed across Wiremold as a complete management system.

Notes

1. Productivity Inc. was founded in Greenwich, CT, in 1979 by Norman Bodek. He formed the company to educate business leaders in Japanese industrial management practices. Its principal activities were publishing newsletters and books, running national conferences and seminars, and organizing study tours in which U.S. business executives would visit Japanese companies to learn how they achieved such remarkable improvements in productivity and quality over the prior 20 years. In 1984, Bodek created a separate company called Productivity Press, Inc., in Cambridge, MA, which was later moved to Portland, OR. Its mission was to bring Japanese management methods to the American business audience. Productivity Press would do this by publishing English translations of Japanese books written by management practitioners and consultants that described the Toyota Production System and other Japanese management practices. Productivity Press Inc. published the classics on Lean management including the works of Dr. Shigeo Shingo, Taiichi Ohno, Seichi Nakjima, and others. Productivity Inc. and Productivity Press, Inc. were combined in 1995 and then sold to The Kraus Organization, Ltd., in 1999. Bodek, in a conversation with Emiliani on 2 January 2002, said that Art Byrne was one of the few managers that fulfilled the mission of Productivity Press by applying the magic of the Toyota Production System at Wiremold. The classic texts by Taiichi Ohno and Shigeo Shingo are available at http://www.productivityinc.com.

2. The complete citations are: *The Toyota Production System*, Taiichi Ohno, Productivity Press, Portland, OR, 1988; *A Revolution in Manufacturing: The SMED System*, Shigeo Shingo, Productivity Press, Portland, OR, 1985; *A Study of the Toyota Production System*, Shigeo Shingo, Productivity Press, Portland, OR, 1989. See the Recommended Reading section for additional titles.

3. Shingijutsu Co., Ltd. was formed in October 1987 by three of Taiichi Ohno's premier students: Mr. Yoshiki Iwata (d. 2001), Mr. Chihiro Nakao, and Mr. Akira Takenaka, reportedly at the behest of Mr. Taiichi Ohno. Its first U.S. consulting engagement was with The Jacobs Chuck Manufacturing Company (Clemson, SC) and its sister company The Jacobs Vehicle Equipment Company (Bloomfield, CT), both units of Danaher Corporation (both reporting to Art Byrne), in summer of 1988. The Japanese word "shingijutsu" means "new technology," reflecting the view that the Toyota Production System was a new management technology. For more information, see http://www.shingijutsu.co.jp/indx_e.htm. Pages 128–131 of the book *Lean Thinking* by J. Womack and D. Jones (Simon & Schuster, 1996) recounts how, in early 1988, Mr. Iwata was one of several teachers for a week-long seminar held at the Hartford Graduate Center in Hartford, CT (the name was changed to "Rensselaer at Hartford" in 1997). Several executives from The Jacobs Chuck Manufacturing Company (now called "The Jacobs Vehicle Systems Company," a Danaher Corp. business unit) attended the workshop. The story goes on to describe how George Koenigsaecker, Bob Pentland, and Art Byrne finally convinced a very reluctant Iwata-san to provide kaizen consulting services to Danaher.

4. A Lean transformation is not dependent on corporate ownership structure: i.e. public or private. In both cases, management must inform shareholders of the broad range of issues and opportunities arising from the Lean transformation. Danaher Corporation's (NYSE: DHR) Lean transformation, for example, involved extensive communication with investment analysts by the CEO, the CFO, and the VP in charge of the Danaher Business System (DBS). They conducted factory tours, gave workshops and presentations, and held investor kaizens where investment analysts would participate as team members. Source: Mark DeLuzio, former Corporate Vice President, Danaher Business System, Danaher Corporation. See http://www.danaher.com.

5. The 5C's are the five essential components of good housekeeping in the workplace. It is an abbreviation used by Hitachi, Ltd. for: clear, categorize, clean, consistent, and continuous (coaching and discipline). It is a variation of the 5S's, which is an essential element of the Toyota Production System, and stands for (in Japanese): seiri (sort), seiton (straighten), seiso (scrub), seiketsu (systematize), and shitsuke (self-discipline). See *Gemba Kaizen*, M. Imai, McGraw-Hill, New York, NY, 1997, Chapter 5. The 5S's, however, are more than just good housekeeping. Involvement in kaizen will provide a deeper understanding of the 5S's and how they favorably impact most of the line items contained in an income statement, statement of cash flows, and balance sheet.

6. Management can create a disincentive for participation in improvement activities if individual manufacturing areas have to incur the cost of kaizen consulting services. Assigning the cost to the CEO's office removes an important barrier; no one can say they didn't want to do kaizen because it would hurt their business results.

7. This is neither an endorsement nor refutation of vision or mission statements. Rather, it is simply to indicate that corporate purpose may not be contained in these types of statements. The Wiremold Company did not have a vision or mission statement while under Art Byrne's leadership.

8. An important examination of Toyota Motor Corporation's corporate purpose is presented in *Corporate Purpose: Why it Matters More Than Strategy*, S. Basu, Garland Publishing, Inc., New York, NY, 1999. Basu

finds that Toyota's corporate purpose is not to make cars or to make money. Rather, their corporate purpose (abridged) is: 1) [to be a] well-balanced corporation; 2) employee care; 3) community care.

9. Where "maximize shareholder value" is interpreted by management in a literal (i.e. purely financial) sense, versus a non-literal interpretation (i.e. a balance of financial, market share, quality, lead-time, customer satisfaction, etc.).

10. See Chapter 5, Note 4.

11. *The Wiremold Company, A Century of Solutions,* J. Smith, published by The Wiremold Company, West Hartford, CT, 2000, pp. 24, 20, 30, 7, and 96, respectively.

12. Called "behavioral waste," also known as the "eighth waste." See "Lean Behaviors," M.L. Emiliani, *Management Decision,* Vol. 36, No. 9, 1998, pp. 615–631.

13. *Toyota Production System,* T. Ohno, Productivity Press, Portland, OR, 1988, p. 4.

14. See "Cracking the Code of Business," M.L. Emiliani, *Management Decision,* Vol. 38, No. 2, 2000, pp. 60–79.

15. In the Lean management system, the key goals are to eliminate waste and create value for end-use customers. Conflict, when it occurs, is normally related to achieving these goals. Conventional management practices are rife with arbitrary conflict due to office politics, bias and prejudice (particularly as it relates to historical inability of different functions to work together such as marketing and manufacturing or engineering and manufacturing), ego-driven decisions, selfishness, inaction, etc.

16. The time-based competition strategy is applicable to a wide variety of industries and results in lower costs, greater pricing power, and higher market share. While most companies in an industry segment do well when business conditions are good, companies that excel at time-based competition typically outperform rivals in a recession. Examples of companies that have successfully deployed time-based strategies and become perennially strong competitors include: Automotive — Toyota and Honda; Air Travel — Southwest Airlines; Computers — Dell Computer; Clothing — Zara; Big-Box Retailing — Wal-Mart; Television News — CNN (though CNN's advantage has eroded in recent years); Auto Insurance — Progressive; and Overnight Parcel Delivery — FedEx (though FedEx's advantage has eroded in recent years)

17. Surprisingly, many batch-and-queue businesses, particularly large publicly owned businesses, do not have a strategy. This is because the overarching goal is to "maximize shareholder value," which can be achieved in the absence of a business strategy. See Table 1 in "Cracking the Code of Business," M.L. Emiliani, *Management Decision,* Vol. 38, No. 2, 2000, pp. 60–79, and see Chapter 5, Note 4.

18. From the late 1940's to around 1970, Toyota's production method was opposed by many people and referred to internally as the "abominable Ohno production system" (see *Just-In-Time for Today and Tomorrow,* T. Ohno and S. Mito, Productivity Press, Portland, OR, 1988, p. 97), as "The Mustache's Methods" (see *Against All Odds,* Y. Togo and W. Wartman, St. Martin's Press, New York, NY, 1993, p. 198), or as simply "Ohno's production system" or "the Ohno system" (see *Workplace Management,* T. Ohno, Productivity press, Cambridge, MA, 1988, p. 77). It was not until the oil crisis in 1973 that the Toyota Production System (TPS) started to become known to people outside of Toyota Motor Corporation. While the name of the production method is "Toyota Production System," it is, in fact, a comprehensive management system (see *Toyota Management System,* Y. Monden, Productivity Press, Portland, OR, 1993). Mr. Ohno frequently referred to TPS as a "management system" (see *Toyota Production System,* T. Ohno, Productivity Press, Portland, OR, 1988, p. xv; *Just-In-Time For Today and Tomorrow,* T. Ohno, Productivity Press, Portland, OR, 1988, p. xi; and T. Ohno in *NPS: New Production System,* I. Shinohara, Productivity Press, Cambridge, MA, 1988, p. 153 and 155). The word "production" in the name makes it difficult for most people to fully understand its true scope and meaning. It also gives managers responsible for non-operating service and support activities a reason to think that TPS does not apply to them. Unfortunately, this narrow view is quite common. However, this simple distinction gives Toyota, and precious few other companies that truly understand TPS, enormous competitive advantage.

19. During the Great Depression (1929–1933), D. Hayes Murphy made a decision that he would not lay off any employees unless he had no choice. Employees washed windows and swept floors to keep busy. This decision resulted in endless goodwill in the community, which then would help Wiremold recover quickly — benefiting customers and investors — when economic conditions improved. This type of leadership behavior is characteristic of, but not limited to family-owned businesses. It is interesting to contemplate why, in the U.S., "family values" are considered so virtuous in a family setting, yet for the most part reviled when applied to a public company business setting — particularly over the last 15–20 years. The incongruity deserves to be critically questioned, particularly in light of the post-1999 economic turmoil, accounting scandals, stock-option overhang, and large-scale business bankruptcies in the U.S. that have had widespread negative impact on key stakeholders such as employees, suppliers, investors, customers, and communities.

Explanation of Exhibit 2-1

The following is a note written by D. Hayes Murphy to "fellow-workers," dated June 19, 1953, and enclosed with the employees' quarterly profit sharing checks. It discusses how errors increase costs, and describes an example of how cooperation between people results in improved outcomes for both employees and customers. If such cooperation is not achieved, then customers may stop sending orders to Wiremold, which will reduce the amount of profit sharing available to employees. He clearly showed what's in it for them.

Mr. Murphy was careful to point out that he was not blaming anyone for errors, as everybody "will occasionally make a slip." Rather, he encouraged greater cooperation between employees to "correct past mistakes and avoid making them in the future," which will result in a higher share of the profits. Importantly, Mr. Murphy saw profit sharing as a key principle for managing a business and an important way to solve world problems, presumably related to the then-growing threat of Communism.

Written almost fifty years ago, this letter still rings true. It demonstrates that the leadership of The Wiremold Company has long understood that focusing on customer satisfaction is how higher profits are achieved, and that waste comes at a very high cost to all key stakeholders.

Exhibit 2-1

THE WIREMOLD COMPANY
Hartford 10, Conn.

June 19, 1953

54th Quarterly Report to Wiremold Profit Sharers

Dear Fellow-Workers:

When you think of the problems of the management of our business, you must wonder how it is possible to pay high wages, high employee benefits (average, 40¢ per hour) and, on top of all this, a share of the profits. The secret is in the immortal words of Woodrow Wilson, "The highest form of efficiency is the spontaneous cooperation of a free people."

This immediately suggests the thought that if we have that kind of efficiency, how does it happen that we make so many mistakes that are so costly - mistakes that take money right out of the Profit Sharing pocket?

Altogether too many mistakes are made, and sometimes we neglect a chance to correct an error before it causes trouble. However, mistakes are not made on purpose and we are trying to learn something from each one we make so as to avoid making the same mistake twice. Unless we do learn this lesson, our customers will buy elsewhere.

We are not pointing a finger at anyone in particular because all humans who are active in getting things done will occasionally make a slip - and this includes every single one of us.

So let us not be discouraged but rather let us, as free people, strive for "spontaneous cooperation" by helping each other to correct past mistakes and avoid making them in the future.

Right in our own shop we have a fine example of how this may be accomplished. Realizing that it is impossible for any inspection department to insure a perfect product without the support and cooperation of all of our people, our foremen have assumed the responsibility of doing more of the basic inspection at the points where the parts are made, where they are assembled, where they are packed and shipped, and they are encouraging the

operators to do the same. This puts everybody into the game, and the results
have already been excellent. Everybody is responding with a will. We are
getting a better finished product, and the inspection job, instead of being a
barrel of headaches, is now a pleasure for those who work at it.

This should mean that our customers will be better pleased than ever
with the things we make. The customer is the boss - keep him happy and he
will keep sending his orders to us.

Here is another things we can be proud of: Although our costs have
been going up for a long time, our prices have not been raised since 1950.
Why? Because we have been working hard to improve our methods and equipment.

Now we are faced with a new hike in costs. Shall we be forced to
increase our prices? If so, will our customers continue to buy?

If we are to continue to succeed, each one of us must be more careful,
more efficient, and more cooperative. The way you handle your job is of vital
importance to the success of our business.

What is there in it for you if you do all these things? Answer:
Peace of mind and a share of the profits.

I am firmly convinced that profit sharing is the right way to manage
a business. I am just as firmly convinced that the profit sharing principle,
if generally applied, would solve the problems that are now keeping the entire
world in misery. . . . . If you agree, please help me to make our Company
a model of efficiency based on Profit Sharing.

For the Profit Sharing quarter ending May 31, your share is enclosed -
5.88% of straight-time earnings.

Yours very truly,

President

DHM:SHH
Enclosure

Withholding and Old Age Benefit
Taxes have been deducted.

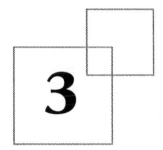

THE FIRST PRIORITY: KAIZEN

Eliminating Waste

Taiichi Ohno (b.1912–d.1990) is credited with developing the Toyota Production System as it is known today. Shigeo Shingo (b.1909–d.1990) made many important contributions, particularly regarding set-up reduction. Ohno's book, *Toyota Production System*, played an important role in shaping Art Byrne's thinking and subsequent leadership at Wiremold. In that book, Mr. Ohno said:

> "The basis of the Toyota production system is the absolute elimination of waste."[1]

Waste, called "muda" in Japanese, is any activity that does not add value to a product or service and can therefore be eliminated.[2] Mr. Ohno showed that there are two types of work: value-added and non-value added (Figure 3-1). Value-added work involves processing, such as changing the shape of raw materials or parts to make products. Non-value added work is work that must be done under present work conditions but does not add value. Mr. Ohno identified seven types of waste:

- Overproduction   *Making more products than can be sold*
- Waiting   *Operators or machines waiting*
- Transportation   *Transporting parts*
- Processing   *Processing itself*
- Inventories   *Raw material, work-in-process, and finished goods*
- Moving   *Operator and machine movement*
- Defects   *Making defective products*

The process for eliminating the seven wastes is "kaizen," the Japanese word for continuous improvement.[3] Kaizen is used to visibly differentiate between value-added work, non-value added but necessary work, and waste, with a goal of performing only value-added work.[4] Eliminating waste improves responsiveness to customer demand, the quality of the product or service, and results in better working conditions.

Figure 3-1 Value-Added Work, Non-Value Added But Necessary Work, and Waste[5]

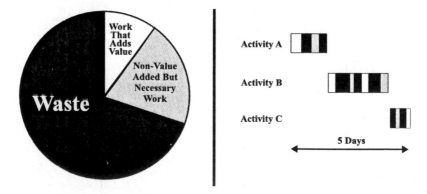

Although the original context is manufacturing, these seven wastes apply to any business and any process. Mr. Ohno realized the Toyota Production System was a management system, not limited simply to manufacturing operations or businesses that manufacture products. He said:

> "The Toyota production system, however, is not just a production system. I am confident it will reveal its strengths as a management system...[6]

> The original concepts behind the Toyota production system were aimed at the entirety — not at a part — of a company's organization... a total management system — across industry boundaries, whether they manufacture goods or handle information — across companies...as large as Toyota or as small as the local dry cleaner...[7]

> Companies make a big mistake in implementing the Toyota production system thinking that it is just a production method. The Toyota production method won't work unless it is used as an overall management system. The Toyota production system is not something that can be used only on the production floors. The belief that it is only a production method is fundamentally wrong... those who decide to implement the Toyota production system must be fully committed. If you try to adopt only the 'good parts,' you'll fail."[8]

People who view Lean as just "a manufacturing thing" suffer a great misunderstanding. It is a dangerous trap that befalls just about every manager, but not Art Byrne. Why not? It is because Art understood, from reading the books by Ohno and Shingo and his practice of Lean at Danaher, that to make this management system work, he and his management team had to behave in a manner consistent with what they espoused — the elimination of waste.

Art understood that inconsistent management behaviors were wasteful and would give associates reasons not to participate in the Lean transformation. Arrogance by senior management would breed animosity and contempt. He and his managers had to behave in less wasteful ways[9] if they were to succeed. Their participation in kaizen would demonstrate to everyone that they were genuinely interested in continuous improvement and life-long learning. According to Tom Goetter:

> "There is a 'don't shoot the messenger policy' here at Wiremold. We continuously enforce it when people bring us bad news. Of course we could jump all over them, but then they will never give us bad news. Instead, people will start padding their sales reports. If they think they can sell 6, they will tell you they can sell 3. So when they sell 4, they're heroes. They'll pad their forecast, their product's cost,

how long it takes to make a part, engineering estimates, product development time, etc. So if you blame people, you create the kind of atmosphere where no one will fail. That's not good.

The stretch-goal mentality at Wiremold says that you are going to fail a large part of the time. You are going to fall short of the stated goal, but that's OK because on average we are leaping farther and faster than most companies. As long as we focus on process, as long as we focus on stretch goals, we are going to continue to out-perform our competitors in the marketplace. The Lean philosophy recognizes that you are not always going to succeed. Therefore, people are going to talk candidly about the bad news and keep on trying."

The First Priority

Art Byrne reflected on the goals that he had in mind for Wiremold (Table 1-3) and considered how to communicate them to associates. Beyond simply articulating the goals, he would personally demonstrate commitment to achieving them through immediate personal involvement.

His first priority was to begin operational improvement at the West Hartford plant. The second was to introduce new products using a fast cycle product development process. The key to both would be to create an operational structure in West Hartford so that improvement would become regular practice. Art was aware that a single kaizen had been attempted a few years earlier and resulted in some improvements in manufacturing. However, after a few weeks, the operation had reverted to its former methods. Orry Fiume recalled the very first kaizen at Wiremold in 1989:

> "In 1989, the Hartford Graduate Center [now known as Rensselaer at Hartford] was sponsoring a seminar with Mr. Imai[10] and Mr. Iwata, where I became familiar with kaizen. And I realized at that point that the kaizen process represented the 'how to' of the Deming philosophy. And so I came back to work saying that kaizen is a good thing. The seminar was five days long. The first couple of days were classroom training, and then they would go into a local company and actually do a kaizen. So I volunteered Wiremold for the next session and we had a kaizen."

In the seminar at the Hartford Graduate Center, Orry would learn about the three super-ordinate principles of kaizen:

- Process and results vs. just results
- Total system focus vs. single function focus
- Non-blaming / non-judgmental vs. blame

Mr. Imai taught him that *kaizen starts with people.* Orry learned that being non-judgmental and focusing on the process rather than people would result in the following benefits: the real issues would emerge, negative blaming would decrease, trust and communication would increase, and associates' capabilities would increase. Orry said this about Wiremold's first experience with kaizen:

> "I was concerned at the time that people were going to say, 'Total Quality Management was the old program of the month and kaizen is the new program of the month.' So I gave a short seminar on kaizen and finished it by saying that these are Deming's 14 principles, and this is the 'how to' within kaizen that matches each principle. I was able to find a match for 13 of Deming's 14 principles. I also tried to get the management group, including middle management, to understand that we were not abandoning TQM.

> But the operations people just didn't latch on to it. They didn't understand how to use it and so it never went anywhere. We continued to try again in 1990, but we just didn't have anybody inside, including myself at that time, that knew how to do kaizen and how to sustain it."

If Wiremold was to make a successful transformation to Lean, Art knew that there would have to be a significant change in how associates viewed their work and the thinking used to solve problems. As a first very visible step, he did away with the traditional August factory shut-down because it was the company's busiest month of the year. Shutting down in August meant that the company had to forecast, in May or June, its sales mix and the volume of demand for August, and build an inventory of products that customers *might* buy.

Not surprisingly, there were numerous complaints from customers because some items they needed immediately were not available from Wiremold's distributors due to stock-outs. Some special orders placed months earlier remained unfilled because the components had not yet been manufactured. Associates in West Hartford were left combing the warehouses in search of inventory to fill these customer orders. At the same time, production supervisors and sales reps had to sort through orders and distributor inventory, consisting of over 1,500 SKUs, in order to determine which items should be given priority when production resumed in September.

Wiremold's West Hartford plant produced a wide range of electrical components used to wire new buildings and to rewire existing buildings. All of its products were UL listed[11] and made of metal. The metal working operations included rolling mills, stamping presses, shaping machines, and punch presses, as well as various paint and assembly operations. All equipment was physically located with other equipment performing the same operation. Hourly associates[12] were assigned to a single functional department such as stamping, and became skilled at operating one type of machinery. Each department produced components needed for all assembled products.

The conventional standard cost and full absorption accounting method required that after a machine had been set up to produce a given SKU, then a large number of those parts should be made in order to ensure a low unit cost. Consequently, the operators had been trained to minimize the number of change-overs from one product type to another. An important result was that at any given time, there was a large amount of work-in-process (WIP) inventory of parts waiting to be assembled into final products, as well as a large finished goods inventory. The result was overproduction, the worst waste of all.

Art Byrne's prior experiences with Lean demonstrated that the way to reduce WIP was to use kaizen to reduce set-up times from hours to minutes.[13] Faster and more frequent set-ups would permit shorter production runs, reduce lead-times, and reduce the amount of WIP and finished goods inventory. This would deliver immediate cash from inventory reductions, cost savings, and higher quality goods. It also would reduce the amount of physical space needed for storing inventory.

To realize the cost savings, there needed to be hundreds of kaizens, most lasting two to five days, over many years. While most managers would see this as a barrier, Art saw it as a great opportunity. Kaizen would deliver not only near-term cost savings, but would become the hands-on learning experience that helps eliminate traditional barriers to change. Kaizen would teach both managers and associates new ways to think about their work and how to effectively solve everyday business problems.

Art Byrne further knew that if the factory floor at Wiremold were reorganized into product families, then each of the new cross-functional product line teams would become responsible for all of the activities required to design, make, and ship every item within the product family. The introduction of U-shaped manufacturing cells, rapid change-overs, and one-piece flow would be essential for accomplishing this goal. Wiremold could then build only those items needed to replenish the stock sold by its distributors. The reorganization of people and equipment would reduce lead times from months to a few days, resulting in lower inventory levels, fewer defects, higher fill rates, and improved customer satisfaction. This change in equipment layout, from single-process islands to multi-process manufacturing cells, would require the relocation of every piece of equipment. Kaizen also would be the process used to determine cell layout.

There were, however, four important preconditions to making these changes:

- Selecting the right opportunities for kaizen
- Conducting the kaizen training
- Selecting team leaders
- Identifying cross-functional team members

Selecting the First Kaizens

The initial kaizens had to be carefully identified because poor selection of improvement opportunities would result in mediocre outcomes that would discourage future participation by managers and associates. Thus, improvement opportunities should be both important and very visible. There should be big problems to solve and big opportunities for success. In other words, the criterion for selecting kaizens was based on opportunities to eliminate waste.[14] Art Byrne reflected on some of the first kaizens that he had participated in at Danaher Corporation, which had not been carefully selected. When the kaizen consultants from Shingijutsu Co., Ltd. — Mr. Iwata, Mr. Nakao, and Mr. Takenaka — walked into the plant and spotted more important opportunities, it created a lot of controversy. Art Byrne described the typical reaction:

> "At that time, Iwata, Nakao, and Takenaka weren't used to working in the United States. They were pretty rough with people. They have since done a great deal more work with Americans and they have changed. But back in the 1980s, they would say things like: 'You are an idiot! You don't know anything! Why are you doing this? You're stupid!' Americans perceived that as insulting, but that was the way they worked."[15]

The managers at Wiremold were very disappointed when they were unable to achieve their goals with Total Quality Management (TQM) and the one kaizen held two years earlier. So, Art Byrne decided to prevent negative emotional responses by identifying the opportunities for kaizen himself for the first few years, though he was open to suggestions, and leading both the kaizen training and all the initial kaizens. Orry Fiume recalled the first kaizen that Art facilitated:

> "The first kaizen that Art led was an administrative process: how do the orders come from the customers, what do we do with them, how do we get them through the system, and how do we get the order to the customer? The idea is that if there is a delay in getting the order into the system, then that is a problem all by itself which needs to be corrected. And then once it is in the system, does the factory have any visibility to it? Recognize that what Art wanted to achieve in the future was the ability to 'sell one, make one.' If the factory doesn't have the ability to see what the orders are, then you can never get to that point. So that was the first kaizen we ever did.
>
> People keep thinking of Lean as a manufacturing thing. The fact that the first kaizen we did was on the order entry process tells you something very significant. It sent a message from the very beginning that this is a way of running a business, not just how to set up a machine or how to set up a manufacturing cell in the factory."

Orry Fiume recalled a talk that he gave several years later at Rensselaer in

Hartford to a group of young employees in a fast-track management program from a local multi-billion dollar manufacturer. They were complaining that they had achieved little improvement in recent kaizens and therefore did not believe that the process actually worked.

> "So I asked them, 'What are you working on?' They gave me some examples of the things they were working on which didn't make a lot of sense. I asked, 'How did you pick those areas?' They said, 'We went around and asked the supervisors and they told us what we should work on.' I said, 'Well, there's your problem.' In most companies people get promoted, in part, based on a perception of how few problems they have, which shows that they're a good manager. So you've got supervisors who have been doing this type of work for their whole life, and their promotions are dependent on demonstrating that they can run an operation without problems. And now you want them to expose their problems? Without fear of retribution? In the past, supervisors got fired if they had a lot of problems. It's crazy. They'll never expose the problems in that environment. They only will put their hand up and say, 'Hey, I've got a problem over here, I need some help' once they understand that they can do that without the fear of being fired or side-tracked. So initially, management has to select the areas to be worked on. Which means you need a management that has a set of eyes that can see the waste. And then you can do a kaizen and get the gains without anybody getting hurt. There has to be no blame."

Selecting the initial kaizens was very important in two key ways. First, Art Byrne wanted to have some early successes. Second, and perhaps more importantly, he wanted to send the message to the entire workforce that management was serious about kaizen and deeply committed to it. Art Byrne explained:

> "Most managers are afraid of change in the first place. As a result, there is a strong tendency to go off in a corner and pick a small, unimportant example so that in case they are asked they can say, 'Oh yes, we are doing it. Want to come over here and see?' Their real hope, of course, is that this whole kaizen idea will go away like all other flavor-of-the-month approaches have, and they would have been politically responsive without having to disrupt their business too much. What we always try to do, on the other hand, is go after the biggest, most important product lines early on. First of all, you get the most gains if you deal with the products that account for 50–70% of your sales or profit. More importantly, you send a strong message to the organization that you are serious; that this is not going to go away and become another flavor-of-the-month. In addition,

because you are aggressively working on the core of your business, everyone knows that you can't afford to mess it up. You get everyone's attention very quickly."

Conducting the Training

Kaizen is designed to achieve multiple objectives simultaneously. Two key objectives are to improve productivity and reduce costs through innovation by using the valuable reservoir of low-cost ideas possessed by the people who do the work, as well as by those who are not familiar with the work. Participants gain explicit knowledge of the methods used to achieve double or triple-digit improvement in productivity. They learn by doing, not by reading about it or listening in a classroom.

The kaizens had a specific set of actionable goals, cross-functional teams to achieve them, and a limited amount of time, usually two to five days, in which to achieve the goals. Each kaizen began with a one- or two-day training session conducted by Art, who was the only person in the company with the knowledge to do it. With the CEO doing the training, it was clear to everyone that management was serious and that kaizen was not the next "flavor of the month" program. Art guided an analysis of the problem to be solved using simple tools[16] (see Exhibits 3-1 to 3-9 at the end of Chapter 3) and measures, and helped establish stretch goals in preparation for kaizen. It is notable that there were no specific cost savings targets, as associates often perceive dollar measures as abstract. So Wiremold set targets based on measures related to the quantity of output and the quantity of resources consumed to improve productivity, rather than dollars.[17] The objective was to get value-added activities to flow without interruption by eliminating waste.[18]

Kaizen also was used to achieve intangible objectives, specifically, to communicate to everyone at Wiremold, through experiential learning, that:

- Business as usual was no longer viable nor sensible
- There would be changes in how work was performed; people's jobs would change
- Kaizen overcomes biases for non-action
- Kaizen would be a positive experience

This communication was better understood when the leader demonstrated it in actual practice. Thus, it was very important for Art to be a visible participant in the early kaizens. The CEO's participation would efficiently convey the tacit knowledge that he learned in previous kaizens, elevate the level of commitment from rhetoric to participation, and allow associates to interact with him on the same level. This opened important avenues of dialogue that would later help sustain interest in continuous improvement.

In reflecting on his prior experiences, Art considered himself to be well enough trained by Shingijutsu *sensei*, the Japanese word for teacher, that he could personally deliver the initial kaizen training.[19] When he considered the delicacy of introducing kaizen in an organization already unsettled by its failure to achieve operating improvements as well as a change in leadership, he decided to conduct the training and facilitate the first kaizens himself. Art Byrne recalled the situation:

> "I didn't want to bring the Japanese consultants in until we had a few kaizens under our belts and people could understand what this was. I was very concerned about the possibility that they might mistakenly perceive that I was hiding behind some consultants who were there for the purpose of insulting them. Then they would really have been turned off. I wanted people to understand kaizen and the big gains that were possible, so in case they were insulted they would not take it the wrong way.

> The guys from Shingijutsu were simply the best I had ever seen — still are for that matter. My game plan was to prepare the way for introducing them to the people at Wiremold. And that happened in a matter of months. All four of those guys, Iwata, Nakao, Takenaka, and Niwa, who I met a little later than the first three, became life-long friends of mine."

Judy Seyler recounted the initial training and kaizen activities:

> "Art did the training. He was the only one in the company who knew what to do. He put together the training notebook. He developed the three-day training program for about 150 of our associates including foremen, supervisors, and others participating in the initial kaizens, including the union leadership. They would know what this was all about. No mystery. And in that first session of training, he did three different classes. At the end of each one, he would lead a kaizen so that we could immediately see what he was teaching in the classroom."

Selecting Product Line Team Leaders

Prior to the first training and kaizen, Wiremold changed from a functional organization to a product line team structure. It took some time to identify all the members of each new product line team, but the team leaders were named quickly and given responsibility and authority for the performance of product families. They also would be intimately involved with converting the factory floor from single-process islands to multi-process manufacturing cells, which supported the new Wiremold organization.[20]

These individuals needed to be named within Art Byrne's first month on the job. Since he had no significant personal knowledge of potential candidates, he used a group nomination and selection process. Art called a meeting of the five senior managers who reported directly to him and described the need for the new organization. The team leader of a product line group would run the product line as if it were his or her business. Each team leader would be measured on defect reduction, inventory turns, working to the rate of customer demand (called "takt time"), on-time delivery, productivity, and visual controls. They also would own the inventory all the way to the customer.

The four key criteria for selecting product line team leaders were:

- Good job performance in the past
- High energy level
- Good people skills
- Ability to work with people above and below them in pay grade or job responsibility

Notably, there was no requirement for previous experience in manufacturing. In fact, this could be a liability since traditional factory foremen often resisted assuming responsibilities beyond keeping everybody busy and enforcing discipline. Art's experience at Danaher taught him that the people who met these four criteria were, in most cases, capable of becoming effective team leaders regardless of their prior functional work experience.

From their knowledge of the company's human resources, Art's direct reports identified six to eight product and support line team leaders, of whom only two or three were working in manufacturing. The others came from marketing, finance, customer service, human resources, and production planning. Art Byrne explained:

> "Personal characteristics were really important in that selection process. Some of the people we selected did not work out too well and had to be replaced. The young man from marketing was one of those. He turned out to have an attitude problem — haughtiness because he was a college graduate — and that he was not going to work on the factory floor. He couldn't help but talk down to our production associates, even though his upwards communications were excellent. Getting people who could work across the organization into these positions was essential to the future success of kaizen and the whole Lean effort."

Selecting Cross-Functional Teams for Kaizen

Three distinct kaizen activities would run simultaneously; two in operations and one in the front office. Each kaizen team had a designated team leader and was staffed with ten to twelve additional associates. The salary and hourly associates participating in the initial kaizens were selected according to a schedule determined by Art Byrne, his direct reports, and the product line team leaders. The three key criteria for selection included a willingness to learn, try new things, and work hard. Several months later, after achieving success in various areas, participation would be spread more widely across the organization. Art Byrne stressed the importance of making sure that no one could refuse to be on a kaizen team:

> "One rule that was established early on was that kaizen partic-ipation was like jury duty — if you were called, you could not say 'no.' This was very important because otherwise people will say that they are too busy to participate in kaizen and put it off and say, 'how about later?' This attitude is self-defeating, as it allows people to say, 'I'm too busy to improve.'"

The selection of people for each kaizen team was an important task. All vice presidents participated in the first kaizen training, and each would be assigned to a kaizen unrelated to his or her functional area — but not as the team leader. For kaizens held in the factory, each team typically would be composed of a senior manager, one or two engineers, one to three operators in the area, a toolmaker, a mechanic, and associates from other support functions such as engineering, sales, and finance to make up the balance. For kaizens in the front office, each team would typically be composed of a senior manager, one or two engineers, one to three associates in the work area, an information systems as-sociate, and associates from the shop floor. It was expected that by year-end, every associate would participate in at least one kaizen. Some people ended up participating in many more. Orry Fiume said:

> "You can't have a successful kaizen when the team is made up of only the people that work in that area. When someone on the kaizen team asks the question, 'Why do you do it that way' to a team that is made up of only people that are working in that area, their ability to understand why they do something is very limited. They do what they do because that's the way they've al-ways done it. An outsider has the luxury of asking dumb ques-tions and also being able to see through a dumb answer. So when somebody says, 'Why do you do it that way,' you get an an-swer and think about it for a minute and say, 'I'm not sure I un-derstand why you do it that way.' By asking 'why' five or six times, you realize that there is no good reason. And that's how you start uncovering waste. By having the kaizen team com-prised of people from different functions and disciplines, it al-lows you to improve much, much faster because the people that don't work in that area are able to see through the static and they're less likely to accept an answer that doesn't make sense. That's true of an administrative kaizen too. If we do a kaizen in the administrative areas, we want people from the factory to participate. Kaizens on the factory floor are easy compared to the ones in the office. You start dealing in paper processes and it's hard to see what is going on sometimes."

Importantly, this approach accelerated the speed of understanding of kaizen across the two levels of the newly flattened organization. Further, associates responsible for processes upstream or downstream of the kaizen gained a clear understanding of how their work processes limited the ability of the operator to do his or her work effectively. This taught people to improve the entire business system, rather than just their individual functional areas.

Recall that one of the purposes of the training session was to identify a problem and gather data. A facilitator helped each team with this pre-kaizen activity and provided assistance in how to use the various new methods for analyzing problems. The facilitator also helped set goals that were documented in a one-page table called the "Kaizen Target Sheet" (see Exhibit 3-5; also called "Target Progress Report"). This table was used throughout the kaizen to track progress day-by-day on such key items as reduction in square footage, inventory/WIP, operator walking distance, part travel distance, lead time (in days), cycle time, defects, manpower, and improvement in productivity.

The teams gathered on the first morning of the kaizen in a conference room and the team leader reported their findings to the sensei, Art Byrne or Bill Moffitt.[21] Art asked questions and made comments to ensure that the kaizen team understood the problem and to provide focus. The team and sensei then proceeded to the work area to begin implementing low-cost solutions to the previously identified problems. Throughout each day of the kaizen, Art moved from team-to-team and provided guidance. His role was not to tell them the answer, but rather to teach them how to solve their own problems. At the end of each day the team leader gave an oral progress report to the sensei, as well as various Wiremold mid- and senior-level managers.

The First Kaizens

Steve Maynard became Vice President of Engineering, the department responsible for the new product development process, in November 1989. He recounted his first kaizen experience in 1991:

> "There was a packed room with all the vice presidents, the new product line team leaders, and other people. Art was up there at the head of the room with slides doing the training. Then we went out onto the factory floor and met Bill Moffitt, a consultant who worked with us. There were about eight people on the team, a mix of people from the factory and people from different departments in the company. I had never looked at set-up times before, and here we were working on a big 150-ton press.
>
> Before Art came, there had been a group working at the particular press our team was looking at. They had gotten the

set-up time down from four hours to two. After five days, our team reduced the set-up time to ten minutes. I had no prior knowledge of a change-over process until the kaizen. When we videotaped the process and wrote down the actual operations, it became very evident what and where the waste was. So we moved as much of the change-over process outside the machine as possible [i.e. when the machine was not in operation] to reduce the amount of time that we had the machine tied-up during the changeover. As we progressed through the week, it became very clear what to do: buy a special wrench for just this machine, put two people on the change-over, put some marks on the fork lift at the right level so we didn't have to waste time adjusting the fork heights, and standardize the shut heights. It was during some of those first kaizens that we realized that the shut heights were all different and that that was costing us a bundle.

I remember I was kind of nervous at the time because I think I wanted to make a good impression as the senior person on the team. I knew that Bill Moffitt was assessing us to see if we were going to buy into this. I guess that's part of what you go through in this transition. As a manager you're trying to learn as fast as possible, but sometimes you are confused and don't want to look stupid. I'll be honest; it's simple, but it takes a while to digest. It took me years and several trips to Japan, working with Shingijutsu, to understand what appeared to be very simple concepts. You don't really understand the concepts until you immerse yourself in kaizen and do a lot of kaizen."

Rich Levesque described the early kaizens as follows:

"When Art first arrived, he said that the West Hartford plant had twice as much space as we needed. And here we were getting ready to buy another building. We were saying, 'This guy is looney.' But Art led the first kaizen event, and we had never seen anything like that; a CEO coming onto the shop floor, getting dirty, and moving machines. So that gave a lot of credibility to what he was talking about. People got the sense that he was probably making good decisions."

Art Byrne described the first kaizens:

"Orry Fiume, who had really bought into the concept of TQM and Deming, was a believer in what we were trying to do, but initially he objected to actually having to participate on a kaizen team. He said something like: 'Why do I want to do that? I don't know anything about set-up. What am I going to do out there?' And I said something like: 'Well, just go and be on the team. You'll be surprised at how much you are going to contribute.' His team went from a 90-minute set-up to a 5-minute set-up in the first week. Since he was an accountant, Orry decided to keep track of how much money it cost to make those changes. He told me it was about $105. So when the members of the management team have the personal experience with just how much can be accomplished in one week, then the enthusiasm for doing kaizen just becomes infectious. In a few months we had people pointing out problems and making suggestions for future kaizens."

Art Byrne knew that the early kaizens would produce big improvements in productivity. In the first two years some work areas were reconfigured as many as three or four times, each time yielding better results. Judy Scyler recalled her participation in one of the first kaizens:

"We were working on rolling mills out in the plant. Those machines would take something like 24 hours for a change-over. There would be a couple of people hanging around waiting for this and doing that. Then we did the kaizen and within 2 to 3 days had the change-over time down to about 2-hours with a group of 4 people. We made a video of it. I always thought it was a classic, because when I watched it, I just thought it was absolutely beautiful. It was almost like a ballet dance the way they took the rolls out and put another set in. As Art described it, it was like putting a videotape into a video cassette recorder; the rolls were all preset, all pre-measured, and they would just slide it in. They would run the first piece and it would be perfect."

Tom Fairbank commented on the importance of set-up reduction in Wiremold's Lean transformation:

"The one thing that affected us significantly was set-up reduction because it ultimately affects inventory and inventory turns. We found that if you can reduce the amount of time that it takes to respond from one customer's need to another customer's needs, the less inventory you have to keep and the higher the customer service level. The ability to reduce set-ups from 4 hours between jobs to 4 minutes is very powerful."

Table 3-1 summarizes the results of early kaizen activities related to set-up reduction.

Table 3-1 Set-Up Reduction Kaizen Results

| | Set-Up Time (minutes) | | |
	Before Kaizen	After Kaizen	% Reduction†
Rolling Mill	720	34	95
150 Ton Press	90	5	94
Punch Press	52	5	90
Hole Cut Mill	64	5	90
2.5 inch Extruder	180	19	89
Injection Molder	120	15	88

† All results were achieved after five days of kaizen and required virtually no capital spending.
  Source: The Wiremold Company

Figures 3-2 to 3-4 show the first three "Kaizen News" memos written by Art Byrne, dated November 1991, six weeks after his arrival. Orry Fiume recalled these early communications:

> "The first kaizen newsletter Art wrote said, 'We need to focus on eliminating waste so that the jobs we do are easier, that we have a cleaner and safer work environment, at the same time we can provide much better service to our customers both internal and external. We have emptied Building 2 in order to eliminate the waste of inventory that was stored there and to provide ourselves some needed turnaround space in anticipation of re-laying out our factory over the next year and a half.' So between the time Art arrived on September 23rd 1991 to November 5th 1991, Building 2 [one of four interconnected buildings at the West Hartford site] was emptied. That was like a tidal wave. It was so big and so visible, he just blew people away that you could even do it and do it that fast. It had an impact on the entire workforce that goes beyond words."

Kaizen also was used to improve non-factory processes. Orry Fiume described how kaizen can be applied to any activity:

> "Kaizen is a methodology of identifying and eliminating waste that will work for any process, whether it is a paper process that transforms information or a physical process that produces a product."

The results of early office kaizens include:

- Order entry   *Reduced time from days to hours*
- Mail room   *Reduced space 62%, JIT delivery of marketing materials, 66% improved brochure request fill rate, reduced consumption of office supplies by over 50%*

- Accounts payable   *Implemented one-piece flow to process most invoices in 24 hours*
- Finance office area   *Relocate office machines to reduce walking distance*
- Financial reporting   *Reduced financial closing time by 25%*
- Human resources   *Combined two forms into one to eliminate rework and relocated the files next to the person performing the activity*

In every circumstance, kaizen is not a one-time activity. It is repeated again and again as waste is identified or as business conditions change. Orry Fiume described the challenge of retaining an improvement:

> "The most difficult thing is to hold on to the gains that were made in the most recent kaizen. Even now, we still time every set-up, keep a record of it, and have those available on the factory floor. If we didn't do that, it would send a message that set-up time wasn't important any more, and 10 seconds would creep in here, and 20 seconds there, and pretty soon, we would be back to 30 minute or more set-up times."

The Shift From Results to Process Focus

In conventionally managed businesses, the primary emphasis is on achieving results because it ensures survival, at least for a while. There is little if anything that can be done within the context of batch-and-queue business practices to break free of the results focused orientation.[22] In general, companies that use this management practice are consumed by internal problems, rather than by creating value for end-use customers. The results focus orientation is deeply embedded, which makes it very difficult for people to understand processes or think about how to improve processes. People simply use whatever tools are available to achieve a "quick hit," which often conflicts with other business objectives.

In contrast, Lean is a much more disciplined management system whose focus is on processes designed to deliver value to end-use customers. While results are obviously very important, the processes used to achieve results are more important because they lead to sustainable results and also eliminate repetitive errors. Kevin Fahey spent much of his career working at companies focused on achieving results. He said this about some of the remarkable things that happen in a management system that enables people to focus on processes:

> "When you shift your focus to process rather than results, that creates a calming effect. And when you have a methodology with which to examine the processes and improve them, that adds

Figure 3-2 Wiremold Kaizen News

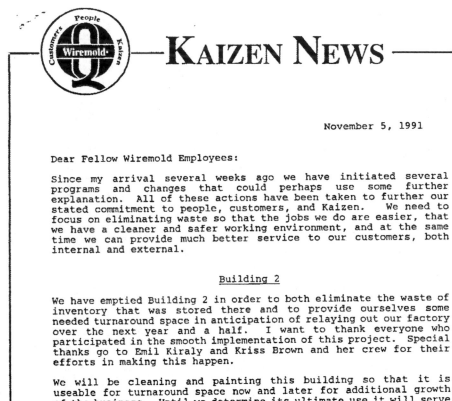

KAIZEN NEWS

November 5, 1991

Dear Fellow Wiremold Employees:

Since my arrival several weeks ago we have initiated several programs and changes that could perhaps use some further explanation. All of these actions have been taken to further our stated commitment to people, customers, and Kaizen. We need to focus on eliminating waste so that the jobs we do are easier, that we have a cleaner and safer working environment, and at the same time we can provide much better service to our customers, both internal and external.

<u>Building 2</u>

We have emptied Building 2 in order to both eliminate the waste of inventory that was stored there and to provide ourselves some needed turnaround space in anticipation of relaying out our factory over the next year and a half. I want to thank everyone who participated in the smooth implementation of this project. Special thanks go to Emil Kiraly and Kriss Brown and her crew for their efforts in making this happen.

We will be cleaning and painting this building so that it is useable for turnaround space now and later for additional growth of the business. Until we determine its ultimate use it will serve as an employee recreation area that should be kept clean at all times. We already have a couple of ping pong tables and a basketball hoop; we'd like your suggestions as to other recreational items that would get good use. Some of you have suggested having a Company-wide Christmas party in this space. That sounds good to me. Again, your ideas and help in organizing this are most welcome.

<u>Rocky Hill</u>

As we reorganize our manufacturing and eliminate the excess work in process inventory in West Hartford, we can consolidate the warehousing, which is currently in Rocky Hill, into the West Hartford facility. I hope that we can accomplish this in the next 6 to 8 months, but it may take longer. By consolidating our warehousing and shipping here in West Hartford, we can eliminate a lot of wasted movement, travel, and cost from our operation. At the same time, our customer service will improve dramatically. The plastic operation will remain, and hopefully grow rapidly, in Rocky Hill.

Figure 3-2 Wiremold Kaizen News, cont'd.

New Team Structure

As you know, we have recently reorganized the business into a team structure by specific product lines. The reason for this is primarily to provide each product team with a complete set of equipment to make its final product. Plugmold, for example, uses raceway from the rolling mill area and plastic parts from Rocky Hill. Under our new organization they will be assigned their own rolling mills and plastic molding machines and thus have total control of their finished product. This new structure should also speed communications as each team will meet with me and my staff once a week to review what has occurred during the preceding week and to make any decisions necessary to help us keep improving. We appear to have plenty of machines and equipment in house and don't anticipate buying a lot of new capital equipment, at least in this first phase.

Kaizen Training

Last Thursday and Friday we initiated our first Kaizen training. We will have a second group go through training this Thursday and Friday. In addition, this Thursday and Friday we will do our first Kaizen sessions on the factory floor. There will be three teams working on the following projects: 1) reducing set up on a press, 2) reducing set up on a rolling mill, and 3) the Plugmold product line. The people in these areas will be provided some initial training to help them understand how the process works. The two-day Kaizen session will be our basic approach to improvement as we move forward. It will serve as both an improvement activity and training for a broad cross section of our people. The focus will be on simplifying how we do things in order to eliminate any waste in our operations.

Open Door Policy

Although I have been on the road quite a bit meeting our customers and distributors, people have really been utilizing my open door policy when I have been here. I really appreciate this and thank you all for the excellent input to date. Please don't be shy -- continue to give me your ideas and suggestions as they are extremely valuable to me.

I apologize for any confusion these changes may have created in the short term. As we move forward, however, I am certain that it will prove to be a much more rational way to run our business.

Art Byrne

Figure 3-3 Wiremold Kaizen News

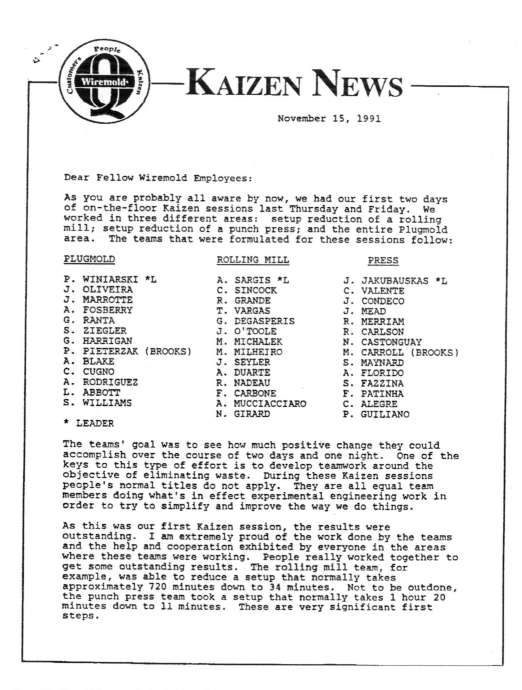

KAIZEN NEWS

November 15, 1991

Dear Fellow Wiremold Employees:

As you are probably all aware by now, we had our first two days
of on-the-floor Kaizen sessions last Thursday and Friday. We
worked in three different areas: setup reduction of a rolling
mill; setup reduction of a punch press; and the entire Plugmold
area. The teams that were formulated for these sessions follow:

PLUGMOLD	ROLLING MILL	PRESS
P. WINIARSKI *L	A. SARGIS *L	J. JAKUBAUSKAS *L
J. OLIVEIRA	C. SINCOCK	C. VALENTE
J. MARROTTE	R. GRANDE	J. CONDECO
A. FOSBERRY	T. VARGAS	J. MEAD
G. RANTA	G. DEGASPERIS	R. MERRIAM
S. ZIEGLER	J. O'TOOLE	R. CARLSON
G. HARRIGAN	M. MICHALEK	N. CASTONGUAY
P. PIETERZAK (BROOKS)	M. MILHEIRO	M. CARROLL (BROOKS)
A. BLAKE	J. SEYLER	S. MAYNARD
C. CUGNO	A. DUARTE	A. FLORIDO
A. RODRIGUEZ	R. NADEAU	S. FAZZINA
L. ABBOTT	F. CARBONE	F. PATINHA
S. WILLIAMS	A. MUCCIACCIARO	C. ALEGRE
	N. GIRARD	P. GUILIANO

* LEADER

The teams' goal was to see how much positive change they could
accomplish over the course of two days and one night. One of the
keys to this type of effort is to develop teamwork around the
objective of eliminating waste. During these Kaizen sessions
people's normal titles do not apply. They are all equal team
members doing what's in effect experimental engineering work in
order to try to simplify and improve the way we do things.

As this was our first Kaizen session, the results were
outstanding. I am extremely proud of the work done by the teams
and the help and cooperation exhibited by everyone in the areas
where these teams were working. People really worked together to
get some outstanding results. The rolling mill team, for
example, was able to reduce a setup that normally takes
approximately 720 minutes down to 34 minutes. Not to be outdone,
the punch press team took a setup that normally takes 1 hour 20
minutes down to 11 minutes. These are very significant first
steps.

Source: The Wiremold Company. Reprinted with permission.

Figure 3-3 Wiremold Kaizen News, cont'd.

KAIZEN NEWS • PAGE 2

-2-

Setup reduction will be very important to our overall improvement efforts in that each time we reduce a setup we increase our capacity and ability to respond to our customers' requests for product. For example, in the case of the punch press the difference between a 120-minute setup and an 11 minute setup is that we can make 11 different parts in the same operating time as before. This means that our inventory levels can go down while our customer service can go up.

The Plugmold team achieved significant results as well. They were able to rearrange the area so that two rolling mills were positioned in front of the PAM machine and a punch press was moved into the area. The next step will be to move two plastic molding machines from Rocky Hill. This will give the Plugmold team total control of their product from beginning to end. In addition, some very good first steps were made to simplify the work in several of Plugmold's manual assembly operations.

Our next on-the-floor Kaizen session will take place November 25 and 26. We will again focus on two setup reductions and one operational area.

These Kaizen sessions are hard work as everyone stays late into the evening on the first day in order to get a good result. At the same time they are great training grounds for all of us. We learn just how much improvement can occur in a short time as a result of eliminating waste and simplifying the jobs we do.

I am certain that our next Kaizen session will have results just as impressive as the first one and once again, I would like to thank everyone for their teamwork, cooperation, and the spirit that was present in our kick off sessions.

Art Byrne

Figure 3-4 Wiremold Kaizen News

KAIZEN NEWS

November 27, 1991

On November 25 and 26 we held our second plant-wide Kaizen session. Three teams were in operation focusing on: 1) setup reduction for the punch press in Plugmold; 2) setup reduction for a rolling mill; and 3) rearrangement and consolidation for the Tele-Power Pole area. A list of team members follows.

Once again each team's results were very impressive. More importantly, the teamwork and cooperation within the teams and the great efforts of our maintenance staff were just terrific. If we can build on this positive momentum, we are certainly capable of becoming a true World Class Company.

There is much follow-up work to be done in each case, but the results achieved in two days (which is a key focus of Kaizen activity; i.e. "what can you actually implement in two days") were as follows:

Rolling Mill Team

The rolling mill team encountered significant problems with machine breakdown. They had to spend over half their time doing nothing but cleaning and repairing the mill itself. This was a good lesson, however, as it pointed out how dirty and ill maintained our fundamental equipment is. We certainly have a lot of work to do in this area. Despite these problems this team was able to take a setup that had previously been done in 16 hours 30 minutes down to 29 minutes. This is a reduction of 97%, which I think you will all admit is a pretty good first step. Even within the 29 minutes, however, there are lots of opportunities for further improvement. Our target will continue to be to get all rolling mill changeovers under 10 minutes.

Punch Press Setup Team

The punch press team in the Poles Department also had a very big challenge. This is an old press that had not really been run yet in the Plugmold area. Despite this, the team was able to make some significant gains. Their first pass at the setup took 52 minutes. After a number of improvements their final result was 5 minutes 9 seconds. This is a setup reduction of 90%.

Pole Team

The Pole Team attacked a significant rearrangement opportunity. They were able to reduce the total floor space from 8,500 sq. feet down to 4,200 square feet - a reduction of over 50%. At the same time they were able to incorporate two rolling mills and three punch presses into the new Pole area. This way the Pole Team will have complete control over all of the parts it utilizes in making the final product. This should really enhance our customer service. The maintenance team did a tremendous job effecting all of these changes.

Source: The Wiremold Company. Reprinted with permission.

Figure 3-4 Wiremold Kaizen News, cont'd.

In addition, the fundamental assembly jobs for the Pole Team were changed such that the new prototype table that was built can incorporate all the pole assembly in one operation. This should allow us to go from six assembly benches in Poles down to three, thus freeing up space and making for a neater, cleaner area.

As we free up space from these Kaizen efforts, it will be important to make certain that we reclaim it for later use. I would therefore appreciate your resisting the urge to dump inventory in the new freed up spaces!

Our next on-the-floor Kaizen sessions, as well as our next Kaizen classroom training sessions, will take place on January 6 and 7, 1992.

Once again I want to thank everyone for your tremendous efforts over the past several days, and I wish everyone a safe and happy Thanksgiving holiday.

Art Byrne

POLES LAYOUT

N. CASTONGUAY, LEADER	
M. PERUSSE	L. ABBOTT
L. MARCEAU	W. MASCHI
S. BLONDIN	B. STEIN
C. VALENTE	F. JORGE
G. BROOKS (BROOKS)	D. GARDNER
H. COOPER (BROOKS)	T. SPAGNOLO
S. BROWN	D. PAQUETTE
M. PELUSO	J. BAUER
D. GOLDEN	R. DUFOUR
V. MANCINI	S. WILLIAMS
F. BIANCAMANO	B. GIRARD
R. KEAN	A. BLAKE
D. CAPOLDO	R. JORGE

ROLLING MILL S/U REDUCTION

T. FAIRBANK, LEADER	
J. JAKUBAUSKAS	M. DUARTE
B. GRANDE	B. GREEN
P. BARROW	A. FOSBERRY
M. MILHEIRO	R. CORNING
K. NOWAKOWSKI	C. PITA
A. MUCCIACCIARO	R. LASKY
R. JOINER	M. HOGAN
G. CHARTIER	

PRESS S/U REDUCTION - PLUGMOLD

D. DONAHUE, LEADER	R. MERRIAM
J. OLIVEIRA	S. NURMI
P. GUILIANO	W. ROGERS
A. FLORIDO	C. SINCOCK
A. RODRIGUES	O. FIUME
J. D'ALESSANDRO	B. RUSH (BROOKS)

another sense of calm because people don't have to say, 'How do I even begin to look at this problem.' You have the opportunity to work with the tools, and obviously the more you work with them that calmness goes up even to another level. You start by simply documenting how we do it today and look to see if there is any waste in that process. It is not an approach that says, 'Let's eliminate the person.' All of that is what I think contributes to a calmness — but I do not associate calmness with complacency.

Maybe peace of mind is a better way of putting it, because I think most people do want to find the most efficient way of getting something done. They don't want to be wasting their time. I think most people do want to feel like they're contributing either directly or indirectly to satisfying customers' needs, whether they are internal or external customers. If they feel that they've got the authority or the ability and the ownership over their processes, and they've got a methodology in which to examine and improve them over time, then it doesn't have to be a final solution; they are not pressured to find the 'silver bullet.'

So if we improve it today, again next month, and again next year, that's okay. That's not saying that the first time that we looked at it we did a bad job and had to look at it again in order to make additional improvement. Again, that contributes to a calmness where people feel more in control of their work and their environment. That translates not only to productivity, but you have less retention problems because people are naturally going to say to themselves, 'Well, this feels pretty good. I feel like I've got ownership and control over my work processes, I'm being compensated for it, and I've got a piece of the pie for the productivity improvements in the form of profit sharing.' Management starts to create a situation where people ask themselves the question, 'Why would I leave?' That information flows out into the communities and creates a pull where people are saying, 'Gee, I think that sounds like a pretty good place to work.'"

Summary

Within a month of beginning the Lean transformation, kaizen activities included the participation of senior managers, salaried associates, and hourly associates. Lean principles and practices were learned by doing, and not just by sitting in a classroom or reading a book. Real-world business problems were addressed at the point where the work actually took place — on the shop floor or in the office. Kaizen knows no boundaries.

Art Byrne retained the entire senior management team and brought in only two new people. He did not look for superstars from outside of Wiremold. He cultivated talent from within; ordinary people learning and doing extraordinary things. Art knew that their way of thinking could be changed if they participated in kaizen. If their thinking changed, he would have both a committed *and* involved management team. His direct reports, in turn, would teach other managers and associates. Their ongoing participation in kaizen would deepen their knowledge of Lean and they would be able to communicate the very valuable tacit knowledge that comes from direct experience. But they could not do any of this if they spent their time competing against each other. Judy Seyler commented on how the senior management team overcame internal competition and office politics:

> "The first thing that Art wanted to accomplish by establishing the teams was to break down functional barriers. Those functional barriers had a lot to do with politics. I remember when I came to Wiremold, somebody said, 'Well a company like this is either run by the finance people, the marketing people, or the operations people.' And that person said that at the moment, the finance people were running Wiremold. He of course believed that the marketing people should run it. So we started to build a team with the goal of getting everybody present to say to themselves: 'I am a Vice President of Wiremold,' not of Engineering, or HR, or Operations. We did everything we could think of to break down those barriers and to be non-competitive, which is where the politics comes in. We were back-up for each other; we could give each other honest feedback about how we were doing, where we could improve, how we could help each other. It really did happen. I think of it as the 'Golden Age' when it was like that; when politics did not dictate what got done, when we wanted to do the right thing for the right reason. It was the happiest work experience I ever had."

There was much more to Wiremold's Lean transformation than just kaizen. The two pillars of The Toyota Way are: "Continuous Improvement" and "Respect for People."[23] From the start, patterns of behavior developed among senior managers that supported the Lean transformation. Led by Art Byrne, they demonstrated "respect for people" through new management policies and in everyday activities such as:

- Applying Lean as a total management system
- Retaining the existing management team
- Eliminating waste in business processes
- Teaching other people
- Behaving in less wasteful ways (e.g. no blame, no lies)

Rather than focusing on solely continuous improvement as most managers do, Wiremold positioned itself to realize the full potential of Lean by recognizing and practicing what was later identified by Toyota Motor Corporation as the two pillars of the "Toyota Way."

Key Points for Senior Managers

- Art did not sweep out the entire management team when he arrived as President. Instead, he trained them in Lean principles and practices.
- Commitment to Lean is important, but participation in kaizen is more important. CEO's must not delegate improvement.
- Kaizen eliminates barriers to change. It also communicates explicit knowledge and conveys more important tacit knowledge.
- Senior managers must behave in a manner consistent with the principles and practices of the Lean management system.
- Focusing on the process yields better outcomes than focusing on results.

Notes

1. *Toyota Production System*, T. Ohno, Productivity Press, Portland, OR, 1988, p. 4. Copyright © 1988 Productivity Inc., http://www.productivityinc.com. Reprinted with permission. Note that Mr. Ohno was greatly influenced by the work of Henry Ford (see pp. 97–109), principally through his book *Today and Tomorrow*, with S. Crowther, Doubleday, Page and Company, Garden City, NY, 1926.

2. D. Hayes Murphy had a basic understanding of waste. In a c.1916 communication to employees on how they can "get more money by making more profits for the Company," he said: "Be saving in the use of materials and supplies around the factory. Don't waste a piece or a pound or a drop of anything. Make everything go as far as possible." *The Wiremold Company, A Century of Solutions*, J. Smith, published by The Wiremold Company, West Hartford, CT, 2000, p. 28.

3. Kaizen is often rigidly viewed as a multi-day activity, typically three to five days in duration. However, kaizen, or continuous improvement, must not be viewed in such a restrictive fashion. People at all levels in the company should use Lean principles and practices to make improvements every day. For example, Total Productive Maintenance normally is structured as a daily improvement activity to ensure that equipment is in good operating condition and available for use when needed. Likewise, root cause analysis should be performed every day. The more elaborate multi-day kaizen activity is used in circumstances that require the dedicated involvement of a small group of people for a short period of time to quickly eliminate waste.

4. John Davis Murphy's personal archives contain an interesting 30-page booklet entitled, "An Error That Took 27 Men, 3 Women, 2 Boys, And 8 Horses To Correct: Needless Mistakes That Swell Overhead And Add To The Cost of Modern Business, With A Graphic Lesson How They Hurt," published in 1919 by McKesson & Robbins, Inc., Manufacturing Chemists, New York, NY, and written by Jerry McQuade. The booklet shows how a small error results in costs that are 108% greater than the value of the initial sale, and describes the negative impact on both McKesson & Robbins and its customer (a pharmacist). It explains the entire process for resolving the error, which people laboring in their respective departments never see. Employees, performing activities in isolation of each other, believe they are doing important value added work — that is until the totality of the process needed to correct the error is presented. The booklet helps people see the system-level impact of an error in a manner that can be easily grasped, and demonstrates that the general concept of waste has long been understood. However, few business people, even to this day, take action to eliminate wasteful errors. This is due, in part, to two factors: 1) a lack of training in root cause analysis in undergraduate or graduate business school curricula, and 2) education that is both functional and results-focused, rather than being focused on the entire business system and business process.

5. Non-value added but necessary work is referred to as "Type 1 muda," while waste is referred to as "Type 2 muda."

6. *Toyota Production System*, T. Ohno, Productivity Press, Portland, OR, 1988, p. xv. Copyright © 1988 by Productivity Inc., http://www.productivityinc.com. Reprinted with permission.

7. *Just-In-Time For Today and Tomorrow*, T. Ohno and S. Mito, Productivity Press, Portland, OR, 1988, p. xi. Copyright © 1988 by Productivity Inc., http://www.productivityinc.com. Reprinted with permission.

8. T. Ohno in *NPS: New Production System*, I. Shinohara, Productivity Press, Cambridge, MA, 1988, p. 153 and 155. Copyright © 1988 by Productivity Inc., http://www.productivityinc.com. Reprinted with permission.

9. In particular, management would have to eliminate not only waste (muda), but unevenness (mura) and unreasonableness (muri) as well. For a complete explanation of the origins, consequences, and solutions to wasteful management behaviors, see "Lean Behaviors," M.L. Emiliani, *Management Decision*, Vol. 36, No. 9, 1998, pp. 615–631; "Continuous Personal Improvement," M.L. Emiliani, J. *Workplace Learning*, Vol. 10, No. 1, 1998, pp. 29–39; and "Cracking the Code of Business," M.L. Emiliani, *Management Decision*, Vol. 38, No. 2, 2000, pp. 60–79. The terms "lean behaviors," "behavioral waste" (the *eighth* waste), and "fat behaviors" were coined by Emiliani in these papers. See http://www.theclbm.com.

10. Mr. Masaaki Imai founded the Kaizen Institute in 1986 and serves as its Chairman (see http://www.kaizen-institute.com). He is the author of *KAIZEN: The Key to Japan's Competitive Success*, Random House, New York, NY, 1986, and *Gemba Kaizen: Commonsense, Low-Cost Approach to Management*, McGraw-Hill, New York, NY, 1997.

11. UL listing means that products have been subjected to testing by the Underwriters Laboratory, an independent product testing and evaluation firm originally established by a consortium of insurance companies offering property and casualty insurance. Most electrical components and equipment are UL listed in the United States. See http://www.ul.com.

12. In fall of 1991, Wiremold's West Hartford plant employed 406 hourly associates who were members of the International Brotherhood of Electrical Workers Union, Local 1040. The total population at the two Connecticut plants, including the field sales force at that time, was 663 people.

13. The definition of "set-up" is the elapsed time between producing the last good piece of part A and the first good piece of part B. The early years of Wiremold's transformation focused extensively on reducing

the time it takes to perform machine set-ups. While the context is principally manufacturing oriented, set-up reduction can be applied to any activity (or operation) — including service and support activities — to eliminate cost that does not add value as perceived by end-use customers. See *A Revolution in Manufacturing: The SMED System*, S. Shingo, Productivity Press, Portland, OR, 1985, pp. 5–31.

14. A common error made by senior managers when embarking on the Lean transformation is to base the selection of kaizen activities upon return on investment (ROI) calculations. Management will use ROI calculations to either justify doing a particular kaizen or assess the results of a kaizen. In many cases, a financial executive will establish the ROI criteria that kaizen teams must follow. The reason this view is erroneous and inconsistent with Lean practice is because ROI-based decisions are made from an internal company perspective. The correct perspective is to base selection of kaizen activities on work that contains large amounts of waste viewed from the end-use customer's perspective. Value stream mapping is a useful method for identifying waste: i.e. overproduction, waiting, transportation, processing, inventory, moving, and defects. As Orry Fiume said, "Don't bean-count Lean," because ROI-based decisions will lead to poor results. Also, ROI or economic value added-based decisions focus on local optimization. This is inconsistent with the intent of Lean, which is to improve the entire business system.

15. Kaizen is facilitated by one of two methods: "suzumura-style" or "Cho-san style." Suzumura style kaizen (apparently named after one of Mr. Ohno's disciples, Mr. Kikuo Suzumura) means "scary style," in which the sensei (teacher) exhibits the following general characteristics: strict, demanding, short-tempered, and insulting or demeaning. Mr. Taiichi Ohno, the creator of the Toyota Production System practiced suzumura style kaizen (See Chapter 5, Note 15). Most of his disciples also practice this style of kaizen. "Cho-san style" means the "human style" of kaizen practiced by Mr. Fujio Cho, President of Toyota Motor Corporation (1999–present), and a former student of Mr. Ohno's. Sensei practicing "human style" kaizen exhibit the following general characteristics: demanding, even-tempered, respect, humility, benevolence, and humor. Many of Mr. Ohno's best students left Toyota after Mr. Ohno retired from Toyota Motor Corporation in 1978, as the principal proponent of "suzumura style" was no longer with the company. Three of them formed Shingijutsu Co., Ltd. (see Chapter 2, Note 3). Cho-san style kaizen prevailed after Mr. Ohno retired, and was an important part of Toyota's global expansion, as other cultures were less tolerant or understanding of "scary style" kaizen. Nippondenso Corporation, now known as Denso Corporation (see http://www.globaldenso.com/), a Toyota Group Company and major Tier 1 auto parts supplier, is said to have always practiced "human style" kaizen. There is an appropriate time and place for each style of kaizen. "Scary style" kaizen may have been the only way to establish the Toyota Production System, since TPS was at odds with how people normally think. People that have a bad experience with "scary style" are advised to recognize that the sensei's intentions are well meaning and purposeful. It is designed to teach people to learn how to think differently; peeling back the onion to understand the true source of problems and apply human creativity to develop low-cost solutions. Source: Personal communication (Emiliani) with Mr. Yoshihisa Doi, President of Kaizen Management Consulting Co., Ltd., 12 February 2002 (see http://www.kaizen-mc.com/index2.html), interpreting by Michael R. Smith (mike1217nj@aol.com).

16. Examples of the tools include: target progress report, 5S form (referred to as 5C's by Wiremold), percent loading chart, time observation chart, standard work chart, standard work combination sheet, set-up observation analysis sheet, kaizen newspaper, skills matrix, etc. See *Gemba Kaizen*, M. Imai, McGraw-Hill, New York, NY, 1997.

17. Conventional management practices typically focus on items related to dollars: e.g. sales dollars, material dollars, labor dollars, and overhead dollars. Instead, Wiremold would set targets related to quantity, which requires physical rearrangement and other types of structural changes. Source: "Management Accounting for Lean Businesses," O. Fiume, The Center for Lean Business Management, LLC workshop, May 2000.

18. The process for creating a visual image that identifies value-added activities and waste is explained in *Learning To See*, M. Rother and J. Shook, The Lean Enterprise Institute, Brookline, MA, 1999. http://www.lean.org.

19. The training materials that Art Byrne used consisted of the following modules: "Change Management," "Introduction to Just-In-Time," "Introduction to Standard Work," and "Constructing a Standard Operation." Some content in the modules came from the training booklet: "How to Implement Kaizen in Manufacturing," published by Shingijutsu Co., Ltd., Gifu-ken, Japan, c. 1990, (see http://www.shingijutsu.co.jp/indx_e.htm) and from Jacobs training manuals.

20. Wiremold used a team-based structure since late 1991 and typically does not depict itself with formal hierarchical organization charts. The organization essentially consists of just two levels: 1) The President's Staff Team and 2) Product Development Team; Product Teams; JIT Promotion Office; Administration Team; Shipping/Warehouse Team; Sales Team; and Factory Support Team. People unfamiliar with Lean spend a lot of time trying to figure out what is the best way to organize the different departments and believe the solution lies in simply producing a new organization chart. This is not useful; the organization chart itself is not what is important. There are three general rules to follow: the organization should be flat, people should be organized into product line teams, and there must be phys-

ical change — i.e. work must be organized to enable flow, which often includes co-locating people. A company can be organized in many different ways and still be consistent with these three general rules. What managers must understand is the root cause of why information does not flow. Changing the organization chart alone will not help overcome this fundamental problem. Managers must also understand that co-locating people will itself not be sufficient to get information to flow because this does not address the root cause of the problem. Eliminate waste (muda), unevenness (mura), and unreasonableness (muri), and information will begin to flow. See Note 9.

21. Bill Moffitt had been an associate of Art Byrne's at Danaher Corporation where he ran the first Just-In-Time (JIT) promotion office. Bill left Danaher in 1991 to form Moffitt Associates, Hilton Head Island, SC, a firm specializing in Lean consulting. Moffitt Associates has provided consulting services to The Wiremold Company since the beginning of their transformation in the fall of 1991.

22. Senior managers accustomed to batch-and-queue business practices, whether in manufacturing or service, find it very difficult to comprehend business processes. The problem is partly due to various negative perceptions related to understanding processes; i.e. that it will take more time, deliver uncertain results, or highlight poor managers or management practices. So instead of understanding processes, senior managers say: "It's results that matter!" This statement seems authoritative, but in reality it is deceptive. This type of thinking encourages managers to manipulate metrics to deliver the desired numbers when real performance falls short. Importantly, this leads to wasteful arbitrary or inconsistent leadership behaviors that other stakeholders find annoying as well as de-motivating. How results are achieved does, in fact, matter.

23. Toyota Motor Corporation characterizes "respect for people" in part as: a) respect for stakeholders (i.e. customers, shareholders, associates, business partners, and the global community), b) mutual trust and mutual responsibility, and c) sincere communication. Source: "Toyota Way 2001," Toyota Motor Corporation, internal document, April 2001. It is important to recognize that Toyota's current capabilities in "continuous improvement" and "respect for people" have evolved and improved over time. In other words, Toyota's management system as it is known today did not start out that way. Toyota Motor Corporation managers learned the importance of these two pillars through the many business challenges they have faced since the late 1930's. See, for example, *My Life with Toyota*, S. Kamiya, Toyota Motor Sales Co., Ltd., Toyota City, Japan, 1976; *My Years with Toyota*, S. Kato, Toyota Motor Sales Co., Ltd., Toyota City, Japan, 1981; *Toyota: 50 Years in Motion*, E. Toyoda, Kodansha International, Tokyo, Japan, 1987; *Toyota: A History of the First 50 Years*, Toyota Motor Corporation, Toyota City, Japan, 1988; *The Origin of Competitive Strength*, A. Kawahara, Springer-Verlag, New York, NY, 1998; *Toyota: People, Ideas and the Challenge of the New*, E. Reingold, Penguin Books, London, England, 1999.

Explanation of Exhibits 3-1 to 3-9

The following exhibits show the types of documents that The Wiremold Company used in preparation for, during, and after kaizen. While information contained in these worksheets are interconnected, they can be categorized as: understanding the problem (Exhibits 3-1 and 3-2), describing the work performed (Exhibits 3-3 and 3-4), setting goals and monitoring progress (Exhibits 3-5, 3-6, and 3-7), summary of accomplishments (Exhibit 3-8), and follow-up activities (Exhibit 3-9, often referred to as the "Kaizen Newspaper"). These simple worksheets also are used for office kaizen activities.

Exhibit 3-1

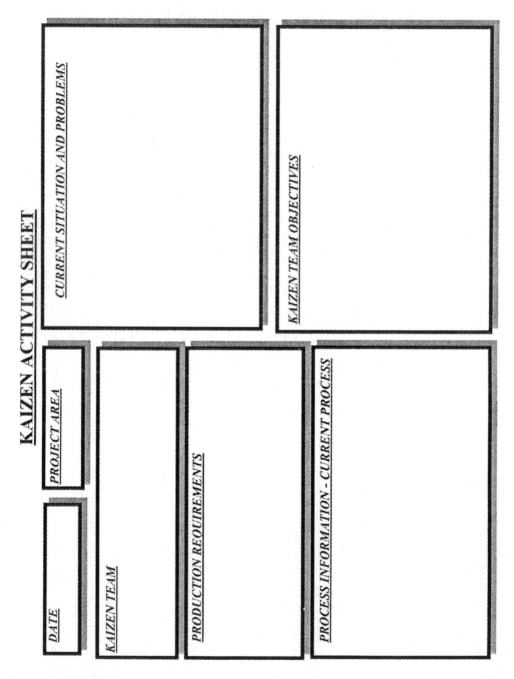

Souorce: The Wiremold Company

Exhibit 3-2

Process for Observation	TIME OBSERVATION FORM 2ND FASTEST REPEATABLE TIME TO BE USED															Date: Operator: Time: Observer:
No.	Component Task	1	2	3	4	5	6	7	8	9	10	11	12	13	14	15	Component Task time	Points Observed
	TIME FOR 1 CYCLE																	

Souorce: The Wiremold Company

Exhibit 3-3

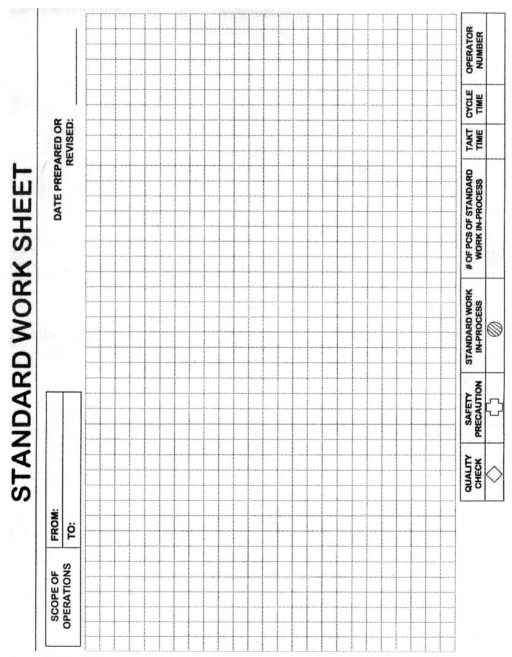

Souorce: The Wiremold Company

Exhibit 3-4

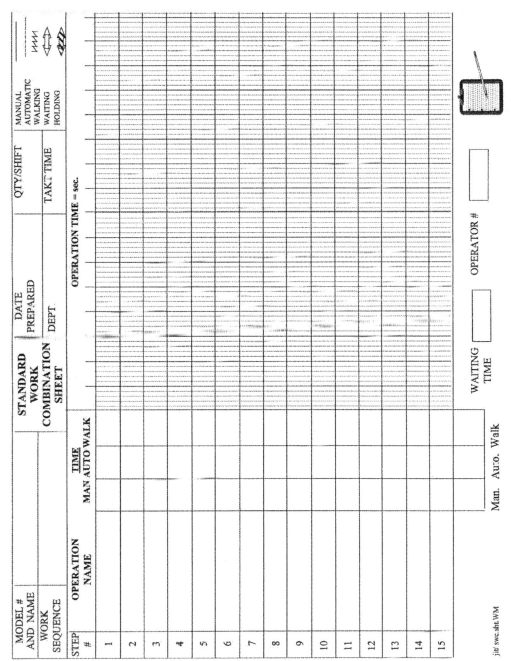

Souorce: The Wiremold Company

Exhibit 3-5

KAIZEN TARGET SHEET

JIT 11-98

PROJECT AREA _____   DATE _____

TEAM # _____   TAKT TIME _____

FILL IN AREAS APPLICABLE TO THE KAIZEN PROJECT

OBJECTIVES	TARGET	START	PROGRESS 1	2	3	4	5	RESULT
INVENTORY								
CYCLE TIME								
SPACE Sq. Ft.								
PRODUCTIVITY								
STAFFING								
STANDARD SHEETS (1 - 5)								
SET-UP TIME								
5C SCORE								
LEAD TIMES								
SAFETY (1 - 5)								
Q C DEFECTS								
VISUAL CONTROLS (1-5)								
PARTS TRAVEL								
WALK DISTANCE								
WIP								

Exhibit 3-6

TEAM _____   **TODAY'S _KAIZEN_ ACCOMPLISHMENTS**   DATE _____

1	
2	
3	
4	
5	
6	
7	
8	
9	
10	
11	
12	
13	

Souorce: The Wiremold Company

Exhibit 3-7

TEAM # _____   **PLANS FOR TOMORROW'S KAIZEN**   DATE _____

1	
2	
3	
4	
5	
6	
7	
8	
9	
10	

Souorce: The Wiremold Company

Exhibit 3-8

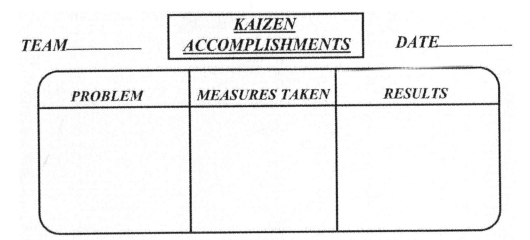

ILLUSTRATIONS

Souorce: The Wiremold Company

Exhibit 3-9

KAIZEN "TO DO" 30 DAY FOLLOW UP

AREA:

DATE:

ITEM	PROBLEM	CORRECTIVE ACTION	PERSON RESPONSIBLE	DUE DATE	% COMPLETE			
1					25	50	75	100
2					25	50	75	100
3					25	50	75	100
4					25	50	75	100
5					25	50	75	100
6					25	50	75	100
7					25	50	75	100
8					25	50	75	100
9					25	50	75	100
10					25	50	75	100
11					25	50	75	100
12					25	50	75	100
13					25	50	75	100
14					25	50	75	100

Souorce: The Wiremold Company

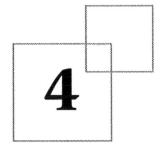

TRANSFORMING THE FACTORY

Factory Layout

The factory would be the first work area to undergo significant change in terms of its physical layout. For many years, parts were processed in typical batch-and-queue fashion: several of the same types of machines were located in a common area[1] to process large batches of material. After a batch of parts was processed, it would move to the next operation, or, more commonly, to a work-in-process storage room to wait until scheduled for the next operation. The following operation was normally some distance away from the preceding operation, which resulted in a large amount of part travel. This was repeated until all operations were completed. Some parts moved as much as 1–2 miles within the factory before they were completed. The waste resulting from large batches, part travel, hours-long machine set-up times, and month-long storage and queue times was enormous. This resulted in long lead-times, quality problems, high scrap rates, and the inability to respond quickly to changes in customer demand.

But before the factory layout could be changed, people had to understand both the types and quantities of products consumed by the marketplace, and the processes used. Cross-functional teams of design and manufacturing engineers reviewed parts and blueprints to determine which could be grouped into product families that were processed in a similar fashion: e.g. roll, punch, stamp, assemble. Gaining a detailed understanding of the specific sequence in which parts were processed was essential, as kaizen teams would use this information to create manufacturing cells dedicated to producing product families. These were typically groups of five to ten part numbers – though sometimes as many as 30 different parts would be processed in the same cell.

The layout of the manufacturing cell would be U-shaped[2] so parts could be processed in the sequence in which value is added. This rearrangement places all equipment needed to process a family of products in close proximity and facilitates material handling. If problems occurred, there would be no place to store the parts. This layout requires people to respond immediately to problems. Identifying the root cause[3] of problems and implementing corrective actions would, over time, enable parts to flow through all processes without interruption.

One-Piece Flow

The first kaizens Shingijutsu consultants facilitated at Wiremold were in January 1992. One objective was to rearrange equipment so that parts could be processed one-at-a-time, called "one-piece flow."[4] In this method, a part moves to the next operation only when the prior operation has been successfully completed. This is in contrast to batch-and-queue, where the parts, including those with defects, move to the next operation only when the entire batch of parts has been processed. One-piece flow greatly reduces waste such as part travel, walking distance, and defects. It also substantially reduces lead-times and the space needed to produce products, while increasing plant capacity.

In one-piece flow production, each part or assembly is processed only as needed. Intuitively, this would seem to increase costs, as set-up times are normally quite long. The conventional manufacturing practice is to produce goods based upon an inventory model called the *economic order quantity* (EOQ). The EOQ formula[5] calculates the optimum level of finished goods inventory based upon unit costs – typically driven by set-up time – and inventory carrying costs. It is usually calculated automatically by a *material requirements planning* (MRP) package within an *enterprise resource planning* (ERP) software system.[6]

Lean practice, however, does not recognize EOQ's because it does not assume that the set-up time is fixed. Reducing set-up times from hours to minutes negates the rationale for using EOQ's and building finished goods inventory in anticipation of future demand.[7] Set-up time is considered waste that must be eliminated, which in turn reduces lead-times and therefore inventory. This reduces costs and improves both quality and on-time delivery to customers.

Most of Wiremold's products are made using stamping presses, rolling mills, plastic extrusion, and injection molding machines, which require periodic die change-overs. Therefore, the early kaizens at Wiremold also were directed to reduce set-up times for each process in a manufacturing cell so that die change-over could be accomplished in minutes. This would enable Wiremold to make "every part every day"[8] using the same group of machines. Figure 4-1 illustrates the impact of set-up reduction on the number of products that can be made in an eight-hour workday. When the set-up is four hours in duration, people will invariably produce four hours worth of a single product, item "A," even though the customer requirement might be for 30 minutes worth of parts. As set-up time is reduced to 30 minutes, the variety of products that can be produced increases eight-fold, items "A" through "H", resulting in greater flexibility to meet changes in market demand. So as set-up is reduced to 30 minutes, all eight parts can be produced in a single day, rather than over eight days. In practice, kaizen teams will strive to reduce set-up times to less than 10 minutes. The impact is enormous, especially for businesses that produce many SKU's.

Figure 4-1 Effect of Set-Up Reduction on Market Responsiveness

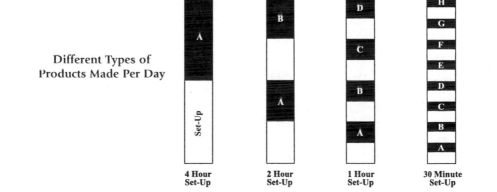

The principal advantage that Wiremold management sought was improved responsiveness to changing market conditions. However, there also was a tremendous cost benefit: the unit cost and inventory holding costs were reduced, as well as indirect cost savings related to the management of WIP and finished goods inventories.[9] However, Wiremold did not focus solely on the cost benefit. This would have limited their understanding of other broad-based benefits, some of which do not have a favorable impact on unit cost but instead reduce total costs.

Recall that one of the books that greatly influenced Art Byrne was *The SMED System* by Shigeo Shingo. Art knew that single minute exchange of dies (SMED) would be critical to accomplishing the turn-around at Wiremold. Orry Fiume recalled the reaction that associates had to set-up reduction:

> "Art would talk to the people on the rolling mills and say, 'We can set up rolling mills in 10 to 15 minutes or less, instead of taking 12 to 18 hours.' Now these guys have done this job for 25 years and they say, 'Art, you're absolutely crazy. I know this job. I've been doing it. You've only been here a couple of months. What the heck do you know? I'm telling you there is no way this machine can get set up in 15 minutes.' But once we did it, well this was another significant emotional event.

> Those first couple of months were critical in terms of creating credibility, and each one of those initial kaizens did that because they were happening in front of people's eyes. And they were the ones doing it. It's not like we brought in a bunch of consultants that did it and then said, 'Okay, we're going to turn it over to you now.' Our associates were doing it. We had no outside consultants at this point, with the exception of a few days of Bill Moffitt's time; it was all Art. He was the consultant."

Frank Giannattasio recalled his first days at Wiremold and an early kaizen:

> "I arrived on March 2, 1992, a few months after Art had begun de-layering the organization. There was a lot of the emotional trauma everywhere. My reaction was that this is a company on the intensive care table right now in terms of the people's emotions. I was part of the rebuilding. My responsibility was rebuilding the factory floor and the rank-and-file work force. I walked in the door and introduced myself as a father of three, that I been doing these different things for the last couple of years, and that I'm here to help. I then proceeded to be here [at the West Hartford Plant] almost around the clock for a while, in the midst of the all the turmoil. And I guess that is what warmed people up to me because they quickly bought into the fact that I was here to help.

The union had some legitimate issues and we took care of those issues very quickly because there was no reason to put them off. And at the same time, they recognized that it was not going to be business as usual. People who didn't want to participate were going to be weeded out. We probably released more people in the factory in the first 18 months than in the entire history of The Wiremold Company. And I would emphasize we did it co-operatively, without grievances or arbitration since it was based on actual performance. We got people to work within some constraints without being dictatorial. I think that people quickly accepted me as someone who was here to help.

The operations leadership and I targeted every kaizen project based on our perception of what was the most raging fire. We had one machine that at that time was considered quick change-over. It's called a raft mill. The changeover was measured in eight-hour shifts, so it took multiple shifts to do the changeover. The process involved using cranes and took up a couple thousand square feet because of all of the stuff laying all over the place. So we went into that kaizen with a goal of doing the change-over in less than 60 minutes. We did quite a bit of reconstruction of the mill during normal down time so that it didn't upset the schedule. When we were all done we had a change-over that was down to about 30 minutes. That was a big break because people came to realize that no matter if the machine was a press or any other type of equipment, that you did the same process of separating internal versus external set-up, standardizing tool heights, getting rid of adjustments, etc. Later, the changeover time was further reduced to about ten minutes."

While manufacturing cells, one-piece flow, and set-up reduction were all very important changes in business practice, there were still many more changes that had to occur. Kaizen would be used to establish an information, or communication, system to provide signals to operators for what items to make next. Another was a means for associates and supervisors to identify problems that were making it difficult to produce at the rate of customer demand.

Visual Controls

A fundamental practice of the Lean management system is to convey information both simply and visually to make it easy to recognize abnormal conditions that result in waste. If waste can be made visible — at a glance — then people can respond quickly to eliminate it using the tools that they learned from kaizen. The objective is to use visual controls so that the workplace is simplified and made easier to understand, even to visitors. Visual controls take information hidden in people's heads, locked in desk drawers, or in computer systems accessible to only a few people, and makes it available to everyone so that they can perform their activities more effectively. During every kaizen, the team considers all of the communication needs of the manufacturing cell and establishes or improves the visual means of conveying information.

Several types of visual controls are used in the Lean system to enable associates to control the flow of activities in accordance with their assigned tasks. These include the line-stop cord, sounds (music or buzzer), and colored flashing lights (called "*andon,*" Figure 4-2). For example, operators are responsible for stopping production if an abnormal condition occurs, such as a defective product or malfunctioning machine. They turn on a flashing red light to signal a problem or delay that requires attention from a supervisor. The supervisor and operators diagnose the problem and apply countermeasures, often within the remaining takt time. When the problem is fixed, a green light is turned on indicating the machine is functioning normally. A yellow light indicates the machine is idle due to a set-up, shift change, or the daily production requirement has been met.

Figure 4-2 Andon Light

Source: The Wiremold Company

Manufacturing cells also contain either a handwritten production performance chart showing plan vs. actual requirement (Figure 4-3), or an electronic display system connected to the equipment in the cell that counts each piece made versus plan, called a *production display board.* The visual display helps associates and supervisors monitor hourly performance to takt time (the rate of customer demand) and to detect variances. Failure to produce the hourly requirement signals the team to identify and correct the problem, which could have been caused by non-conforming raw materials or late delivery of parts from other manufacturing cells. Production problems and their sources are posted on bulletin boards so operators and supervisors have a record of the causes of specific deviations from production. Recurring problems become the subject of future kaizens.

Figure 4-3 Production Performance Chart

DAILY PRODUCTION PERFORMANCE

Cell: _Shanklin_   Shift: 1st.__ 2nd__   Date: _2-1/9/02_

1st. SHIFT 2nd. SHITT	Total Min. this hour	Clock Number	PART No.	QTY. Required	ACTUAL Qty. produced	CUM. Required	CUM. Actual produced	Minutes on this job	Code for down Time	Scrap
6:00/7:00	60	1107	2/5747-2		180			60		
3:00/4:00	60			360		360	180			
7:00/8:00	50		N57445		210			40		
			C.N5744S pc		50			20		
4:00/5:00	60			360		720	440			
8:00/9:00	80		9/57445		200			50		
5:00/6:00	50			300		1020	740			
9:00/10:00	60		N57445		330			55		
6:00/7:00	55			330		1350	1070			
10:00/11:00	50		N5744		300			60		
7:30/8:30	60			360		1710	1370			
11:00/12:00	55		N5744		300			50		
8:30/9:30	50			360		2070	1670			
12:30/1:30	60		N5748-2		260			60		
9:30-10:30	60			360		2370	1930			
1:30/2:30	50		N5748-2		260			50		
10:30/11:30	50			300		2670	2190			
						Total %	82 %			

Down Time Reason Codes:

1. Air System	9. Conveyor / Run -Off Table	17. Electrical Prob.	25. Motor	33. Sensors
2. Another job	10. Conveyor Jam	18. Fin. Goods Hand.	26. Oil Leaks	34. Set up
3. Bad Materials	11. Cut-Off Press	19. Incorrect Materials	27. Out of materials	35. Tapper
4. Bottom Out /Die #	12. Cutter wire	20. Jam up	28. Polish / Clean	36. Tool tryout
5. Box Taping Machine	13. Damaged Material	21. K/O Unit	29. Quality problems	37. Tote Handling
6. Broken Equipment	14. Die / Number	22. Light Curtain / Guarding	30. Rework	38. Training
7. Changing Colors	15. Die Handling	23. Machine Controls	31. Scrap Removal	39. Waiting for dies
8. Clutch / Brake	16. Disorganized Mat.	24. Misfeed problems	32. Scrap removal	40. Waiting for steel
				41. Welder

Source: The Wiremold Company

Other examples include marks on the shop floor to identify a specific area or location of an activity, standard work charts,[10] standard work combination sheets,[11] signs, empty parts bins, an empty shelf, kanban cards, and production leveling boxes (called *heijunka*, Japanese for "load smoothing"). Installing these different types of visual controls became important elements of Wiremold's early kaizen activities, and enabled them to "unplug" processes designed to manage the old batch-and-queue production system.

A particular focus was the portion of the MRP computer system that forecasted and planned daily production, as this was an obvious source of conflict with the Lean transformation activities. If set-up times were significantly reduced, then Wiremold would not need to use forecasts to guide daily execution. Instead, they would limit the use of forecasting to planning long-term capacity and sales objectives. Eliminating the execution portion of the MRP system turned out to be a very big hurdle because everyone believed they could not work effectively without this information. However, twice a year, Wiremold sent groups of people to Japan to learn from Toyota how to use kanban cards and heijunka boxes, which resulted in more accurate, lower cost, and less confusing information flows. First they would have to understand how to level, or smooth, customer demand.

Leveling Customer Demand

The foundation of the Toyota Production System is heijunka, or smoothing the peaks and valleys in the quantities and types of products customers demand. The purpose is to level production to create an even workload, which in turn eliminates waste (muda), unevenness (mura), and unreasonableness (muri). This is accomplished by calculating the takt time, or rate of customer demand. "Takt" is a German word that means the beat or pace of an activity, such as in musical timing or rhythm. It is calculated by dividing the total available daily operating time by the total daily production requirement.

For example, a manufacturer with 900 minutes of available operating time over two shifts and a daily demand of 400 units must produce one unit every 135 seconds to satisfy market demand. The same principle applies to service businesses. For example, The Internal Revenue Service provides its customers with employer identification numbers (EIN). If the IRS service center branch has 450 minutes of available operating time over one shift and a daily demand of 550 EIN's, then it must provide one EIN every 49 seconds. An increase in customer demand results in a shorter takt time. To satisfy the new higher rate of customer demand, the process must be improved, the amount of available operating time must be increased through overtime, or people must be added to the process.

Takt time differs from both *cycle time* and *lead-time.* Cycle time is the time to complete one cycle of an operation performed by a machine, for example. Lead-time is the total elapsed time between when a customer places an order to when they receive the product. These same terms apply to service activities.

A key Wiremold objective was to work to takt time – the actual rate of customer demand – versus making products to forecasted demand. Kaizen was the process used to eliminate imbalances in cycle time between operations and reduce long lead-times, thus improving their ability to satisfy customer demand. Another key objective was to implement one-piece flow for product families where it was possible to do so. Again kaizen was the process used to create manufacturing cells configured for one-piece flow.

Recall that before Art Byrne arrived at Wiremold, the factory shut down for two weeks in August, the month of highest demand. The shut down made it impossible to respond to customer demand during that period and in the few months thereafter. So if Wiremold were to fulfill a key objective of working to takt time, the plant-wide shut down had to be eliminated. Likewise, set-ups that took tens of hours to complete had to be reduced to minutes if they had any hope of working to takt time. Takt time, production leveling, and set-up reduction were among the mechanisms used to impart market discipline upon the business. By reducing set-up times and leveling both the quantity and mix of products, Wiremold could produce just what the market wanted, when it wanted it, and in the quantities wanted.

The Kanban System

Mr. Ohno developed what is called the Kanban System,[12] based upon the Just-In-Time (JIT) concept created by the founder of Toyota Motor Corporation, Mr. Kiichiro Toyoda.[13] Just-In-Time is one of the two pillars of the Toyota Production System (the other is "Autonomation," or automation with a human touch). It is not a zero inventory system.

Kanban is the Japanese word for "sign." It is the method for realizing Just-In-Time, or "pull" production systems, using visual controls (Figure 4-4). It cannot be used in isolation of the other principles and practices in the Toyota Production System, such as production leveling. Kanban is a visual system for controlling activities in the workplace. The signal for replenishment is typically a paper card that contains many different types of information such as the part number, box capacity, part name, storage location, delivery time, producer identification symbol or number, previous process, and next process. Kanban systems deliver the right material to the right place, in the quantity needed, just when needed. While kanban is an impressive system for reliably and accurately communicating up the value stream, it also offers significant financial benefits such as higher inventory turnover, reduced working capital, and increased cash flow.

A simple example of a kanban system is found in the bread aisle of a supermarket. Customers picking loaves of bread create voids on the shelf that serve as a signal that bread has been sold. This signal starts the next upstream process, bread delivery, to replenish items removed from the shelf. This then signals the next earlier process, bread making, which in turn signals the next earlier process, delivery of raw materials: flour, eggs, and yeast. Therefore, in a kanban system, it is always the later process that gives the signal to initiate the next earlier process to provide the right material to the right place, in the quantity needed, just when needed. However, the reverse happens in batch-and-queue businesses: the MRP system[14] schedules material to the next later process whether it needs it or not, which results in a build-up of inventory and confusion over which item should be processed next.

Figure 4-4   Kanban Cards

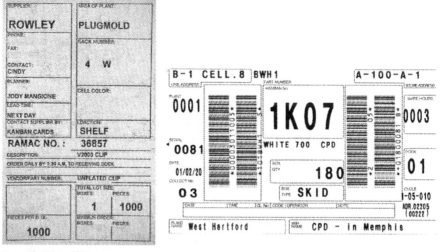

Source: The Wiremold Company

The establishment of a kanban system would also include "supermarkets," which is the location where materials are drawn from in order to satisfy demand (Figure 4-5). Supermarkets are typically small in size, holding only a few hours or days worth of material. The kanban system and supermarkets were established immediately during the first kaizens and quickly replaced the MRP forecasting and scheduling system. Steve Maynard recalled early efforts to establish the kanban system at Wiremold and that it required a change in the way people managed information:

> "We had to figure out how to run without MRP. When you set up supermarkets, you try to reduce your finished goods down to a reasonable level – two or three days of demand. You shut off the master scheduling function in MRP, but retain the bill-of-materials, the parts master, the purchasing system – including payables, the order entry/invoicing system, the general ledger, and the shipping modules. People ask me, 'What do I do? You want me to throw out my MRP system?' I say, 'Be careful. What we mean is to shut off the forecast-driven master scheduling module in the system and run your factory using kanban or pull system.' Most MRP packages today include all of your critical business processes, and these processes are needed to run your business.
>
> What happens when you unplug the MRP system? You go temporarily blind; people no longer have visibility on the computer as to what is being produced, as the inventory module fed from move tickets is disabled. One of the problems in the old culture

is that people are sitting in an office somewhere looking at computer screens; they are not located in the factory. This is where the culture shift came in. A buyer-planner was assigned to each product team and located in the factory in the manufacturing cell. They got to know the product intimately, and they could see what was going on in the cell. They no longer needed a computer screen to see it, they just got out of their chair and walked over and looked at the raw materials supermarket or the finished goods kanban rack. This is a huge shift in culture. The computer screen is replaced with a visual system on the factory floor that each team manages."

Figure 4-5 A Supermarket

Source: The Wiremold Company

Kanbans must be properly sized to accommodate the amount of product that will be sold between the time when the kanban is empty and when it is filled. Steve Maynard describes how this was done:

"If you have a long transportation time between your plant and your warehouse, then you will need a big buffer to be able to provide a high level of customer service. If you are five days away, you need at least five days worth of demand there. Unless, you can guarantee a steady state model with a day's worth of demand on the road for each of the five days, you have to be very careful. Variation in demand affects the kanban system."

The kanban cards resided at Wiremold's distribution centers in Memphis, Tennessee and Sparks, Nevada,[15] and were placed adjacent to each finished product. The receipt of customer orders would initiate activity by pickers who would select the products and package them for delivery. When the amount of product picked was equal to or greater than the amount shown on the kanban card, the card(s) were sent by truck back to the Wiremold plant in West Hartford. Wiremold operates its own small fleet of trucks that make daily "milk runs" between its distribution centers and the West Hartford plant. Kanban cards are typically received within 24 hours.[16] The kanban cards were then delivered to the appropriate manufacturing cell, which signaled the need for replenishment of products.

However, not every cell made completely finished products, and some products had low or erratic demand. This meant that some parts had to be processed by more than one manufacturing cell, and that the kanban cards had to communicate the internal production sequence. Art Byrne knew the preferred approach was to provide each cell with everything it needed to make its own products. However, working within the physical constraints of a factory that was built in stages beginning in 1929 made this impossible. In addition, in some cases, investment in new equipment was just not worth it, so different, lower cost solutions would be used. Some associates were assigned the task of transporting material from one cell to another. These people are called "water spiders," whose name is derived from the insect that moves quickly from point-to-point on the surface of a pond. Art Byrne described the situation:

> "Initially, not all of the cells had a complete set of equipment to build their particular product. Team leader A had to rely on team leaders B, C, and D to get parts and pieces to him or her in order to make their product line work. And of course, that was always the biggest problem because team leader B, C, and D were always making their stuff first and then they would help team leader A. As you would expect, humans are humans, and so you had to reinforce the importance of working together. We eventually created kanban systems to help make that smoother, but our main thrust was always to eliminate that kind of behavior by making sure that each person had 100% of their own equipment. Now, we still have cases today [summer 2001] where A has to help B, and B has to help C and D and make parts for them because in some cases you only had one machine. You didn't really need to buy another machine. So what we did is to say, if 80% of what comes off that machine is used by team A, then team A owns it and the other 20% that goes to B and C, they have to supply B and C. And A has to be a good supplier to them. We don't want B and C saying that A won't

give me any parts. So we set up kanban systems between A, B, C, and D, and used water spiders to transport material between processes. Training the organization to receive the first kaizens and have responsibility for the measurements that we wanted to set was critical in our thinking and in getting these things done."

The Heijunka Box

While kanban cards appear to be similar to job order tickets, there are some very important differences. Job order tickets are generated by a centralized materials requirement planning system in a conventional batch-and-queue business, and work is initiated at the beginning of the production process. These job order tickets typically reflect a combination of actual and forecasted material requirements that are *pushed* into the manufacturing process. The quantity of material may be automatically adjusted up or down based upon economic order calculations embedded in the software. Alternatively, the quantity may be manually adjusted up or down by an authorized material requirements planner based on current business information, which is often not accurate. These adjustments in quantity are usually made with good intentions: to ensure that future customer requirements can be met. However, managing material requirements in this way leads to demand amplification[17] throughout the value stream, resulting in chronic production errors such as shortages of some SKU's and an oversupply of other SKU's.

Kanban cards, on the other hand, are visual instructions issued by the order entry system. They serve as a signal to manufacture a specific SKU, or combination of SKU's, which replenishes inventory that has been sold. The cards initiate work from the point of sale backwards into the preceding production process, resulting in a *pull* system. By reflecting only the quantities and types of materials actually sold, the kanban system greatly dampens demand amplification and synchronizes the rate of production with the actual rate of customer demand.

However, kanban cards alone will not result in a balanced or leveled production system. To do that requires production leveling, or heijunka, which is facilitated by a heijunka box. Recall that the two pillars of the Toyota Production System are Just-In-Time and Autonomation (also called *jidoka* in Japanese). These two pillars rest upon a foundation called heijunka (Figure 4-6), which is essential in order to flexibly respond to fluctuations in customer demand for diverse products. The heijunka box, similar in appearance to a pigeon-hole mail box, is used to smooth the production load – i.e. lowering the peaks and raising the valleys – thus reducing variation in production output. Production smoothing, however, can only be achieved if set-up times are minutes in duration, which enables a reduction in lot sizes. This results in shorter lead-times, higher product quality, lower cost, and further illustrates the interconnectedness of the Lean management system.

Figure 4-6 The Toyota Production System

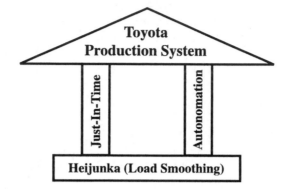

Kanban cards received from the distribution center are placed in a central heijunka box located within the factory (Figure 4-7). The slots in the heijunka box sequence work that is to be performed in each manufacturing cell on an hourly, daily, or weekly basis, depending upon rate of demand of each SKU. The cards are withdrawn, typically several times a day by a water spider, and delivered to each manufacturing cell. Steve Maynard recalled how the installation of heijunka boxes in West Hartford smoothed customer demand, resulting in a balanced and responsive production system:

> "If you look in the plant, you will see a bunch of heijunka boxes. This is the place where the kanban cards are stored. We call it the 'post office.' If you allow the raw customer demand to hit the cells, it creates spikes in demand, which the cell cannot handle. The cell has only a finite amount of raw material or semi-finished components based upon the size of its internal supermarkets. We had to figure out a way to 'level' or 'dampen' the demand that was hitting the cell. The heijunka box accomplished this by only presenting to the cell a day's worth – and no more – of demand for a part's kanban cards. The upstream supermarkets are sized to accommodate a day's worth of demand. The system works very smoothly. The heijunka box also serves a 'wheel' function, which cycles the cell from one item to the next, so that all of the products can be produced throughout the day."

Getting Rid of Parts Hotels

A hallmark of the batch-and-queue production system is the large quantities of inventories – raw materials, work-in-process, and finished goods – that it produces. These are stored on racks or pallets at various locations within the plant, in warehouses, or at distribution centers. Factory personnel are continu-

Figure 4-7 Heijunka Box

Source: The Wiremold Company

ously challenged to reduce inventories due to the financial burden associated with managing unsold finished goods, which includes the cost of storage racks, pallets, unproductive floor space, computer systems, printers, bar code scanners, materials handling equipment, etc. However, batch-and-queue businesses are usually unsuccessful at reducing inventories for several reasons:

- Inaccurate production information due to demand amplification
- Long lead-times
- Quality problems
- The need to maintain high customer service levels
- Economic order quantities
- Safety stocks
- Unplanned machine downtime

Because of these systemic problems, managers often decide to sell inventories to third parties that specialize in inventory management and distribution logistics.

In the Lean business system, inventory is considered the root of all evil because it hides waste. One of the responsibilities of the kaizen teams was to eliminate the racks that stored these inventories, called "parts hotels"[18] (Figure 4-8). Art Byrne assigned a person the task of eliminating parts hotels for a given area. Inventories were moved to where they belonged: stacked up adjacent to their respective manufacturing cells. Moving inventories from remote locations in the factory to the exact spot where they are produced gave operators a simple visual signal indicating which parts were on hand and which parts needed to be made. As Orry Fiume recalled:

"The principle that we used as we took the storerooms apart was that if it was a purchased part, it went to the operation that was going to use it so that they could understand how much they had overbought. If it was an internally manufactured part, it went back to the people who made it so that they could see how much they overproduced. As a result, when you went to the factory floor, people were just surrounded by mountains of inventory. It was ugly, but it sent an important message. One of the things that people talk about in the factory environment is that they like to see a lot of inventory waiting to be worked on because it gives them a sense that we are still in business; that they've got work to do. When you send back all the stuff that they already worked on that hasn't been used yet, they have not only the stack of inventory sitting in front of the machine that needs work, but now in back of the machine they have a stack of inventory that has already been finished at their operation. They were surrounded by all this stuff. It's very visual."

Figure 4-8 Parts Hotel

Source: The Wiremold Company

When Wiremold acquired Walker Systems in 1993, storage racks 30–40 feet high occupied about half the floor space. The racks were referred to as "ICA's," or inventory control areas, where work-in-process material was stored. Art Byrne describes the process that he used to eliminate the storage racks:

"These were big huge racks completely filled with WIP. So I got a pad of paper, a marker, and some masking tape and walked over to the work-in-process inventory area. I wrote, 'Parts Hotel Closing. This Rack Goes Away by", and I wrote a date that was about 30 days later [see Figure 4-9]. I taped the sign on the rack and wrote other signs that were about a month apart for the other racks. Barbie was a pretty aggressive person, and she said to me, 'Hey, get over here. What are you doing?' I said, 'I'm putting these signs on here because we have to get rid of all this stuff. This is just waste, so it all has to come down.' I said, 'Why do you ask?' She said, 'My people are all upset that you're putting these signs on the racks saying that this rack has to go away. They see this as their jobs, and they are worried that their jobs are going to go away.' So I said, 'Tell them not to worry about their jobs. They won't be out on the street, but they just can't be doing this anymore because it is waste.'

So I said to Barbie, 'You are in charge of this area. I want you to do whatever the sign says. I want you to get this rack down, get this stuff out of here, and get rid of the inventory by the target date on each sign. I don't want you to just keep it someplace else. I want you to get rid of it. When you take the rack down I want you to send me my sign back.' She looked at me kind of funny, but she agreed to do what I asked. So Barbie and her people would get stuff out of the WIP racks and they would take it back to the manufacturing cell that made it. The machine operators wanted her to put it back up on the rack, but she said, 'Sorry, I've got to close this rack out. Art says it has got to come down. You can't put it back here, so you better use it up.'

About a month later, she sent me the first sign that I had made [Figure 4-9] and also wrote me a poem about the rack and the sign [Figure 4-10]. I went down to Walker about a month later to lead another kaizen, and she said to me, 'Where is my poem?' I didn't know that Barbie had expected a poem in return from me. So I sat down and wrote a poem while I was waiting for the kaizen teams to wrap up their presentations. After the presentations, I stood up and I read her poem, and then I read my poem [Figure 4-11]. Every time a rack came down she sent me a poem, and every time I sent her back a poem of my own. The poems are pretty funny, and they helped people understand what was waste and how to eliminate it. It shows that you can work hard and have a lot of fun at the same time."

The fun did not end there. Art collected the poems he and Barbie wrote and made copies to hand out at an upcoming meeting of Wiremold's Board of Directors. Art asked Barbie to attend the board meeting to explain how she got rid of all the parts hotels. Barbie showed up dressed entirely in black and

Figure 4-9 Art's Sign

Figure 4-10 Barbie's Poem

ODE TO ART

"Inventory is Evil" said King Arthur of Kaizen
So he Came to Dame Barbie With His Plan.
You Must Make These Horrid Racks Go Away Or
February 25th is Your Banishment Day.

Dame Barbie Cried And Wrung Her Hands
But King Arthur Had Made His Noble Stand
So She Gathered Her Trusty Knights Around
And Now Racks K & L Can't Be Found.

Source: The Wiremold Company. Reprinted with permission.

Figure 4-11 Art's Poem

THE PARTS HOTEL

WELCOME TO THE PARTS HOTEL
IT'S REALLY QUITE THE PLACE!
WE LOVE OUR PARTS SO VERY MUCH
WE GIVE THEM LOTS OF SPACE

THEY COME ON IN TO GET A REST
WE TREAT THEM ALL THE BEST
THEY LAY ABOUT FOR WEEKS OR MONTHS
JUST WAITING TO GO OUT

WE LOVE FOR THEM TO GATHER DUST
IN THIS WE REALLY TRUST
AND SOMETIMES IF WE'RE LUCKY
THEY STAY LONG ENOUGH TO RUST!

THEY HAVE A LOT OF FUN HERE
THEY MAKE A LOT OF BUDDIES
WE FEEL WE CAN SELL THEM FOR MORE MONEY
IF THEY GET A LITTLE CRUDDY

THE HOTEL IS REALLY SPACIOUS
THE RACKS GO TO THE SKY
IF WE UNDERSTOOD THE WASTE HERE
WE'D ALL BREAK DOWN AND CRY

THE PARTS FLY IN BUT DON'T GO OUT
THEY HOPE THAT THEY'LL GROW OLD
I'M SURE YOU'LL UNDERSTAND THIS
THEIR ONLY OTHER OPTION IS TO FINALLY GET SOLD

THEY REALLY LIKE THE STAFF HERE
THEY TREAT THEM WITH SUCH CARE
ESPECIALLY DAME BARBIE
AND THE HAT THAT HIDES HER HAIR

THE LOCATION IS ALSO SPECIAL
IT'S DARK AND OUT OF THE WAY
IT'S REALLY PRETTY FAMOUS
THEY CALL IT THE ICA

BUT NOW THE MASSIVE PARTS HOTEL
WITH ITS RACKS UP TO THE CEILING
HAS BEEN EXPOSED AS MASSIVE WASTE
AND HAS THAT SHRINKING FEELING

DAME BARBIE HAS RESPONDED WELL
THE RACKS ARE COMING DOWN
SOON THERE WILL BE NO PARTS HOTEL
AND NO EXTRA PARTS DOING NOTHING BUT LYING AROUND

Source: The Wiremold Company. Reprinted with permission.

Figure 4-12 Barbie's Poem to the Board

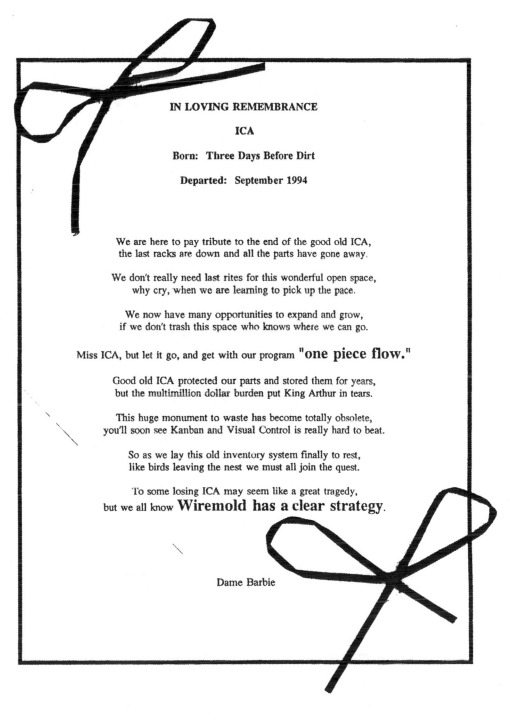

IN LOVING REMEMBRANCE

ICA

Born: Three Days Before Dirt

Departed: September 1994

We are here to pay tribute to the end of the good old ICA,
the last racks are down and all the parts have gone away.

We don't really need last rites for this wonderful open space,
why cry, when we are learning to pick up the pace.

We now have many opportunities to expand and grow,
if we don't trash this space who knows where we can go.

Miss ICA, but let it go, and get with our program **"one piece flow."**

Good old ICA protected our parts and stored them for years,
but the multimillion dollar burden put King Arthur in tears.

This huge monument to waste has become totally obsolete,
you'll soon see Kanban and Visual Control is really hard to beat.

So as we lay this old inventory system finally to rest,
like birds leaving the nest we must all join the quest.

To some losing ICA may seem like a great tragedy,
but we all know **Wiremold has a clear strategy**.

Dame Barbie

wearing a black veil. The directors thought Barbie was a disgruntled employee or was there to tell a tragic story. She went on to read a poem titled, "In Loving Remembrance: ICA," which memorialized the inventory control areas (Figure 4-12). Her accomplishment inspired one director, Millard Pryor, to pen a poem of his own. The signs were a physical reminder of Art's instructions and put pressure on people to think differently about the racks – to begin to see how they did nothing more than hide waste. The signs and poems served as a teaching tool both at that time and into the future.

Art knew there were important financial and operational benefits to eliminating the parts hotels and reducing inventories as quickly as possible, including:

- A reduction in total costs of carrying inventory (direct and indirect expense)
- Increased cash flow
- Increased factory floor space to support future growth
- Waste would become visible
- Commitment to one-piece flow

However, this created a problem. Reducing inventories would result in a negative impact on gross profit for several quarters as the inventories were depleted and converted to sales or written-off as obsolete or damaged items. The apparent increase in the cost of sales could turn a gross profit into a loss if inventory was dramatically reduced within a very short period of time, as illustrated in Table 4-1.

Table 4-1 Effect of Inventory Reduction on Profits and Cash Flow

		B&Q	Lean
Net Sales		4,250,000	4.250,000
Cost of Sales:			
Beginning Inventory		980,000	980,000
Material Purchases		1,570,800	1,160,800
Wages and Benefits		1,628,600	1,628,600
Other Manufacturing Costs		790,500	790,500
	Subtotal	4,969,900	4,559,900
Ending Inventory		(980,000)	(300,000)
Cost of Sales		3,989,900	4,259,900
Gross Profit		260,100	(9,900)
Depreciation		75,000	75,000
Cash Flow from Manufacturing		335,100	745,100

In this example, the number of inventory turns – cost of sales divided by ending inventory – have increased from 4 to 14. This improvement would occur over time, likely a few years. At the same time there would be improvements in productivity and sales growth that would offset the charge to income for prior periods labor and overhead that were capitalized as part of inventory.

The near-term negative impact on profitability can be a disincentive that most managers will find difficult to overcome. However, it should not be a barrier because it is only a transitional issue – a short-term price to pay for past errors. There is no other way around it.[19] Orry Fiume commented on this problem:

> "In a traditional, standard cost absorption accounting system, you set your overhead rates based on some budgeted number of hours and then on a month-to-month basis you absorb based on actual hours. If your actual hours are more than that budget amount, you have a favorable absorption variance. If they are less than that budget amount, you get an unfavorable variance. What happens is, as you bring inventory down, let's say sales stay flat, now what you're doing is satisfying the customer out of inventory, not out of current production. So you're not creating any hours, and that creates huge unfavorable variances which kills the P&L. That's where the CEO who doesn't understand what's going on says: 'I don't know what you're doing, but stop it, it's killing us.' It happens all the time."

Once the company gets through the near-term negative impact on profits, it emerges in much stronger financial position. Notice the substantial increase in cash flow from manufacturing. This allowed Wiremold to begin to realize its growth strategy by providing an internal source of funding for acquisitions and new product development.[20]

Consolidating the Supply Base

While the management team did much to improve internal operations, it also had to make some changes in relationships with suppliers who provided materials to the factory. In 1991, the West Hartford plant did business with over 340 production materials suppliers. It was simply far too many to manage effectively. In addition, purchase volumes were fragmented across numerous suppliers with variable levels of service and quality performance. Dozens of suppliers were there just in case they were needed to respond to occasional part shortages. When asked what caused the proliferation of suppliers and fragmented purchasing volumes, Frank Giannattasio said:

> "Suppliers have a mission to sell you something. For example, we'd have four different engineers working on six different projects and they were all looking for a solution to their problems. Different suppliers would come in and tell each engineer that they needed their full line of screws, when all we needed was just two types of screws for each project. That's how we ended up doing business with hundreds of

companies, each supplying us with a few types of similar products. We had a centralized purchasing organization at the time, and they did not do their part to control the growth of the supply base."

Orry Fiume characterized the importance of suppliers' products to Wiremold's processes:

> "We used to play one steel supplier against another to get a better price. But in reality, this was costing us more in terms of poor quality and rework. When you buy steel, you give the suppliers a specification that contains upper and lower tolerances. If you set your machine up and Supplier A delivers steel at the high end of the tolerance, while Supplier B delivers steel at the low end of the tolerance, and then you start switching rolls of steel, the variation in tolerances causes expensive quality problems."

The first step was to consolidate the supply base by eliminating poor performers and redundant capabilities. Orry Fiume described the process:

> "We look at our Tier 1 suppliers as partners.[21] You have to be good partners, which means you don't play games like pitting one supplier against the other, not paying them on time, or stretching out payment terms. Those are not the things that partners do to each other. Instead, we educated them. We invited them in to see what we are doing, conducted training sessions, invited them on kaizen teams, etc. We wanted our suppliers to understand what we were trying to accomplish and the reasons for it, so that when you start asking them to behave differently, they understand why it's important to them. They also understand that if we are going to reduce the number of suppliers by 90%, there will be winners and losers in that process. If they want to be a winner, they have to get on board. But once they do, they win the work for a long period of time."

Frank Giannattasio provided details of how the supply base was reduced:

> "The first 150 suppliers that were cut just never got a purchase order from us again. Going from 150 to 100, then 100 to 75, was a 'make the cut' type of process. We invited suppliers to participate in kaizen. Some suppliers quickly demonstrated that they had no interest in working with a company that was going to place those kinds of demands on them, and so they didn't make the cut. Then there were some suppliers that sent in their top management and quickly saw merit in what they

were participating in and embraced it. Those suppliers were part of the last 75. The next 25 that were cut offered us the least value in their overall package. They were good suppliers, but they lacked technical capabilities to participate in our product development, or we were such a small part of their business that we didn't get enough attention.

You can have suppliers involved up-front as participants in your improvement effort. But getting the pull system to function properly is the important last step. You cannot demand world-class performance from your suppliers without showing them how it's done. A lot of people think JIT is just a material supply thing; that you just beat the daylights out of the supplier to get them to deliver material several times a day, even when they are producing the material in large batches."

Frank described some specific changes that occurred when Wiremold interacted with fewer numbers of suppliers:

"Our communication with suppliers is much more timely than in the prior centralized purchasing process. The problem that we first inflicted on them was that we probably talked to them eight times a day with four different people, which of course became very cumbersome and sent a confusing message regarding their performance. So we developed a standard work process so that all communication was contained in messages delivered two times per day. Where we used to project only annual demand, we now update 12-month demand on a quarterly basis and commit to 3 months worth of material. We obviously don't bring 3 months worth of material into the plant, we just commit to that amount. The material is either immediately available at the supplier's plant or it can be quickly converted to suit our needs.

Instead of squeezing supplier margins, we try to take cost out of the supplier's operations by doing kaizen to improve their processes. We've always used price increase discussions to say we want them to come in because we want to understand why labor costs are going up. Inevitably, we've gone in and helped them contain cost and in many cases averted the price increase. Generally the only price increases that we are willing to sign-up for is when the basic commodity material is going up in a documented way. When steel, copper, or aluminum is going up in the commodity markets, we understand that and we have to participate in those price increases. We've taken cost out of supplier's products by working on packaging. When you're getting product turning over at the rate we do, we spend a lot of time unpacking material. We look to see if the packaging is necessary for the protection of the product in transit, or is this something that was made for a different customer who has it sitting in inventory for 3 months. So we reduced steel banding and outside protective materials because some things don't have time to rust – we use the material right away."

As part of the change in purchasing practices, the purchasing department was combined with production planning and then decentralized to support product line teams.[22] Frank Giannattasio described the daily activities of buyer-planners:

"The buyer-planner is a materials management position. They will help make sure that we're buying competitively, that the incoming material is good quality, and represent us as one company to our supply base. They'll do material sourcing and planning capacity to meet the expected demand. Their job takes them out on the floor throughout the day because they physically collect and move kanban cards to order parts and plan short-term material requirements with suppliers. They go and review production or productivity data to evaluate whether or not the capacity is there that they planned to have. They have to do some analysis of why output may not be what they planned it to be. For example, if a cell is coming up 15% short, they are the person who gets into that analysis and determines what two or three parts we're not able to produce at cycle time. They may dig deeper and find out that there's a quality issue with a particular supplier part that's causing the shortfall. They will go out and ask the initial questions to the associates on the line to find out why we are not performing to plan.

Those that have more experience may have a primary supplier management role. We have 12 very critical partners, and of those 12 we have 4 or 5 that are even more critical: the steel supplier, corrugated supplier, packaging supplier, non-metallic material supplier, and aluminum supplier, which represent most of the material that is delivered to the Connecticut plants. So we try to divide those responsibilities so that different people can gain experience in coordinating the plants or the company's efforts with them. It's hard to separate the key 12 suppliers from our organization; they all have somebody in here daily or at least several times a week. Some of them participate in our Voice of the Customer activities with our new product development teams."

Art Byrne explained how consolidating the supply base resulted in benefits for Wiremold's internal operations, their suppliers, and Wiremold's customers:

> "We took our supplier base from about 340 companies down to 40 or so. Some of them weren't too happy because they lost what business they had, but the other ones that were willing to work with us and support our way of doing business have enjoyed a lot more business. Quite a few of our suppliers have actually done kaizen in their operations to try to help them to keep up with where we wanted to go. So they get some gain from that. Most of them haven't taken what we have showed them and moved it on much further, but they did accept some training. So we got some gains from that. The real question is how do you take these gains to your customers? That is where you are going to gain market share, where you get growth, where you're going to distinguish yourself from your competition. You have to be able to translate the gains to your customers."

Summary

The transformation to Lean starts with a commitment by the CEO to learn and practice a completely different type of management system – one that focuses on business processes and process discipline in order to repeat favorable results again and again. Embarking upon the never-ending path of continuous improvement means management recognizes that its prior knowledge and experiences may be based upon flawed assumptions and that conventional solutions to business problems are actually ineffective. Kaizen is the process for making visible the large amount of waste that exists in all business processes. It helps people overcome biases[23] against thinking or acting upon the types of positive change that must occur in order to create value for end-use customers, while simultaneously avoiding destructive tradeoffs between key stakeholders.

Orry Fiume characterized the leadership challenge for the Lean transformation as follows:

> "The leadership has to be willing to invest the time and effort to learn what Lean really is. They have to be willing to abandon any past learning experiences they've had without guilt. They have to just accept the fact that they did it that way in the past because it was the best they knew at the time and not get invested in that past experience to the point of making it a barrier to change. But they're learning a better way. You have to have a totally open mind and pursue this without feeling bad about what you did in the past. You have to mean it and want it more than just words. You have to mean it in actions. Your actions have to be totally consistent. You have to be totally

honest. If people ask you difficult questions, you have to give an honest answer even if it's an unpleasant one, which managers are not prone to do. How many managers are asked the question, 'Are you going to have a layoff?', and they say 'No,' and then three days later they announce a layoff. You do that and you've lost your credibility. The leadership has to take the time to understand Lean. They can't delegate the practice or the understanding of it to somebody else."

The leadership challenge is great and multi-faceted. It includes realizing that people are not waste and managers must behave in ways that demonstrate this recognition. Lean leaders know that it is the business processes that contain immense amounts of waste and it is process waste that must be eliminated, not people. The challenge for senior managers is to recognize where the opportunities really are, as noted by Tom Fairbank:

"Most senior managers can not see the opportunities for improvement in their business, even though they are very evident. So instead of trying to improve their operations in the United States, they'll decide to move to another country where wages are much lower. But in most cases, they haven't done anything to improve the process; they've just lowered their cost. What we're saying is that Lean is very inexpensive to do and you can still keep your business in the United States. The unit cost of labor isn't a big issue if you can double your sales without increasing your workforce. It's a totally different way of doing business."

Key Points for Senior Managers

- The factory layout must be changed in order to effectively eliminate waste.
- Set-up reduction – for any activity – is a key to reducing lead-times, improving quality, and reducing cost.
- Implementing one-piece flow requires the use of visual controls, production leveling, and the kanban system.[24]
- The reduction in inventory has a short-term negative impact on profitability but a positive impact on cash flow.
- The cash flow generated by reducing inventories can serve as a source of internal funding for new product development and acquisitions, in support of future growth.
- The supply base must be consolidated and taught how to respond to pull systems.
- CEO's leading the Lean transformation must understand that business processes contain waste, and people are not waste.

Notes

1. In industrial settings, people have a natural preference to locate similar types of machines together. For example, all of the lathes will be grouped in one area, all milling machines will be grouped in another area, and all stamping machines will be grouped in yet another area. Assembly operations will be located in an area far away from the lathes, milling, and stamping machines. (A similar approach is used in office settings). The people who design factories obviously believe this type of layout is more efficient; otherwise they would not have designed it that way. As Art Byrne says, "Do the stamping presses like to be together? Do they like to work and sleep together?" Now let's use this same logic for locating the equipment found in the home. All sofas should be put together in one room, all beds in another room, all chairs in another room, all tables in another room, all telephones in another room, and all televisions in yet another room. This obviously makes no sense; it is grossly inefficient and ineffective, as the quality of life at home would be terrible. Yet this is the accepted practice in manufacturing businesses! For the home to be both functional and efficient for its inhabitants, different pieces of equipment must be arranged in close proximity so that they can be used in *combination* with each other. Locating the same types of equipment together in a factory simply demonstrates that: 1) no thought was given to how equipment is used or how work flows, and 2) management's observation skills are very poor. This is the reason why re-arranging the factory layout is a fundamental aspect of Lean management practice. Likewise, businesses must use different functions in combination with each other. Lean businesses do this better than batch-and-queue businesses.

2. Manufacturing cells are U-shaped to use floor space efficiently, reduce operator walking, promote visual management, and improve communication. Also, the material flow in a manufacturing cell is counterclockwise since most people are right-handed, which facilitates parts transfer from one person or process to the next.

3. The simplest and most important root cause analysis tool is called the "5 Why's." When a problem arises, the root cause can be determined by asking why five *or more* times. This will reveal the true nature of the problem, and countermeasures can then be applied to avoid repeat occurrences. The "5 Why's" technique will solve perhaps 95% of problems. More elaborate methods such as six-sigma may be needed for the remaining 5%. The "5 Why's" should be used by every person in the company – including senior management – on a regular basis, as it is a highly effective method for eliminating waste. See *Toyota Production System*, T. Ohno, Productivity Press, Portland, OR, 1988, pp. 17–18 and 123.

4. The term "one piece flow" leads some people to think literally that one complete piece is being made at a time (which is related to the misconception that Lean is a zero inventory system). This interpretation can be a barrier. What is really happening is that one piece is being processed at a time. So, if there are six processes in the manufacturing cell, then there will be a small number of pieces of material in process. The minimum number of pieces to ensure flow is called the "standard work in process" (SWIP), which depends upon the takt time. In contrast, the batch-and-queue system would require hundreds or thousands of pieces at each process, which results in high WIP inventory expense. The difference is remarkable. For example: 10 pieces x 6 processes = 60 pieces of SWIP for Lean, versus 1000 pieces x 6 processes = 6,000 pieces of WIP for batch-and-queue. The same method can be applied for performing service work such as processing insurance claims.

5. The basic economic order quantity (EOQ) formula is expressed as $Q^* = (2K\lambda/h)^{1/2}$, where Q^* is the economic order quantity, K is the set-up cost, λ is the demand rate (assumes demand rate is known and a constant units per unit time), and h is the holding cost. See *Production and Operations Analysis*, S. Nahmias, Irwin, Chicago, IL, 1997, Chapter 4. The EOQ model is not recognized in Lean practice because set-up times are not fixed and holding costs are typically grossly underestimated. The EOQ provides the illusion of precision and control while encouraging exactly the wrong behaviors.

6. As might be expected, Wiremold's approach to managing information and processing data using computer systems closely follows Lean principles and practices. Their information technology (IT) investment philosophy can be described as "fast follower" rather than "early adopter." They try to avoid purchasing and implementing IT technology in "batch" mode. Rather, they try to keep up with technology by investing smaller amounts of money more frequently. In addition, Wiremold makes sure that it does not automate wasteful business processes. Instead, they will first improve the processes using kaizen and then automate the remaining process steps where it makes sense to do so.

7. In Lean terminology, inventory is often referred to as "money sleeping" because it is an investment that does not generate a return as products have been made and stored in advance of customer orders. In addition, inventory loses value over time, hides waste, and thus increases costs. Lean is not a zero inventory system. In other words, some level of inventory is needed to run the business in the best manner possible at any point in time, consistent with end-use customer service level requirements. For example, Japanese automobile dealer networks operate a business system with an average of 20–30 days worth of finished goods inventory, while US automakers typically have 45–90 days worth of inventory. Some in-process inventory may be needed as de-couplers or WIP "supermarkets" when continuous flow is not possible. Standard work in process (SWIP) is needed within manufacturing cells to separate the operator from the machine and to maintain continuous flow. Wiremold's objective was to create a replenishment system, which requires some inventory. However, the level of inventory would be much lower than the competition because their response

time was becoming much faster. Eliminating waste would further improve Wiremold's response time, and thus reduce the level of inventory (assuming the number of SKU's remain constant). What the Lean management system demonstrates is that the level of inventory actually needed is far less than what we normally think is needed. The key is to reduce lead-times through set-up reduction. See Note 4.

8. One of Wiremold's goals is to make "every part every day," which has been achieved by numerous manufacturing cells. By making every part number's daily requirement every day, Wiremold has been able to dramatically reduce finished goods inventories as well as reduce upstream WIP "supermarket" inventories, thereby realizing higher inventory turns and increased customer fill rates.

9. It also embodies the "respect for people" principle in two important ways: 1) better financial performance helps stabilize employment, as reductions in workforce are often the result of inventory corrections due to a severe mismatch between supply and demand – i.e. overproduction; and 2) management has a responsibility to ensure that people are not wasting time making things that end-use customers have not actually purchased.

10. A standard work chart is a single page diagram posted in each manufacturing cell that shows the sequence in which work is performed. It includes symbols that depict the location in which quality checks are performed, safety warnings, and the standard inventory (quantity of parts in process), takt time, and cycle time. See Exhibit 3-3.

11. A standard work combination sheet (SWCS) is a detailed visual description of how a part is processed for each operation in a manufacturing cell. It includes the time (usually in seconds) associated with three types of activities: manual (human), machine, and walking. Other information contained on the SWCS sheet includes the part number, work sequence (or operation number), and takt time. The SWCS is the basis for future improvement by kaizen. To some, the term "standard work" implies that the work sequence does not change. This is incorrect. The SWCS is changed in response to new ideas by the team, changes in the rate of customer demand, by improving the process, or by changing the manpower. See Exhibit 3-4.

12. For additional information on the kanban system, see: *Kanban: Just-In-Time at Toyota*, M. Lu (Translator), Productivity Press, Portland, OR, 1986, and *Toyota Production System*, Y. Monden, Engineering and Management Press, Norcross, GA, 1998.

13. The term "Just-In-Time" was coined by Mr. Kiichiro Toyoda c. 1936, which he described as: "Just make what is needed in time, but don't make too much." See *Toyota: 50 Years in Motion*, E. Toyoda, Kodansha International, Tokyo, Japan, 1987, p. 58. Also, Mr. Toyoda was influenced by the work of Henry Ford, principally through his book *My Life and Work* (with S. Crowther, Garden City Publishing Co., Inc., Garden City, NY, 1922), as cited in *Toyota: A History of the First 50 Years*, Toyota Motor Corporation, Toyota City, Japan, 1988, p. 42.

14. ERP software now usually has associated with it a demand management software module that may include kanban card creation routines. While the software may generate a kanban card, it does not create a complete kanban system – in part because it does not include production leveling (heijunka). Such ERP systems simply generate move tickets that look like kanban cards, which is nothing more than the common practice used in batch-and-queue production.

15. Wiremold consolidated distribution to the Memphis, TN, facility in 1989, and then moved its distribution center to Middlesex Township, PA, in 2002.

16. Starting in 1999, kanban signals would be sent electronically to each of Wiremold's plant sites.

17. Demand amplification, also known as the "bullwhip effect," occurs when small variations in demand at the retail end of the supply chain become amplified due to each supplier's efforts to process (i.e. adjust) the demand information it receives from the preceding tier. Companies will often try to dampen demand amplification by increasing buffer inventories, which normally leads to higher costs and does not address the root cause of demand fluctuations.

18. The term "parts hotel" is used disparagingly to describe places where parts rest in queue between operations or as finished goods. The term is used to make people aware that parts do not need to rest. The idea is to create manufacturing cells and implement one-piece flow to eliminate costly parts hotels. The cost is not only in WIP and finished goods inventories, but also in using productive floor-space for unproductive purposes, storage racks, pallets, boxes, totes, labeling machines and labels, materials handling equipment, parts re-inspection, spoilage, etc.

19. Unless, of course, as the Enron bankruptcy has taught us, a special purpose entity (i.e. off-balance sheet partnership) was created to remove these "assets" from the balance sheet. Not recommended!

20. See *Toyota Management System*, Y. Monden, Productivity Press, Portland, OR, 1993, pp. 1–28, for further discussion on sources and uses of funds.

21. Important information on how Lean businesses manage key supplier relationships can be found in: *The Machine that Changed The World*, J. Womack, D. Jones, and D. Roos, Rawson Associates, New York, NY, 1990, Chapter 6; "Supplying the Toyota Production System: Intercorporate Organizational Evolution and Supplier Subsystems," W. Fruin and T. Nishiguchi in *Country Competitiveness*, B. Kogut, Ed., Oxford

University Press, New York, NY, 1993, pp. 225–246; *Strategic Industrial Sourcing*, T. Nishiguchi, Oxford University Press, New York, NY, 1994; "Toyota Supplier Development," G. Bounds in *Cases in Quality*, G. Bounds, Editor, R.D. Irwin Co., Chicago, IL, pp. 3–25, 1996; "Partnering the Honda Way," G. Bounds, A. Shaw, and J. Gillard, in *Cases in Quality*, G. Bounds, Editor, R.D. Irwin Co., Chicago, IL, pp. 26–56; *The Evolution of a Manufacturing System at Toyota*, T. Fujimoto, Oxford University Press, New York, NY, 1999, Chapter 5 and 6; *Supply Chain Development for the Lean Enterprise*, R. Cooper and R. Slagmulder, Productivity Press, Portland, OR, 1999; "Creating and Managing a High Performance Knowledge-Sharing Network: The Toyota Case," J. Dyer and K. Nobeoka, *Strategic Management Journal*, Vol. 21, No. 3, pp. 345–367, 2000; and "Supplier Development at Honda, Nissan and Toyota: A Historical Case Study of Organizational Capability Enhancement," working paper, October 1998, M. Sako, http://www.sbs.ox. ac.uk/html/faculty_profile_research.asp?ID=5137. Compare these descriptions of collaborative problem solving and capability development, which yield long-term competitive advantage, to the online reverse auction tool used by many large companies (see http://www.theclbm.com/publications.html), including at least one of Wiremold's key competitors, to drive short-term cost savings.

22. Having 340 suppliers requires a large purchasing department, while having 40 does not.

23. Biases against change are typically rooted in the fear of being criticized for past decisions that were made in relation to people (hiring, promotions, etc.) or money (expensive investments in machines, software, facilities, new products or services, etc.). Specific types of bias include: anchoring, status quo, sunk-cost, confirming evidence, framing, and estimating and forecasting (See "The Hidden Traps in Decision Making," J. Hammond, R. Keeney, and H. Raffia, *Harvard Business Review*, Vol. 76, No. 5, 1998, pp. 47–58). Kaizen and root cause analysis are highly effective at eliminating these types of biases in business decision-making. Also, they must be practiced in a no-blame environment in order to overcome the biases related to past decisions and ineffective modes of thinking.

24. Note that kanbans are temporary measures to solve the problem of not being able to achieve true one-piece flow between shared resources – i.e. situations where processes are not connected.

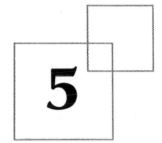

5

LEAN IS A PEOPLE SYSTEM

How Management Views People

In conventional management practice, people are often viewed as a burden or cost to be eliminated. This belief is characteristic of managers that have been trained in batch-and-queue management practices.[1] Most managers think the way to solve problems is by spending money, and will seek new technologies that replace people. Their determined efforts are a simplistic and frequently ineffective approach to cost reduction. For example, in the 1980's, management focused capital investments on factory automation systems. In the 1990's, managers shifted capital investment decisions to computer hardware and sophisticated software. In many cases, these technologies turned out to be expensive investments that fell short of expectations. Management clearly did not understand the root cause of the problems that it was trying to fix. It was very easy, however, to purchase expensive "silver bullet" solutions.[2]

The essence of recent management practice is a strong emphasis on achieving results, with little or no interest in the processes used to achieve the results. To do this, a general set of management behaviors are used which demonstrates that people are not respected.[3] For example, management will lay people off, close plants, and squeeze suppliers' margins in an effort to maintain price competitiveness or to fulfill the corporation's primary purpose: maximize shareholder value.[4] Dividing stakeholders is commonly seen as acceptable leadership practice, and that success often is best achieved by making tradeoffs between such key stakeholders as employees, suppliers, customers, the community, and the environment. Giving consideration to these stakeholders is typically seen as a cost that reduces profitability, and hence shareholder value, and has no quantifiable economic benefit.

Managers operating batch-and-queue businesses drive employees to optimize the individual parts of the business hoping that the sum of these efforts will result in overall improved competitiveness. However, employees that are strongly focused on internal local optimization lose sight of their customers and other key stakeholders. Invariably, most of an employee's time is spent on non-value added work and waste.

Senior managers, who on the surface appear very strongly focused on costs and profitability, will inadvertently destabilize their business and achieve inconsistent financial performance.[5] This then requires management to make additional tradeoffs among key stakeholders and leads to greater dissatisfaction. The batch-and-queue management system must, by its very design, exact a high toll on all forms of resources available to a business: time, people (employees, customers, suppliers, and investors), money, physical resources (buildings and machines), corporate image, the community, and the environment.

The Lean leader has a completely different perspective on the value of people in business.[6] Fundamentally, the view is that people are valuable, not waste, and that it is business processes that contain waste. They recognize the importance of people and that technology can be very useful if it is carefully understood and selectively applied. Through direct experience, management knows that people possess a vast supply of creativity and will contribute their ideas to eliminate waste and create value for end-use customers if given the opportunity to do so.[7] Management takes very seriously its responsibility to manage human resources effectively and to help people realize their full potential.[8] Scott Bartosch explains:

> "Lean is not just about being more efficient or figuring out how many people you need to get a job done. It's also about understanding what people really want to do. We have three people now who are probably some of the best billing and credit people that I know of. They hate being on the phone to customers. They don't want to take an order; that's not their thing. But prior to this they were on the phone taking orders from customers. Were we using them to their maximum potential? No, we weren't. You have to participate in figuring out what they are best at doing.

> It's like the concept of having leaders at every level within a company. Not everybody wants to be a team leader. Not everybody has the capacity to be a team leader. But you have certain people within a company that are tremendous individual contributors, and you have to learn how to identify a person who's an individual contributor. For example, Sue [not her real name] was our inside sales manager. She managed our customer service department and did a very good job. But as we grew and as we began to make the kind of changes that we were making here, Sue was in over her head. This was not what she wanted to do. If you looked at Sue's strengths, nobody knew our order entry and customer system better than Sue. She could tell you about it inside, backwards, forwards and sideways. Sometimes you just have to go and lay your cards on the table. So I said to Sue, 'I don't think you're doing what you want to be doing.' She said, 'Well, what am I going to do?' I said, 'We are going to set up an electronic data interchange [EDI] system with our customers. How would you like to have that responsibility.' She was delighted and was a great individual contributor."

> We both needed to make a change. She's a talented lady; she may have left the company if she got stuck in that leadership position. But we took the time to say 'What does she really like to do?' When you watch somebody jump into it, just get immersed into it right up to their ears, then it's all worthwhile."

The Lean leader understands that the purpose of business is to fulfill socio-economic objectives,[9] and that managing a business in purely economic terms will result in destructive tradeoffs and therefore wasteful imbalances. People are considered a precious resource. Associates are hired carefully and not discharged easily, and viewed as resources to develop. Ed Miller explains:

> "When we add a person, it's very carefully thought out, but we try very hard not to add a person. Instead, we try to grow people by giving them different assignments and expanding their capabilities."

Customers are seen as resources that provide important feedback for improving products, reducing costs, and improving quality, rather than simply purchasers of goods and services. Suppliers are viewed as resources that help create value for end-use customers, rather than simply instruments with which to bargain for lower prices. The environment is seen as a resource to conserve rather than exploit, and business should contribute to the development of the community. The trust placed by investors in management is demonstrated by achieving stable long-term equity growth and consistent payment of dividends. In this way, management leverages the interests and capabilities of key stakeholders, rather than dividing them. The term "corporate responsibility" is thus understood and applied in a more meaningful and balanced way.

The Lean leader is acutely aware of the importance of generating profits reliably throughout the business cycle, without having to resort to deceptive accounting practices.[10] Well-defined processes are used to plan corporate profit targets and manage costs at the source, including target costing, kaizen costing, and value engineering.[11] The Lean management system, operated correctly, is both highly disciplined and process-focused, which in turn yields consistent results. An important outcome is the establishment of inter-organizational learning routines that respond rapidly to common business problems, as well as capability building over time, which results in improved competitiveness.[12] People make the Lean management system work.

A Lean business can be created two different ways: by establishing a new, or greenfield operation, or by converting a brownfield business, such as The Wiremold Company. A greenfield Lean business has the opportunity to carefully select people for employment who meet such specific criteria as the ability to work on teams, willingness to try new ideas, interest in cross-functional experiences, and are self-motivated. However, in a brownfield business, the transformation to a Lean management system usually begins with the recognition by senior management that the business is overstaffed. This situation is entirely due, unfortunately, to past batch-and-queue business practices.

Art Byrne knew from walking around the West Hartford plant during his initial interviews that Wiremold was overstaffed because productivity was low. He also knew that something would have to be done about that before they could embark on the Lean journey. Whatever actions were planned would have to be done carefully since Art viewed people as his most valuable resource.

People's Reaction to Lean

Based upon prior experience with the Lean management system, Art knew that people's response would typically follow a normal distribution curve. There would be a small group, 5–10% at the beginning of the curve, who would eagerly embrace the change. Then there would be a larger group of people, 40–45% that would adapt fairly quickly because they saw benefits for themselves as well as the company. Jobs would become more interesting, the working environment would become cleaner and less complicated, and profit sharing would increase as company profitability improved. Another large group, 35–40%, would watch the second group, and ask a lot of questions, but they would eventually support the change because they didn't want to leave the company. Finally, there would be 5% or so that would resist the changes. In most cases, resisters would become very dissatisfied with the new environment and leave on their own. This source of attrition was beneficial to Wiremold as it was clearly overstaffed in 1991.

Art Byrne also was aware of some general relationships between head counts in various departments, sales levels, and productivity. The senior management team concluded that they needed to reduce the total workforce by 15 percent. The questions then became, what was the best way to reduce the work force? The senior management team decided that they could afford the cost of a voluntary early retirement program (VERP). If enough eligible salaried and hourly associates took advantage of the VERP, there would be no need for layoffs. The criteria that senior management used to select people for the voluntary early retirement was simple: age plus number of years of service. If layoffs became necessary, then the senior management team would evaluate categories of jobs and specific positions judged to be non-value added.

Art announced the voluntary early retirement program at the West Hartford facility in late December 1991. As Orry Fiume recalled:

> "On November 1, 1991, we had 406 hourly and 257 salaried people for a total of 663. We had 72 candidates or 17% of the hourly workforce and 17 people or 6% of the salaried workforce accept the offer. When it ended, 82% of those eligible for the VERP took it. But only 41% of those eligible in the salary work force took it. Overall we had about a 13% reduction."

Wiremold had a reduction in workforce within the first four months of Art's arrival. While sufficient numbers of hourly associates accepted the offer, not enough of the eligible salaried associates took advantage of the voluntary early retirement program, which then resulted in a small number of layoffs. In 1992, there was another reduction in force in response to poor economic conditions. Judy Seyler recalled what happened next:

> "We had another voluntary early retirement program in 1993, and again, not enough salary people took it. So we had another reduc-

tion in force. At that point we reduced the salary force by 36 people and that brought us to a total of 15% reduction in salary force."

So Wiremold ended up having two reductions in workforce in the first two years. While most of the reduction was achieved through voluntary early retirements, some layoffs were necessary. Art Byrne commented on the initial round of voluntary early retirements and involuntary separations:

> "What associates asking about a potential layoff are really saying is, 'I'm about ready to buy a new car and commit myself to $300 per month in car payments. If I have this job and can count on it, then I can get through the 3 or 4-year period of the loan on this car and I'm fine. On the other hand, if we are definitely going to have a layoff, and I'm probably going out the door because I have low seniority, I don't want to commit to this or that, a new car or a new roof on my house or whatever it happens to be.' Your answer will affect their behavior and their lives and their kid's lives and everything else, so we have always taken the approach that you just have to be flat out honest with people and tell them the way things are as best we know it."

Art Byrne was able to see differently the question that most managers view as simple-minded and unnecessarily provocative in a group setting: "Will there be a layoff?" He understood that this question had deeper meaning in the minds of those who asked it, as well as those who did not. He was aware of their concerns and thus able to put the pending workforce reduction into a context that people would understand and come to accept. Associates would understand how work at Wiremold would change in the future, with kaizen playing a prominent role. Art Byrne explained:

> "So it was very important that we provide an honest message about the voluntary early retirement and the layoff, along with information about what it would be like to work here in the future. That's why we wanted to give as many people as possible a kaizen experience. The hope was that people who didn't want to work in a Lean environment would leave of their own accord. And that was pretty much what happened."

Most of the people that couldn't adjust took the initiative to find employment elsewhere.

Kaizen was a key process, not only for improving operations; it was also connected to evolving human resource policies and practices. Associates who responded positively to kaizen would have many different types of opportunities to learn, make valuable contributions, develop their skills through job rotations, and advance their careers. Scott Bartosch explained how the senior management team developed human resources:

"We wanted to put people in new and challenging growth situations. We also wanted them to learn how the 'other half' lives. It's vital that they understand it. We started a little ad hoc program six or seven years ago. We wanted to get some of the talent we had in the factory out in the field to face the customer. And we wanted to get some talent we had in the field into the factory to see how the other half lived. What we wanted to achieve was to develop people internally that could operate this business because I'm not going to be here forever. The issue is that whoever does take my job, will not come straight from the sales force without experience in manufacturing because there's too many things intertwined as a company to say, 'Okay, this is the sales operation, this is the manufacturing operation.' We would not be successful if our thinking was that way.

So Frank Giannattasio, Ed Miller, and I decided that we'd swap people who were interested in a new experience. So I took a salesman and gave him to Frank for two years, and he took Tom Fairbank, who is now our plant manager here [in West Hartford], and he gave him to me for two years. I put Tom out selling, just put him out on the street, said 'Here's your bag, Tom.' And we put Rob Riccitelli, who's now our southeastern regional sales manager, in the factory. He was a foreman in the rolling mill area. We told them both, 'If you can't tolerate this, you have got to tell us. You can go back to where you were and it's as if nothing happened; you keep right on with your career. They both came to us and said, 'Are you guys sure you know what the heck you're doing?' But if you look at the two of them today, their potential is absolutely extraordinary. Today [summer 2001] there are probably about 30 people involved in the leadership development program throughout the company.

We have people doing things that they never dreamed they were going to be doing, and in a completely different discipline than where they were 5 years ago or 2 years ago or 10 years ago. It's about trying to teach people that they more than likely have talent they never even thought about using. Rob Riccitelli is a regional manager and he's out in the field and he's talking to the customer. The customer starts asking him, 'What about the Model 4000 raceway product?' Rob will say, 'Well, when I was a foreman in 4000 raceway...' Or, if all of a sudden you wind up talking to Rich Levesque about a product, he can help you understand an installation problem because he used to be the head of maintenance at West Hartford. He can tell you how our product works because he installed them. This does a couple of things for you. First of all, it puts your high potential people on a path to learn the whole business. It also gives people coming in the door an understanding that there are other places they can go to. And it motivates people, whether they want to do another job in another location or if they prefer not to move. You have to have that type of people, too. It motivates them to help the person who is gaining cross-functional experience succeed."

Kevin Fahey was stunned to learn in his first few weeks on the job how willing the senior management team was to move people across functions:

"People like Scott Bartosch, Ed Miller, and Frank Giannattasio would willingly sit down together, without even needing Human Resources to prod them, and say, 'I've got a regional manager here who wants to run a business somewhere down the road and he or she is ready for the next step.' These folks just had the common sense and the good judgment to know that they could either take the conventional approach found in many other organizations and selfishly hold on to their best players because it's going to help drive the performance within their function; or I can put my business hat on and really take seriously my role in helping to develop this organization. That means I've got to be willing to give up my key players and take somebody else's. Of course not every one of those moves has worked, but the majority of them have. And the ones that have not worked, I think we have gotten better at owning up to the fact that they weren't working and in most cases we repositioned the person back into an area where they can be successful."

Tom Fairbank commented on how Wiremold has changed and the importance of internal job rotations:

"The pace of work has certainly changed. It's much more intense now because a lot of the safety nets that we used to have are now gone. The focus of management has also changed; the way we run the company is a lot different. We've got accountants running manufacturing cells, we've got people from sales getting trained as product line team leaders, we've got people going out into field sales to learn that part of the business. That has allowed differences of opinion to emerge and the ability for change to happen."

The Qualified Job Guarantee

In most Lean transformations, participation in kaizen and the resulting productivity improvements result in layoffs. Senior managers that lack a proper understanding of the Lean management system do not know how to use the extra people, and so they usually take advantage of the situation to increase short-term earnings and raise share price performance. As mentioned previously, this is a gross misapplication of Lean principles and practices — a trap that Wiremold did not fall into. Participation in kaizen was never a factor determining who would be eligible for the VERP or who would be laid off. In fact, quite the opposite was true.

In late 1991 and early 1992, Art Byrne told all associates, both salary and hourly, that nobody would lose their job due to the productivity improvements that resulted from kaizen. It was a verbal agreement, resting on the trust that Art had in the workforce to respond positively to change, and further developed a trusting relationship between associates and management. The agreement remained verbal for sixteen months until it was incorporated into the 1993 IBEW contract, which read:

> No Union Associate employed on the effective date of this Agreement shall be subject to layoff, as a direct result of any continuous improvement project or other change in manufacturing method designed to improve quality or efficiency. Nothing herein shall restrict the rights of the Company to adjust its workforce in response to business conditions, provided such rights are not exercised in a manner which violates any other provisions of this Agreement.

According to Judy Seyler, the correct way to reduce headcount at the onset of the Lean transformation, is as follows (in order):

- Offer voluntary early retirement program if you can afford it
- Then, if needed, layoff to meet target; use value-added model to determine who and where
- Offer a qualified job guarantee

"Timing is everything," Judy said. Workforce reductions should be completed within the first few months, prior to announcing the qualified job guarantee.

Most CEO's will strenuously resist making such a commitment. But why? It's because they believe that nobody can guarantee employment. Well, even Art Byrne agrees with that. Notice that he did not guarantee employment. The qualified job guarantee simply gives associates an assurance that they will not lose their job due to their participation in continuous improvement activities. And if these activities are successful, which they invariably are, the company grows and prospers without having to resort to layoffs to increase earnings. Further, the qualified job guarantee motivates associates to learn new ways of doing business. Without it, the amount of improvement that can be achieved is very limited, and the company's competitiveness will be negatively impacted. In addition, the qualified job guarantee is a very important expression of the value management places in people willing to learn and contribute to its success.

The Employee Attitude Survey

One of Art Byrne's concerns from the outset was the information he received from people inside of Wiremold. It was apparent to him in conversations with associates that people withheld some of the facts. As most do with a new President, in the absence of trust, people say what they think he or she wants to hear. Art could not accept that. For change to occur and take root, the senior management team had to have an accurate understanding of associates' issues and concerns.

The process used to understand associates' attitude would be a survey instrument conducted annually starting in early 1992. Art knew that he had to be careful when using surveys, as they are often lengthy and complex, and can yield results that are not actionable by senior management. As might be expected, Art preferred a survey instrument that was easy to use and concise, yet capable of yielding useful data in three key areas: associate-supervisor relationships, associate-management relationships, and overall employee satisfaction with the workplace and benefits program. Wiremold decided to adopt the simple 20-item[13] survey used for many years by Federal Express. Judy Seyler described what happened:

> "In the fall when Art arrived, he told me that he wasn't hearing the truth. He didn't think that he was getting the truth from the people and so he said: 'I want you to go to Memphis, Tennessee, and visit Federal Express and talk to their people about their survey.' The president of Federal Express has been doing this for many years, the same survey, and it was pretty good. So I went and spent a day with the senior vice president of Human Resources at Federal Express and he showed me their survey. I came back with it and we implemented it in 1992.
>
> The employee attitude survey was first so that Art could hear the voice of the people directly from them to him, and not through any intermediary. We developed a process where that could be confidential and absolute. Art is just an incredible leader in the sense that he not only listened to all that feedback, but he did something about it. A couple of months after we got the results I would schedule every team for him to sit and talk with them; anywhere from 45–90 minutes in groups of 6, 8, or 10 associates. He would say, 'You know, this survey tells me that there is a problem here. I want to hear about it.'

Then we would sit and look at all the things that they had to say and see what we could change, what we could make better. Art would do about 50 separate sessions per year, and has done so every year since we started the survey back in 1992."

A key result from the survey was information about relationships between associates, their supervisors, and managers. The management team wanted to ensure that leaders were in place at every level. More importantly, they wanted to identify people in leadership positions who were not behaving as leaders. The survey instrument gave management precise information on who these people were and what the problem was — but not for the purpose of blaming them or to use the information as grounds for immediate dismissal. Rather, the survey was used to identify areas where ineffective leaders could improve. Judy Seyler described the process:

> "These were the people that had been foremen and supervisors, and we had a part of the survey which was indexed to give a rating on the leader. We let the leaders know in no uncertain terms that if their scores were below an acceptable level, then they would have to come up with a personal action plan for improvement. If they didn't get their scores up acceptably in two years, then the understanding was very clear that they would not be a leader anymore. We did terminate some people who were definitely not in favor of the program and were not in favor of being leaders instead of heavy-handed bosses. But we also did an awful lot of reassignments. Those people who were valuable contributors or had valuable knowledge moved into non-leadership positions. That led to a new kind of job structure and a new kind of compensation program. It was an evolution. I guess on the outside it looked like a revolution, but to me it seemed like we were going through a very logical process that ended up eventually changing every single personnel process that we had."

Importantly, the survey instrument was coupled with a leadership development process that gave ineffective leaders an opportunity to improve. As a result, the process was judged by associates to be fair and was also effective at either improving leadership skills or assigning valuable people to non-leadership positions. This resulted in the creation of dual career ladders for leaders and individual contributors, which lead to the introduction of job rotations for skill development. Figure 5-1 shows the results of this employee attitude survey during the first five years of Wiremold's Lean transformation. These 1996 results ranked Wiremold in the 90th percentile of the hundreds of companies participating in the survey nationally.

Figure 5-1 Wiremold's Employee Attitude Survey Results

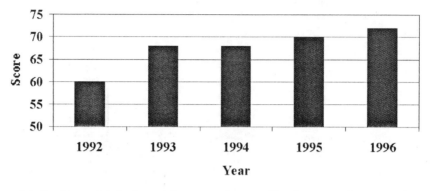

Note: "Score" is non-dimensional measure that represents the average of "agree" responses to the twenty questions.
Source: The Wiremold Company.

The Code of Conduct

Art Byrne brought with him a sense of the management behaviors needed to support the strategy and Lean management system.[15] He knew that a management system that espoused the elimination of waste would require the senior management team to behave differently. They couldn't behave like the results-oriented managers running batch-and-queue businesses. They would instead focus on the business processes from which results flow. Since inconsistent behaviors are de-motivating and cause confusion among the associates, Art modeled the kind of behaviors that senior managers must exhibit in a Lean business. The rest of the senior management team followed his lead.

For several years, that was good enough. Then Art asked his senior management team to develop a code of conduct to articulate explicitly the behaviors that everyone should follow, not just the senior management team. The result was the Wiremold "Code of Conduct" (Figure 5-2). Anyone who violated any of the seven principles would be placed on probation and work with their supervisor to develop a corrective action plan. Ultimately, an associate could be terminated if the violations were repeated or if the corrective action plan and management feedback process proved unsuccessful.

Orry Fiume recalled how the Code of Conduct was developed:

> "One of the things that Art used to talk about when he first came here was the concept that he wanted a one-page human resource policy manual because he hated bureaucracy. We played with that over time and started developing a code of conduct. The first one we drafted was probably two or three pages long, and while we were wordsmithing it one day we sat back and said, 'You know, we're not even sure anyone's going to read this, and if they read it we're not sure anyone will re-

member it.' So we threw it away, and we made a basic rule that said if you can't say it in three words or less, it's not worth saying. And that's what we came up with. If you look at most other companies, they have a large document that tries to address those issues. But it's so cumbersome, so convoluted, and couched in so many ambiguous terms that it's meaningless. Every word you add adds three or four different possibilities for misinterpretation."

Judy Seyler described the Code of Conduct:

"It wasn't until 1996 or 1997 that Art told us he wanted to come up with some kind of a code of conduct for everyone, president on down. So the senior team took a pass at it, and then we got the presidents of our other companies to take a pass at it, and then we put it out to the workforce. It was very simple. There were seven items on it. We had them printed up and the people realized that things were really different; that they could go up to a leader and say, 'It says here on the code of conduct, *Keep Your Promises*.' And the leader would say, 'You are right.' Any leader that was caught doing something like getting back at someone was grounds for losing that position if not their job. That is a good example of where we got to in terms of giving and sharing information, and trusting each other."

Figure 5-2 The Wiremold "Code of Conduct"

Source: The Wiremold Company

The logo at the bottom of the Code of Conduct card is Wiremold's "Core Values." The words surrounding the symbol "Q" (for Quality), people, customers, and kaizen, are a logical extension of the words "people and products" contained in the Total Quality Process booklet published in January 1990.

Art defined these core values shortly after his arrival and they have remained a constant for Wiremold ever since. They mirror some of the early values espoused by D. Hayes Murphy, the company founder. They came from a strong belief that companies are simply collections of people competing against other groups of people in other companies to satisfy the same customer. If you have the best people, motivate them well, and grow their skills, then you will always win. As a result, people have always been the principal focus at Wiremold, with kaizen used as the process enabler that ties everything together and provides the best results for customers. Art Byrne explained this in more detail:

> "Making the change from a traditional batch-and-queue company to Lean, in the end, is all about people. You have to change their attitudes and show them a new way to do things that they can embrace and run with. Let's take a simple example. Let's say that one day I call the set-up operators into a room. They have been with the company 20–25 years on average, and their best set-up times during their whole time with the company averaged around three hours each. I say, 'Hi, I'm Art, and we have to improve to be competitive, so I want you to get the average set-up time down to under 10 minutes.' Well, what do you think they'll say? After they say I'm nuts, they will be able to provide a very detailed list of reasons, all of which make sense, as to why this can't be done. At that point, most companies get stuck; they want to reduce set-up time, but can't. There are too many good reasons why it can't be done coming from the people who do it. On the other hand, if I work with them, show them how to do this, and give them the backing to get it done, then the release of energy and ideas is overwhelming, and they'll do it under five minutes.
>
> So for us, the key focus in moving to Lean has always been on people. You sometimes have to push people to try new things, but watching them grow is very rewarding. Watching them start to win against much larger competitors on a consistent basis is even better."

Top and Bottom 10 Percent

As part of the people development process, the senior management team instituted annual reviews for all associates, which included performance appraisal and career planning. They also established peer reviews at the conclusion of team activities and used external resources to deliver leadership skills development and training.

The final element of the evolving human resource practice was application of an annual forced ranking of all associates. Art Byrne used this practice at General Electric and felt the senior management team should as well. Managers were asked to identify their top and bottom ten percent of all associates using paired comparisons based upon the following criteria:

Individual Contributor	**Leadership**
• Communication	• Communication
• Teaming	• Teaming
• Decisions	• Decisions
• Flexibility	• Flexibility
• Resourcefulness	• Resourcefulness
• Strategic thinking and analytical skills	• Leadership
• Technical competence	• Strategic thinking and analytical skills

The top ten percent were considered to be future leaders and given opportunities to develop through job rotation and leadership training. The bottom ten percent would work with their supervisor to identify specific areas for improvement and develop an action plan. If there were no progress after a period of time, typically six months to one year, the associate would be subject to involuntary separation. Associates that were found stealing or responsible for other serious types of misbehavior were subject to immediate dismissal.

The process that Wiremold senior management used for the bottom ten percent is in stark contrast to how batch-and-queue businesses typically handle such matters: upon completion of a forced ranking, management simply lets people go without giving the affected person an understanding of his or her deficiencies. Thus, the Lean management system, practiced correctly, strives to ensure fairness among stakeholders. While there may be some instances in which it is impossible to ensure a fair outcome, they should be very rare, as the Lean management system does not tolerate frequent violations in philosophy and practice. That, of course, would be wasteful.

Wiremold senior management thus made a clear distinction between the criteria and processes used to reduce headcount to adjust the workforce at the onset of the Lean transformation. The process for adjusting headcount after making the qualified job guarantee is different. While it certainly still includes voluntary early retirement programs and attrition, the focus is now performance-based and includes annual reviews, top and bottom ten percent forced ranking, and associated feedback mechanisms.

The Lines of Defense

When business conditions were good, Wiremold was very careful to limit growth of the permanent workforce because senior management knew that good times don't last forever. Instead they rely on a part-time workforce, typically 15% of the total, which is hired knowing that the condition of employment was that the job might not be needed at some point in the future. Ongoing kaizens ensure that existing internal resources are available in times of increased demand.

What should a business that practices Lean management do when the economy deteriorates? Can management rely solely on voluntary early retirement programs and attrition? Definitely not. Should layoffs be the first course of action, like most companies? Not Wiremold. If economic conditions deteriorate, then Wiremold could invoke its five "lines of defense" (in order):[16]

- Insource work
- Reduce overtime
- Release part-time associates
- Reduce the workweek
- Voluntary early retirement program

Thus, Wiremold has developed a comprehensive system for effectively managing human resources throughout the business cycle. These practices are consistent with the principal of eliminating waste by ensuring that valuable human resources are used effectively.

The Profit Sharing Plan

D. Hayes Murphy began experimenting with profit sharing in 1914 and established a profit sharing plan for all associates in 1916. By tradition, profit sharing was paid by check at the end of each quarter according to the following formula: 15% of pre-tax consolidated income divided by total straight time wages for the quarter. As Wiremold began to acquire companies in the 1990's, the formula was changed. The pool was calculated as 15% of consolidated pre-tax income. Then, the pool was allocated to all Wiremold divisions that report a positive profit for the quarter on a pro rata basis of divisional profits. The division's profit sharing pool was distributed to all associates in the division in proportion to their straight time wages and salaries for the quarter.

Meetings were held each quarter with all associates to report the company's financial and non-financial progress, and the amount of profit sharing that had been paid. Judy Seyler recalled how associates were informed of profit sharing results:

> "Profit sharing had always been paid quarterly in cash as a separate check from your paycheck. Warren Packard always had a

quarterly meeting but it was only with the managers and officers, and they got the results. But the people in the plant got their checks. When Art came in, he had apparently seen or tried or inherited several different kinds of profit sharing plans over the years. When he saw this one he thought it was the best one he had ever seen. Therefore, he didn't change it at all. He just built on that.

The key change that Art made was to hold those quarterly profit sharing meetings in the plant with everybody. So he would make a presentation. He would have the charts. He would show the sales volume. He would show the defect rates. He would show the delay times in shipping. He would show everything that was contributing to the formula. Then he would say, 'Now, the next quarter here is what we have to do. We are going to increase the inventory turns by another two times in the next several months, etc.' And he would say, 'Now it is not shipping's fault, but here is what we have to do,' and that is why people were so intensely involved and knowledgeable about it. Every month we would put a report up on the bulletin boards so that people were looking at profit sharing results month-to-month and say, 'We are going to have a really good third month' or 'We are not going to have as much as we had last time;' that was the conversation. You would go out to post the things out on the bulletin board and people would practically swamp you. You've heard about those crushes at soccer games; that was about the way it was in the plant on profit sharing day."

The profit sharing plan gave all associates a stake in the performance of both the entire company as well as their division. This discouraged actions that would improve department or cell results at the expense of overall company or division performance. It also provided an incentive for management to translate productivity and quality gains into improved financial performance through sales growth.

Wiremold created a 401(k) plan for salary associates in 1985 and matched contributions in company stock. By 1992, associates were seeing a rise in the value of their 401(k) accounts due to the positive effects of kaizen. Their participation in kaizen, in the Lean transformation, paid off both short-term through profit sharing and long-term through the 401(k) plan. Judy Seyler described the performance of the 401(k) plan:

"Almost every person in the plant participated in the 401(k) plan. They were seeing a steady increase in the value of the stock, which increased the matched share in 401(k) plan for the future. They had the short-term reward in profit sharing and they were also watching the long-term reward. Between the time I was hired in 1989 and when I retired in 1999, the stock price had increased over six times. People participating in the 401(k) plan had acquired a considerable asset."

Gaining Union Support For Lean

Wiremold's relationship with the IBEW was adversarial prior to Judy Seyler's promotion in 1990 to Vice President of Human Resources. However, Judy and the IBEW representative, Lorraine Tinsley, worked together to successfully improve that relationship. Judy recalled the situation:

"When I was promoted to Vice President of Human Resources, Warren Packard said to me, 'I don't care how you do it, but I want you to change this adversarial climate that we have here.' So Orry sent me off to Harvard University's school for negotiation[17] and I came back with all these bright ideas. I was talking with the union business manager, Lorraine Tinsley, and she looked over on my bookshelf and she saw the book *Getting to Yes*.[18] She said, 'Oh, where did you get that?' I told her that I had gone to this course. And she said, 'My union sent me to that.' She said, 'Would you be willing to try?' I said 'You bet.' That happened before Art came. Instead of looking to be adversarial, we tried to find a win-win solution. The year prior to my taking over we had something like eleven arbitrations; in my first year we had one. In my whole tenure we only had three arbitrations in nine years."

Art knew from his prior experience with Lean that there would be resistance from all quarters. The union's reaction to the unknown — participating in kaizen — would be essentially no different from that of any other internal stakeholder. They would be concerned about job loss, among other things. This was a fundamental and legitimate concern that management had to address in order to gain acceptance of Lean and work towards achieving the strategy.

In addition to the concern over job security, the union contract contained work rules that specified who could perform various types of work. Senior management expected union representatives to resist any changes to who performed the work, as this would constitute a violation of the contract. Further, the contract and its inflexible work rules were not up for re-negotiation for another 18 months. The barriers to change were formidable.

During the first kaizens, hourly associates alerted their union representatives that salaried associates and managers were doing union jobs. As might be expected, this precipitated some conversations between Art Byrne and the union representatives. Shortly thereafter, they reached a verbal understanding: union rules would be suspended for the duration of the kaizen. Art re-stated his commitment that no associate would be laid off due to the productivity improvements resulting from kaizen, although their jobs might change. Displaced workers would be re-deployed to areas of the company that needed additional labor. Judy Seyler recalled when Art Byrne gave associates a qualified job guarantee in 1992:

> "After we had the initial voluntary early retirement, Art gave them virtually a job guarantee. He said, 'From now on nobody in this company will ever lose their job because of kaizen.' He gave it to both salaried and hourly people. This didn't apply to people who were not pulling their own weight, or where there was a discipline problem or cause for dismissal. But as far as process improvement, nobody will lose his or her job. You might have to be trained for another job or you might work in another section of the plant or the company. What was interesting is that people took his word on it. In 1993 we had a different union negotiator and they requested that guarantee in writing."

A more challenging issue was the need to collapse the many pay grades and job descriptions throughout the organization, for both union and non-union jobs. The 10 pay grades for hourly associates were subdivided into 19 classifications and 48 work assignments,[19] while there were 20 pay ranges for salary associates. The finely divided pay grades that had proliferated over the years contributed to the inability to flexibly respond to changing business conditions, and made it impossible to get work to flow smoothly without interruption. Frank Giannattasio recalled the difficulty of having multiple job classifications:

> "We had nineteen different job classifications. As our production process became one-piece flow, one operator could do the work contained in 4 or 5 different classifications. People at different pay grades were working side by side, which created a bit of a problem. We worked out a solution to consolidate to seven job classifications. This made reassignment of associates much more practical in order to satisfy changing takt times."

Thus, human resource policy issues were at the forefront of the transformation to Lean and had to be addressed concurrently with the introduction of kaizen. Art knew that applying Lean principles and practices would result in many changes to all functional areas, and that Human Resources would be among the first to experience change. Judy Seyler described the situation:

> "We had to do things immediately on the people side to support what we were going to try to do in the plant. I was a member of a union when I was in training for my first job many years ago, and what I found is that you have a large group of people that you have to be sure receive equity, fairness and so

on. How do you establish a relationship that will fairly and honestly represent all those people? We can't negotiate with 400 people. We have to negotiate with union representatives. As long as they are good people doing their jobs right, I didn't see why we couldn't work it out together.

In situations where there was no elected representation, we used many alternative feedback systems such as the employee survey, employee focus groups, employee suggestion programs, and lots of one-on-one interviews and counseling sessions. Leaders were not just encouraged but recognized for establishing good rapport and communication with their team members."

In 1993, Wiremold acquired six businesses. The largest was Walker Systems in West Virginia, a maker of in-floor electrical distribution products. The hourly associates at Walker belonged to the International Association of Machinists and Aerospace Workers (IAMAW) Lodge 2077. The relationship with Walker's management was much more adversarial than the IBEW-Wiremold relationship at the West Hartford plant prior to Art Byrne's arrival. The transfer of West Hartford's Lean management system to Walker was essential to realize the benefits of the acquisition and create value for end-use customers. Rather than view the historical relationship as a barrier, Art and Judy used persistence and creativity to find a solution. Judy Seyler described the situation:

"I didn't really become involved in any of the acquisitions until we got to Walker. Art said to me, 'Walker has a union and they have a contract that is totally inflexible. I want you to go in there and get that contract changed so we can do kaizen.' I went with Art for the signing of the papers in December 1993. That very afternoon, Art and I met with the union leadership. It was quite an experience. Art put up a chart that laid out what a traditional management-union relationship is about and then showed them how Wiremold does business. Their mouths were hanging wide open. They couldn't believe what he was saying. You could see their minds just shut down. Art said, 'Now there's a lot to learn and a lot to be gained from this. So I'm going to send Judy down to talk with you.' But they indicated that they were not going to meet with me.

The union didn't want to get involved in any of this Lean stuff. They didn't want to, and they didn't have to. So Art and I had a caucus, and I said to the union leadership, 'I will be at Walker every Tuesday at 9:00 a.m. I will be in this room, and I will talk to anybody who comes to see me. All I'm going to do is talk, and if nobody comes, that's fine. I'll be there the next Tuesday.'

I went to Walker every Tuesday in December and January. By about February 15th, we had negotiated changes in the contract. We took about 53 job classifications to just 7, made the appropriate rate changes for that to happen, and made some other changes in the contract.

The only training that I had was with win-win negotiating. That is all I knew, and obviously that had never happened in West Virginia before. They'd never even heard of it. They really didn't know what to do with me."

In an interesting twist, the controller at Walker Systems, Don Beaver, who was part of the management team that could not overcome the adversarial relationship between management and the IAMAW leadership, became the interim Human Resources manager and later the General Manager of Walker. Judy recalled the situation:

"They had a labor relations person who, when the acquisition was about to happen, did not want to join Wiremold, and so he left and went back to the parent company. Art knew that he was not going to have anybody there to do the human resources job, and that is why he took me along. Then as soon as we got the contract signed, we obviously had to have somebody there in place. The finance person who helped me with numbers said that he found the whole process very interesting, and that he would talk to the then-president of Walker about becoming the human resources manager. They agreed that he would do it for six months until they could hire somebody for that job. It turned out that he liked the job very much. And that person was Don Beaver.

Don liked everything about how we did the negotiating. He and I talked a lot. He was sharing with me the books that he was reading on his own. He was a change agent, he had an open mind, and is very smart, and he did a fantastic job and later became general manager of Walker."

Steve Maynard recalled another example of how Wiremold senior management interaction with union members overcame barriers:

"A year or two after we started kaizen, something happened that everyone still talks about. Art and Frank Giannattasio were walking around the plant and two of the ladies building Tele-Power® poles stopped them and said, 'This is a terrible process.' Art and Frank said, 'What's wrong with it?' Art asked if they would show him what was wrong, and they let Art and Frank try building the Tele-Power® poles. It was a hand operation, so Art and Frank stood at the table that was used for that assembly work. They built Tele-Power® poles for a day and a half. Everybody in the whole plant came by to see them doing it. They weren't very good, and are still debating who was worse. Art agreed that it was a terrible process and that they would schedule it for a kaizen. People still talk about Art and Frank building Tele-Power® poles. The union never filed a grievance on them for doing 'union work' because they understood that management was trying to understand what the workers were going through, and to make the job better.

Kaizen is a work in process all the time; it is a continuous activity. The president has to lead kaizen; it can't be delegated. All the vice presidents know that it is an on-going part of their jobs. It isn't a program of the month. Professional people learn, early in their careers here, that kaizen is a part of our culture. If they want to work here, they have to learn it, become an advocate for it, and do the best they can with it. If they are uncomfortable with it, it is best for them if they leave and work somewhere else, because kaizen is part of our culture; it is not an option.

In the early days, some people did leave because they didn't like the new environment. But the best part about it is that we are all working shoulder-to-shoulder. Management is encouraging the workers. And kaizen knocks down a lot of walls that are created in traditional environments."

Art and Frank's willingness to learn the work of union members, treat the union as an important stakeholder, and find innovative solutions to restrictive contract terms accomplished two things. First, it further confirmed their commitment to continuous improvement and second, demonstrated respect for people. According to Orry Fiume:

"You've got to get out there and get your hands dirty, and there aren't a lot of CEOs that I know who have ever spent any time in a factory. People recognized that Lean was not something he was espousing because he read it in *Harvard Business Review* last week, and that this was some new idea that he wanted to try out on everybody. Art lives, eats, sleeps, and breathes this stuff. And people know that."

Frank Giannattasio described some of the key leadership characteristics needed for the Lean transformation:

"You're going from a low inventory turn, long lead time, high defect, variable customer service business to one that's more cost efficient, shorter lead time, higher inventory turnover, and better customer service. Rest assured there will be plenty of bumps on the road. We knew that up front, but we're committed and we just dealt with the problems as they came up. Commitment to Lean is the number one leadership characteristic. Number two is that you're committed to listening to members of the team, recognizing that the bumps in the road are people issues, and that they are legitimate issues. You resolve the issues one by one. If the leader is committed to the team and committed to Lean, then trust will come. Trust is the third characteristic. That's important because when it is not apparent that this is in their best interest, they'll have some reason not to trust you. You have to deliver on resolving their issues, even when they're in doubt that Lean is the right thing to do.

Fairness would have to come next. The leader is making a lot of decisions; establishing a lot of rules as you go along, as you take apart and rebuild things. So a lot of these rules have no precedent and are not going to be covered in the union contract. Or in some cases they will be in conflict with the contract, so it will have to be rewritten. If people trust you, it makes that a lot easier. That you are fair goes along way. You have to be a judge, not judgmental, and ready to make fair decisions, anywhere from who stays in a job or leaves a job assignment; what that job is going to be paid; which suppliers are going to stay on and which will get cut loose; what teams are going to be responsible for a product; what product development project gets funded and which don't; which customer stays and which customers goes as you consolidate marketplaces. Commitment to Lean, trust, fairness... you have to develop a track record of consistency and dependability that people can see."

Tom Goetter makes the following observations about the leadership team:

"I've never seen a leadership team that has as little ego as this company does. I remember at another company where I worked in the 1970's, the vice presidents would come through and they just had an air about them. I joke about the fact that I didn't say anything to them other than 'Yes Sir' and 'No Sir.' People on the shop floor have absolutely no compunction about coming up to any vice president or Art and saying whatever is on their mind. It is because we encourage that kind of dialogue. Associates will seek me out to say, 'This product was designed poorly from the start. The product does not belong on the manufacturing floor, and that's your fault Tom because you lead Product Development.' I can't imagine telling a vice president at my old company that I thought he or she was doing a terrible job. When people tell me that I say, 'Thanks for your input. I'll talk to the designer. I'll look into it and see what I can do.' People are comfortable talking to senior management because they are actually interacting with senior managers in kaizen. They learn that we have got a job to do just as they do. We are no different than they are. We all have a job to do and we all contribute to Wiremold."

Frank Giannattasio said this about the ways in which Wiremold operated as a team:

> "We all have the same objectives, we all have the same end goals in mind. There's functional goals as well, but whatever they might be, they are definitely subordinated to the company's end goals."

Summary

Art Byrne did three very important things during his first few months on the job: 1) he was involved in kaizen training and facilitation; 2) he gave associates a qualified job guarantee; and, 3) he sustained the profit sharing program and involved every associate in quarterly profit sharing meetings. The power of these three actions was remarkable, as it removed the three main concerns that employees had about the new leadership:

- Is the CEO genuine? Will he walk the talk?
- Will I lose my job if I participate in kaizen?
- How will this benefit me?

With these concerns removed, associates could focus their attention to participating in kaizen and learn the new processes and tools needed to restore Wiremold's competitiveness. Art Byrne's actions thus helped eliminate waste (muda), unevenness (mura), and unreasonableness (muri) as it related to human interactions.

The human resource policies of a Lean business, practiced correctly as Wiremold did, stand in stark contrast to conventional human resource policies and practices. People are respected so that mechanisms are created to allow associates that must leave the company to do so with self-respect. People who preferred a different work environment were given time and the opportunity to make their own transitions. Art Byrne demonstrated respect for people by separating the criteria and processes used to adjust workforce levels before and after making the qualified job guarantee.

The leadership challenge related to understanding what "respect for people" truly means goes to even deeper levels, such as helping people realize their full potential through cross-functional assignments. A key principle in kaizen is to "spend ideas, not dollars." By adhering to this principle, management taps into the vast reservoir of latent creativity possessed by all people in the workplace that can be used to solve common business problems quickly and inexpensively. Production leveling (heijunka), Autonomation (jidoka), and Just-In-Time are operating practices that not only enable consistently successful outcomes, but also help eliminate wasteful blaming and rework. These are structural practices that intrinsically demonstrate respect for people.[20]

Key Points for Senior Managers

- Lean leaders view people as valuable resources to develop.
- Significant changes must be made to human resource policies to support the Lean transformation.
- The processes for adjusting workforce levels before and after the Lean transformation are different.
- The Code of Conduct established the behaviors needed to support the strategy.
- Profit sharing is an essential component of the Lean transformation.
- Management has at its disposal several "lines of defense" that can be invoked before having to lay people off.
- Labor unions need not be a barrier to the Lean transformation.

Notes

1. In general, undergraduate and graduate business school curricula are deeply rooted in batch-and-queue thinking and business practices. The conventional way to perform an activity — whether in or out of a business setting — is almost always batch-and- queue (see, for example, *Lean Thinking*, J. Womack and D. Jones, Simon & Schuster, New York, NY, 1996, p. 22). Batch-and-queue business practices abound in non-manufacturing activities such as: finance (learning curves, annual budgeting), purchasing (range quoting, economic order quantities), engineering (engineering changes, new product development), human resources (annual employee reviews, hiring process), sales and marketing (order release, quantity discounts), management information systems (data processing, software change-over), legal (terms and conditions, document review), distribution (unpack/re-pack, over-inspection), and general management (periodic initiatives, management reviews). Business measurements in each of these areas support batch-and-queue thinking (i.e. purchase price variance metric, standard costs, earned hours, function-based incentive compensation, etc.).

2. Conventional management practice is often consumed with finding magical solutions to common business problems. The "silver bullet," "quick hits," "bang for the buck," and "home run" mentality ignores business processes and reinforces the results-at-any-cost paradigm. People will eagerly spend lots of money on new computers or equipment to solve problems, instead of on inexpensive ideas. Or, they may look to outsourcing as a solution to problems management was never able to fix. Managers desperately seek shortcuts; a prime example is the recent popularity of online reverse auctions, which usually fail to deliver the intended results (see "Realizing Savings from Online Reverse Auctions," M.L. Emiliani and D.J. Stec, *Supply Chain Management — An International Journal*, Vol. 7, No. 1, pp. 12–23, 2002 and http://www.theclbm.com/publications.html).

3. Additional specific examples of management actions that demonstrate disrespect for people include: not listening or acting upon employee suggestions; ignoring a team's recommendations; canceling vacation days; age/sex/race or other biases; ignoring supplier suggestions; mandating supplier price cuts; incomplete or misleading disclosure to investors or other key stakeholders; blaming others; work that causes physical or mental injuries; quality problems; anticompetitive practices; speaking in abstract terms; polluting the environment; not keeping promises; not doing your share, etc.

4. Business leaders, particularly those managing large publicly owned businesses, generally believe that the sole purpose of the corporation is to maximize shareholder value. Consequently, senior management's activities and decision are directed at achieving this objective, despite the fact that this belief is accepted without ever being tested. A formal test is presented in: "A Mathematical Logic Approach to the Shareholder vs. Stakeholder Debate," M.L. Emiliani, *Management Decision*, Vol. 39, No. 8, 2001, pp. 618–622. This proof indicates that companies do not intrinsically exist to maximize shareholder value. The same method can be used to examine if companies can logically be based on the stakeholder business model. The key is to understand the difference between *intrinsic* (i.e. natural) and *extrinsic* (i.e. man-made) corporate purpose, as well as *literal* (i.e. pure financial) and *non-literal* (i.e. balance of financial plus quality, market share, etc.) interpretations of the term "maximize shareholder value." Decision-making by directors and senior managers will improve if they accept both intrinsic corporate purpose and a non-literal interpretation of "maximize shareholder value" — without losing sight of certain important requirements associated with extrinsic corporate responsibilities — and also focus on long-term stable growth. See Chapter 2, Note 19 and Chapter 5, Note 9.

5. *Profit Beyond Measure*, H. Johnson and A. Bröms, The Free Press, New York, NY, 2000.

6. *Stakeholding: The Japanese Bottom Line*, R. Ballon and K. Honda, The Japan Times, Tokyo, Japan, 2000, and *Inside Corporate Japan*, D. Lu, Productivity Press, Cambridge, MA, 1987.

7. *40 Years, 20 Million Ideas: The Toyota Suggestion System*, Y. Yasuda, Productivity Press, Cambridge, MA, 1991, and *The Service Industry Idea Book*, Japan Human Relations Association, Productivity Press, Cambridge, MA, 1990.

8. *Manager Revolution!*, Y. Hatakeyama, Productivity Press, Cambridge, MA, 1985, and *Human Motivation*, Y. Kondo, Ed., 3A Corporation, Tokyo, Japan, 1989.

9. A thoughtful and persuasive argument in support of the socio-economic (i.e. intrinsic) purpose of business is presented in *The Divine Right of Capital*, M. Kelly, Berrett-Koehler Publishers Inc., San Francisco, CA, 2001. See also *Corporate Irresponsibility: America's Newest Export*, L. Mitchell, Yale University Press, New Haven, CT, 2001; *Corporate Purpose: Why it Matters More than Strategy*, S. Basu, Garland Publishing Inc., New York, NY, 1999; the 1999–2002 annual reports for Toyota Motor Corporation; and the Caux Round Table *Principles for Business* at http://www.cauxroundtable.org/ENGLISH.HTM.

10. "Redefining the Focus of Investment Analysts," M.L. Emiliani, *The TQM Magazine*, Vol. 13, No. 1, 2001, pp. 34-50.

11. *Cost Reduction Systems: Target Costing and Kaizen Costing*, Y. Monden, Productivity Press, Portland, OR, 1995, and *Toyota Management System*, Y. Monden, Productivity Press, Portland, OR, 1993.

12. *Strategic Industrial Sourcing,* T. Nishiguchi, Oxford University Press, New York, NY, 1994; "Supplying the Toyota Production System: Intercorporate Organizational Evolution and Supplier Subsystems," W. Fruin and T. Nishiguchi in *Country Competitiveness,* B. Kogut, Ed., Oxford University Press, New York, NY, 1993; *The Evolution of a Manufacturing System at Toyota,* T. Fujimoto, Oxford University Press, New York, NY, 1999; and, "Case Study: The Toyota Group and the Aisin Fire," T. Nishiguchi and A. Beaudet, *Sloan Management Review,* Vol. 40, No. 1, 1998, pp. 49-59.

13. The twenty items are: 1) My work is satisfying to me; 2) There is *not* enough cooperation between my work group and others we work with; 3) There are opportunities for those who want to get ahead; 4) For the jobs in my area, working conditions are OK; 5) We *don't* get enough information about how well our work group is doing; 6) I have confidence in the fairness of management; 7) Our retirement plan (401k, profit sharing, etc.) is OK; 8) I can be sure of a job as long as I do good work; 9) There are *too many* rules and procedures to follow; 10) I have as much freedom as I need to do my job well; 11) I feel free to tell my supervisor what I think; 12) I am proud to work here; 13) I am paid fairly for the kind of work I do; 14) During the past six months I have looked for a job on the outside; 15) Favoritism is a problem in my area; 16) Most employees I know are in jobs that make good use of their abilities; 17) My job seems to be leading to the kind of future I want; 18) This is a better place to work than last year; 19) I understand what is expected of me in my work; 20) Compared with other organizations, our insurance benefits are good. Bold and italics are in original. The survey response choices are: "Agree," "Disagree," and "?" (meaning "I don't know"). Source: Center for Values Research, Inc., Dallas, Texas, at http://www.cvrdallas.com. Copyright by the Center for Values Research, Inc. Reprinted with permission.

14. An important part of the leadership development process included "Value Systems" training for every salaried employee starting in 1992. The purpose of the training was to improve relationships among people and align stakeholders: i.e. create one team focused on Wiremold's new business strategy, rather than having people or departments pushing forward separate agendas. The dramatic change that the Lean transformation represents meant that management had to better understand people's different value systems to communicate with them more effectively. The value systems training was also used to help improve hiring, coaching/counseling, performance reviews, and leadership development processes, and create a more flexible cross-functional workforce. The value systems training was connected to the annual employee attitude survey in the following way: survey feedback provided managers and supervisors with data on improvement opportunities whose solution may lie within the value systems training. The value systems training is given presently to new hires, and offered twice per year. See http://www.cvrdallas.com.

15. In his book *Toyota Production System* (Productivity Press, Portland, OR, 1988), Mr. Ohno makes many references to management's behaviors and responsibilities when practicing the Toyota Production System. This includes, for example: respect for humanity (pp. xiii, 7); patience (pp. 11, 34); listening (p. 13); root cause analysis (p. 17); eliminating waste (pp. 18, 41); utilizing human resources effectively (pp. 20, 62); teaching others (pp. 22, 34); teamwork (p. 23); practice and training (p. 25); thinking deeply about problems (p. 30), etc. See also *Workplace Management,* T. Ohno, Productivity Press, 1988. Various colleagues and disciples have said that Mr. Ohno was extremely demanding, ill tempered, and sometimes demeaning. Mr. Ohno also makes reference to his behaviors in his writings. For example, Mr. Ohno said: "When I confirmed the validity of the system and tried to implement it, everyone objected vehemently. To overcome this resistance, I had to quarrel and fight. And since the numbers [of people] were against me, I had no choice — I went crazy." (see *Just-In-Time for Today and Tomorrow,* T. Ohno and S. Mito, Productivity Press, Cambridge, MA, 1988, p. 97. Copyright © 1988 by Productivity Inc., http://www.productivityinc.com. Reprinted with permission). Mr. Ohno was obviously very open-minded regarding change, while at the same time extremely close-minded when people defended conventional wisdom (see Chapter 3, Note 15). Any incongruity between his writings and his actual leadership behaviors is easily rectified by recognizing that innovative ideas leading to important structural change for the first time often require aggressive tactics. Referring to Figure 3-1, Mr. Ohno's behaviors can be considered "non-value added but necessary" (see Chapter 3, Note 9). Further, Mr. Ohno's disciples are quick to point out that his behaviors were purposeful, not indiscriminate, and the benefits of his teachings are immeasurable on at least three levels: personal, company, and society. See, for example, "The Real Face of Fujio Cho, New Head of Toyota" in *President Magazine* (Japan), September 1999, at http://www.president.co.jp/pre/9909/e_01.html. Wiremold's Lean transformation is an important example of how widespread acceptance of new ideas can be achieved when the CEO exhibits value-added behaviors.

16. On page 140 of the book *Lean Thinking* by J. Womack and D. Jones, Wiremold's five lines of defense are: 1) reduce overtime, 2) put extra people on kaizen, 3) insource work, 4) cut the work week, and 5) develop new products. Two of the items listed in this book are different from that presented in *Lean Thinking* because they reflect an evolution in Wiremold management's thinking regarding effectiveness in responding to rapid changes in market conditions. For example, putting people on kaizen teams can be a helpful means of coping with normal fluctuations in business conditions (e.g. ±5% change in sales). However, layoffs (voluntary or otherwise) may be inevitable if sales suddenly drop 20–30% and the outlook for recovery is poor, such as in the 2001 recession. Developing new products may be an ineffective solution if the marketplace is not receptive to buying new products, despite the fact that

Wiremold's new product development cycle time is much shorter than it used to be. Note that there are many more lines of defense that a company could have; as many or 25 or 30, depending upon the ideas and creativity of the team charged with determining the lines of defense.

17. Called "The Program on Negotiation at Harvard Law School." See http://www.pon.harvard.edu.

18. *Getting to Yes: Negotiating Agreement without Giving In*, R. Fisher, W. Ury, and B. Patton, Penguin Books, New York, NY, 1991.

19. In the mid-1980's, Wiremold had 20 pay grades and about 120 work assignments for hourly associates. Wiremold management worked with Union leadership to reduce these to 10 pay grades, 19 classifications, and 48 work assignments, over two 3-year contract periods by the time Art Byrne arrived in September, 1991.

20. Other practices in the Lean management system that support the "respect for people" (i.e. employees, customers, suppliers, investors, community, etc.) principle include: 5 Why's, spaghetti chart, total productive maintenance, 5S (or 5C's, as Wiremold calls it), standard work, standard work combination sheets, visual workplace, one-piece flow, set-up reduction, fast development cycle times, value stream mapping, etc. In contrast, conventional batch-and-queue business practices demonstrate disrespect for people due to lengthy queue times, confusion, rework, learning curves, economic order quantities, large schedule variations, standard costs, purchase price variance metrics, machine utilization, office politics, budgeting process, capital appropriations, ROI, IRR, or other economic value added calculations, "flavor-of-the-month" training programs, direct/indirect labor metrics, ignoring employee or supplier suggestions, etc.

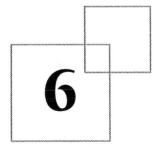

GROWTH THROUGH NEW PRODUCTS

New Product Development Process

In September 1991, there were approximately 35 new products under development in the 30-person Engineering Department headed by Steve Maynard. Many of them were special projects undertaken at the request of a single customer or a company officer. The engineers were accustomed to responding to different requests for urgent action. Hence, little was accomplished on any one project and projects were cancelled once the urgency faded. The product development process in use was the traditional sequential approach. The development cycle was long, two to four years in duration, and yielded only a few completed projects each year. This process would not be effective in helping to grow the business quickly.

Art Byrne knew that the transformation to Lean would require the company to grow. Kaizen was yielding tremendous improvements in productivity. Work that previously required ten people was now done with just four or five people. The productive capacity had expanded rapidly and created a major problem: too many people and not enough work. Figure 6-1 illustrates why Lean is not just a "manufacturing thing". The entire company — all functions — must get involved in kaizen to improve their processes and take advantage of the increase in available capacity created in operations. However, in most businesses, this does not happen. Instead, management cuts both people and capacity in relation to the size of the marketplace.[1]

Figure 6-1 Change in Capacity Due to Kaizen

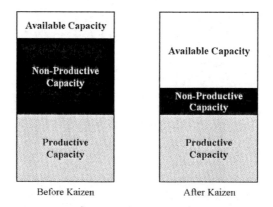

Before Kaizen   After Kaizen

Laying people off due to increased productivity would violate the commitment Art made to the workforce and would have been a misapplication of Lean principles and practices. Furthermore, layoffs would have created wasteful turmoil and slowed down or even halted Wiremold's Lean transformation. Orry Fiume explained the situation:

"We knew we had too many people, particularly in the factory. If you've got low attrition, which we have always had, and you start getting big productivity gains, then you have one or two choices: you either let people go because you don't need them or you keep them. Those are the only two choices you've got. If you let them go, that is the last time you'll be able to get that type of a gain. You can't put together a manufacturing cell and go from eight people to four, and then lay four people off, and expect the remaining four people to repeat that again. People will not cooperate with you in putting themselves out of a job. And so the only choice that you really have is to keep them, and we made a commitment that there would be no loss of employment as a result of productivity gains.

If you're going to keep them, then you have to keep them productively employed, which means you've got to grow the business. Think about what happens: if you increase productivity 20% a year, you have to grow the business at 20% a year to keep those people gainfully employed. That puts an enormous amount of pressure on management. When we tell CEOs that visit us that you have to make that commitment, they are stunned. They recognize pretty quickly what it means in the long run to them as a manager of that business; in order to keep those people gainfully employed, they have got to work a heck of a lot harder.

We knew our product development process wasn't very good early on. We were only introducing new products at the rate of a couple per year at best, so we weren't going to grow the business that way. And we weren't going to get significant additional market share because we were already the market leader.

We also knew resistance to these types of changes would most likely come from people that had been doing the same job for many, many years. The reason why that's important is because in a typically union factory, if you want to reduce the workforce, you have a layoff. When you have a layoff, who goes out the door? It's the newest people; the ones that are probably most likely to be receptive to new ideas. So we chose, even though it's a union environment, to have an early retirement program and incur the cost of that in order to allow those people that would have difficulty accepting this type of change to retire gracefully. Right out of the box we had 89 people retire, 72 of them from the factory, and we had not yet made one improvement in the factory to speak of. That put us in a huge overtime condition. So over the next couple of years, all the productivity gains came out of reducing overtime, which gave us some time to improve our product development process and produce many new products."

Growing the business would not be easy, as customers were dissatisfied with Wiremold's past performance. This became one of the greatest challenges for the management team in the first few years of the Lean transformation. If they could grow sales, then they would be able to re-deploy displaced associates into new value-added activities. However, this could only be accomplished if sales, marketing, and engineering applied Lean principles and practices to their processes to reduce cycle times and become responsive to the time-based competition strategy. In other words, the team would have to work together to meet the business challenge that the kaizen activities in manufacturing had created for them.

Part of the growth strategy called for a reduction in new product development cycle time and to concentrate resources in fewer projects. Art Byrne suggested that Quality Function Deployment[2] (QFD) could be used, though he did not have much direct experience with it. Quality function deployment, whose roots are in Total Quality Management, is a process for integrating both internal and external stakeholders at the start of product development. It integrates both the needs and desires of customers and gives specific and actionable direction to such stakeholders as product designers, production engineers, toolmakers, marketing, and suppliers. To do this, customer requirements must be converted into measurable parameters.

The senior management team agreed that the development and introduction of 35 new products in two years would be expensive. Further, it was not likely that the needs of customers would be met. After extensive discussions, two senior engineers and Dick Ryan, VP of Sales and Marketing, accompanied Steve Maynard to the American Supplier Institute[3] in Detroit to learn about Quality Function Deployment. Steve Maynard recalled:

> "I was in the role of Vice President of Engineering when Art Byrne came on board and I can remember the very first meeting we had face to face. He said 'What do you know about Quality Function Deployment?' I said well, we had actually started learning about it. I broached the topic to management about a year before, and they had kind of shot it down, but we set up a 'skunk works' operation, and we had a guy from MIT come to help us understand how to actually do this, in the evenings outside of our normal work. So we were all excited when Art knew about QFD. He sent us to the American Supplier Institute in Detroit where we were formally trained in

QFD. Then we trained the whole staff and brought that in as part of our culture. It became part of the methodology for doing product development.

QFD is a structured methodology that was being used in Japan. Basically it takes the voice of a customer and it uses a cross-functional team to understand their wants and needs. And I mean a real co-located cross-functional team. Some key concepts that came out of this really forced us to change. We co-located the marketing folks with the engineering folks. We physically moved the departments together so that they sat together."

Filling Gaps in the Product Line

Upon their return from the American Supplier Institute, the team prepared a product map that contained each of Wiremold's product families, including new products under development. The map contained base products, line extensions, and combinations of products assembled to meet the needs of a major customer. All products on the map were in production. The information about each product included the base technology used in the product, the customer need it satisfied, sales volume, sales channel, prices, and customer mix. New products under development, with comparable projected information about them, were included on the map in a different color. Finally, the map showed similar products available from Wiremold's top three competitors in the product family. Steve Maynard's recollection:

"At the very beginning we started with a product map. We actually took catalogs of all of our competitors' products and our own products, and we stuck them up on a big piece of brown paper on a wall. It looked like a large matrix with product families on one axis and competitors and us on the other axis. We stuck pictures of what each company had in the different product families. This pointed out big holes in product lines that we didn't even have in our product offering. If we wanted to be the leading manufacturer of wire management products, we had to address some of those holes. Some of the holes became the targets of acquisitions, while others became targets for internal product development. The hard part of this process is prioritizing the project list and deselecting the projects that you're not going to do. You have to have a very clear business strategy as a management team to do this process.

For all new product designs, we encouraged upper management to participate in our development process, asking that they attend the

product reviews. They were now trained in QFD and they understood that the voice of the customer was driving the team's discussions during the development process. The customer was constantly 'screwing our head on right' and eliminating pre-conceived
ideas and correcting our perspective on what was important. They
told us things, and we saw things by visiting job sites, that you simply could never get from internally driven development. We
learned that you had to actually talk to the customer to understand
what drives their decision-making. What are the things that are really important to them?"

Upon examining the map, a number of things became apparent. First, there
were several projects underway for items similar to existing products. The team
thought that customer's needs could be satisfied in other ways, and so they
agreed to cancel those projects. Sales representatives would work with customers to try to satisfy their needs with products already in production.

Second, there was one new non-electrical product under development
that was related to personal computers. When asked why, Dick Ryan and
Steve Maynard responded that many new office installations required both
electrical and data connections. The discussion then moved to assessing the
information related to competitor's products that included data connections. The team noted that there were several areas in which Wiremold was
not competitive. This led to a discussion about the future demand for data
connection products, and whether or not Wiremold should fill those gaps in
its product line.

The gaps could be filled in two ways: through internal product development or acquisition of companies that already made those products. The team
discussed which gaps could be effectively filled through internal development
and which ones would be best filled through acquisition. The cash that was
generated through inventory reductions could be used to acquire companies
that made the products Wiremold needed. In some cases, it would be faster to
acquire companies whose products were already accepted in the marketplace
and convert them to Lean, rather than create new products in which Wiremold
did not possess strong design and manufacturing capability.

So, within a few months of Art Byrne's arrival, the management team had set-
tled on a structured process to bring the voice of the customer into the new product development process to articulate desired product features, performance, and
price — parameters that were previously controlled by individual internal departments such as marketing, engineering, or manufacturing. Also established
were the basic parameters for acquiring companies with products complementary
to Wiremold's but outside the scope of their current capabilities.[4]

Who is the Customer?

One of the first things Wiremold had to do was make sure that they understood who was their customer. There are five fundamental principles in Lean practice that define the essence of what the people in a company do.[5] They are:

- Specify value   *from the end-use customer's perspective*
- Identify the value stream   *activities that create value*
- Flow   *make value flow*
- Pull   *respond to customer demand*
- Perfection   *zero waste*

The first principle, specify value, is very important because if a company does not understand how to do this, then it runs the risk of producing products or services that customers do not want to buy or selling products or services that dissatisfy customers. Quality function deployment is a process for specifying value to ensure that company resources are applied effectively to potential opportunities. The key question is, whose perspective of value should be considered?

Value can only be specified by the *end-use* or *ultimate customer*,[6] and not by various internal or intermediate external customer relationships. The end-use customer is the person who pays for and uses the product or service. However, often the person who buys the product may be different from the person who pays for it, both of whom could differ from the person who uses the product or service. The end-use customer therefore can be more than one person. In all cases, end-use customers will be located close to or at the end of the value stream.[7]

For example, in industrial and commercial markets, Wiremold sells directly to electrical and communications supply distributors, who in turn sell to electrical contractors and communications installers hired by construction companies to work on new projects or renovations. However, the people specifying Wiremold's products are architects and engineers.[8] So the "buying" is done by two entities, the architects and engineers who specify wire and cable management systems on the blueprints as well as the contractors who physically purchase the products. But who is paying for the product: the bank or the building owner? The next question is, who uses Wiremold's products? They are the electrical contractors who install Wiremold's products as well as the people who come into contact with Wiremold's products every day. In an industrial setting, other important users could include the building manager or owner. From a practical standpoint, Wiremold considered architects, engineers, contractors, and the actual end-use customer as the people who have the most influence on the purchase decision. As a result, all cross-functional new product development teams speak to at least these people.

The situation is different in the do-it-yourself (DIY) consumer market. Wiremold sells to big-box home improvement stores whose primary customers are homeowners. The homeowner purchases the product, installs, and uses it. In most cases, the end-use customer in the DIY market is the homeowner. Therefore, it is the homeowner's perspective of value that Wiremold's new product development teams must understand. However, the big-box home improvement stores also sell to small contractors. In this case, the purchaser is the contractor and the user is the homeowner. In order to understand whether Wiremold's products deliver value, it was necessary for people from engineering, marketing, manufacturing, sales, etc., to talk to both small contractors who use the product during installation and homeowners who use the product everyday. Also, the big-box stores have huge buying power and surely consider themselves to be important customers. So Wiremold must understand their perception of value as well.

Determining who pays for and who uses the product or service can be confusing at first. However, Wiremold overcame this confusion by having cross-functional teams talk to constituents throughout the value stream,[9] including, for example, the architect at the building design stage, the consulting engineer at the specification stage, the installer, the end-user, and the person who services the system afterwards. Steve Maynard explained the Voice of the Customer process used by Wiremold:

> "Rather than just mail out a survey, we actually did a lot of visits to customer sites, like a hospital, where our products were being used. And we watched the contractors install the products. It was important to observe how they used our products. We also talked to them, but the visual information was very different from what people say. It really improved the communication because we saw things that they didn't see or realize. For example, like two people struggling with a piece of raceway because it was too long, how many tools they needed to install something, how easily things got damaged, or how our products were stored on the job site. These are important things that you wouldn't get in a mail or telephone survey. We actually did a combination of all three. We visited distributors to see how our products were being stored on the shelves, how they wanted it to be stored, and what kind of labeling they wanted. We then followed-up with telephone interviews and mail surveys as well. A lot depended on the type of product that you were developing and how novel it was.
>
> We even visited competitor sites to see how the competitor's product looked when they were being installed in the same buildings as our products. We would show up with our team and go rummage around a new job. It really was fun. It would get the whole team inspired to move forward."

The QFD Process

The QFD process begins with a systematic approach for developing a shared understanding of how the end-use customer perceives value among all the functions participating on the team. It ensures that the most important needs are translated into product specifications, and that no important customer needs are missed. For the QFD process to work correctly, Wiremold had to ensure that it obtained data that accurately reflected the end-use customer's perception of value. Specifying value can be accomplished in a variety of ways including focus groups, one-on-one interviews at trade shows, written surveys, or by observing intermediate or end-use customers using the product. The data obtained may be qualitative, semi-quantitative, or quantitative.

Field interviews are used often to specify end-use customer value, which can broadly be classified using the Kano Model (Figure 6-2):[10]

- Basic (or expected) — What customers expect the product will do. Teams normally determine the basic expectations in advance of customer visits.
- Performance (or normal) — What customers say they want the product to do. This is key information that the team obtains in field visits.
- Excitement (or delighter) — Needs that will, if fulfilled, surprise and delight the customer. These needs are often derived from indirect customer feedback.

Figure 6-2 The Kano Quality-Feature Model

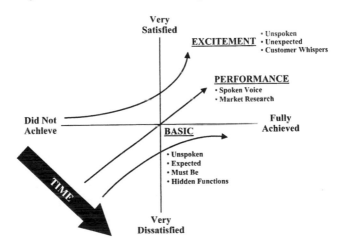

Source: The Wiremold Company

The customer needs are then arranged in a hierarchy of primary, secondary and tertiary value, and prioritized. In addition, customer perceptions of the value of competitors' products are assessed. The primary, secondary and tertiary needs are cascading levels of detailed customer voice that help to define the root want. The team makes a decision as to what level of detail to put on the House of Quality chart.

Figure 6-3 QFD Product Planning Matrix

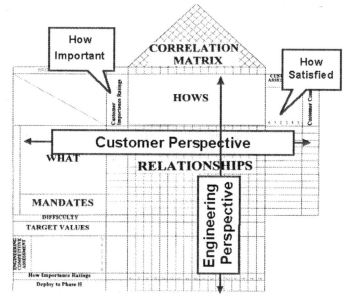

Source: The Wiremold Company

The QFD process begins after the end-use customer's perspective of value is specified. The first House of Quality matrix, Product Planning, is comprised of a series of customer wants that run down the left side of the diagram (Figure 6-3). Crossing each of these rows is a series of columns for engineering characteristics or performance requirements that address the desired customer attributes. The roof of the house develops when the columns are extended to cross over each other to provide a space for the team to note the potential conflicts between various engineering characteristics. This is where tradeoff issues are identified. Relationships are identified through the middle of the House of Quality. This relationship section provides checks and balances to the process and helps prioritize focus areas for the project. Target values for each engineering characteristic are identified that will delight the customer. Upon completion, the House of Quality provides a visual map that clearly connects the end-use customer's perception of value to specific performance requirements.

Creating the first House of Quality is only the beginning. There are three more phases: Design Deployment, Process Planning, and Production (Figure 6-4). The matrix used for each phase is filled out with the help of an experienced facilitator. Once the customer attributes are translated into engineering characteristics, the engineering characteristics are then translated into parts characteristics in the Design Deployment matrix. These parts characteristics provide the rows for the third matrix, the Process Planning matrix. The parts characteristics are translated into key process operations that become the rows of the fourth matrix, the Production Planning matrix. In the

Production Planning matrix, the key process operations are translated into production requirements.

Figure 6-4 Four Phases of Product Development Using QFD

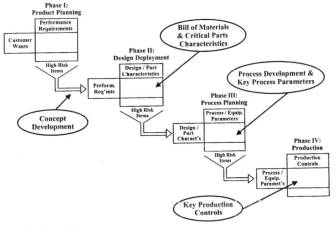

Source: The Wiremold Company

Importantly, all members of the team go though each phase of the product development process together, from product planning through production. According to Steve Maynard:

> "The real difference with QFD is that the people work as a team. They all go out and do the market research work together, they do the design work together, they build the manufacturing cell together, the marketing roll out, the planning for the warehouses, labels, etc. No matter what hat you wear, you're out there doing the market survey. Although the core expertise of a design engineer obviously is in the area of the design, the team participates in all phases of the process. That was a real shift from how we did things. In some areas it was very difficult to get people to come along because they felt that it was a waste of a tool designer's time to be out doing market research. So we'd say, 'They're going to learn something new, they are going to learn a lot more about our customers, and they're going see the product used in real life.' It was a very powerful process because people came at it from all different perspectives when they got out of the plant and talked to customers. They all wanted to know how the product worked out in the field, and they would end up having a lot of fun."

Orry Fiume described the importance of listening to customers:

"Once end-users start understanding that you're listening to them and the things that they are looking for are being built into the products that you're bringing out, they'll support you a lot more compared to the competition."

Ed Miller described how QFD helps people understand end-use customer needs:

"QFD is a very tedious process. But the good thing about it is you actually get the end-customer involved with the design team. So they're working with our engineers and marketers in defining the functions, features, and form. What you need to be able to do is understand the needs of the end-use customer better than anybody else. You have to keep asking why, why, why, and keep peeling the onion back, eventually you'll get to a true need. And if you understand that, you can come up with a solution. You have to have that basic understanding in place before you get started with QFD. It allows you to define on one sheet of paper the whole product spec and the priorities. A design engineer will have to make tradeoffs sometimes. If I do this, then it may cost too much. Well then, which features can I tradeoff? QFD prioritizes them so that you can clearly see which features you can't tradeoff, which ones are less important that you might need to tradeoff, and which ones are nice to have but you can trade them off if it costs more. The House of Quality allows us to do that; it has the competitors on it, has the customer on it. It has a lot of parameters on one sheet of paper."

The Wiremold Product Development System

Steve Maynard and his team established the basic framework of Wiremold's new product development system between 1991 and 1995. Tom Goetter, who became Vice President of Engineering in 1996, later improved and formalized the process, and introduced the Wiremold Product Development System (WPDS). Over ten years, Wiremold added approximately 1,500 new products to the 1,500 or so SKU's that had existed in 1991.

Figure 6-5 shows Wiremold's Product Development System. The cross-functional team consists of representatives from engineering, manufacturing, marketing, tooling, product line support, and distribution. The process begins with the "Strategy and Concept" activity, which introduces the Voice of the Customer, concept definition, an analysis of the various concepts that were developed using the Pugh Analysis[11] and the creation of the product planning QFD matrix. Tom Goetter emphasizes the importance of the customer's voice in the new product development process:

"QFD provides us with a mechanism to listen to the customer.

Figure 6-5 Wiremold Product Development System

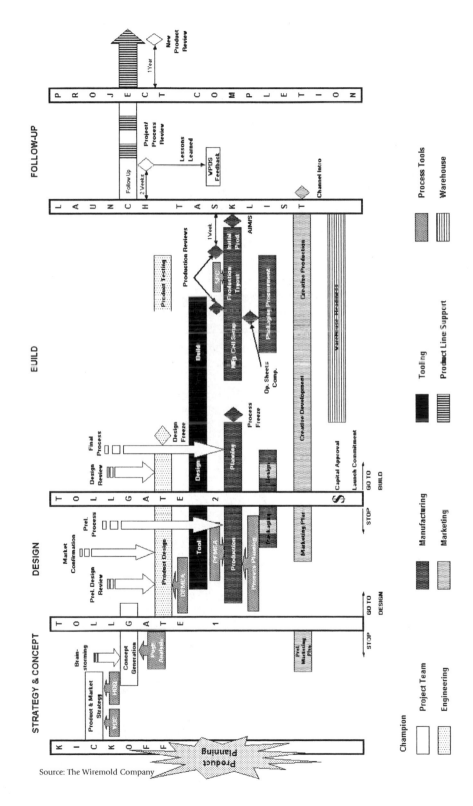

Source: The Wiremold Company

When product development teams are at their first tollgate, the process forces them in a direction that they discover by listening to the customer. In addition to understanding what the customer values, the teams learn the importance the customer places on quality. They also uncover what the customer is willing to pay for this value and quality. This allows the team to calculate a target cost,[12] by knowing in advance the selling price and what the company requires for a profit margin. The target cost then becomes part of the design specification.

We will sometimes use research firms to help us get customer data, especially when we do blind focus groups, to help us make sure that the questions are objective and not push them down the path that confirms what we think they want. Sometimes customers will say completely the opposite of what the designers on the project team wanted. You can have real problems convincing people that this is really what the customer wants. It's a real plus when you've got manufacturing people fighting for marketing ideas and vice versa. That's when you know you are winning. Now everybody is focused on what the customer wants. It forces people to come up with new ideas.

This is how we avoid the typical engineering mindset of what I call 'W6' designs: we 'design what we want the way we want;' designs that end up costing a lot to produce and fail to meet customer needs."

The first tollgate is a "go/no go" decision about whether or not to proceed to the "Design" activity. If a decision is made to proceed, then several activities occur in parallel including preliminary design, market confirmation, tool design, production planning, process planning, packaging, and development of the marketing plan. The Design Deployment QFD matrix is created in this portion of the process. The next tollgate is a key go/no go decision. This is where a commitment is made to allocate capital to the project and launch production. The duration of the "Strategy and Concept" and "Design" activities depends on the type of project: i.e. — new platform or derivative. About one-third of the development timeline is devoted to the strategy and concept, which shows commitment to the product planning process versus the traditional design and then check process.

The next activity is "Build," where the design is reviewed and frozen, detailed process planning is completed, packaging is designed, and the creative aspects of the marketing plan are developed and produced. This is also the point where the final QFD matrices, Process Planning and Production, are completed. The team then designs the manufacturing cell, conducts production tryouts, and tests the products, while the warehouse makes preparations to receive the new product. After packaging and marketing materials are procured, the manufacturing cell begins initial production and the product is launched into the marketplace.

The final tollgate is reached following product launch. The project and product line teams perform "Follow-Up" activities to assess the successes of the project and process. The feedback activity is performed within a few weeks to capture lessons learned while still fresh in peoples' mind. Twelve months after the product is in production, the product line team conducts a product review to assess how the product met the needs of the end-use customer.

Of course, not all product development projects go smoothly. Rich Levesque commented on how management interacts with teams when problems are encountered:

> "There is a fine line between getting involved in details and micro-managing. Although you empower the team to make decisions, there are times when they are going to struggle or they are going to fall. You need to be there to help pick them up. The only way you are going to do that is by getting into the details and understanding what the issues are. So in order to be successful you have to listen to people. You have to listen to what they are saying. You have to help them when they need it. You can't just say, 'Why don't you go see so and so.' We are teachers, and they can rely on us for giving them the perspective of being a teacher rather than a decision-maker for them."

Impact on the Business

Wiremold's experience with QFD was successful because management treated each new product development project as an important investment. Basic resources were provided to the product development team and management behaved in a manner that gave them confidence to work together as a team. As a result, the teams were able to access their own valuable reservoir of ideas and creativity to find low cost solutions to challenging product development problems. There was also strong commitment to the process from management and the product development team members. Team members learned that creating products that delivered value to customers was both more important and rewarding than perpetuating the historical barriers between functions.[13] It is significant that Wiremold's average annual sales growth rate between 1995 and 1999 for the Wire Management group was nearly double the industry average sales growth rate, principally due to the new products created using the QFD process.[14] So QFD clearly had a tremendous impact on the business as well as on end-use customers.

To the casual observer, QFD might appear to be a rigid process that stifles the creativity of participants. But in fact, the opposite is true. Wiremold, like other companies that use QFD correctly, found that people exhibited greater creativity when the entire cross-functional team was given

the opportunity to participate in specifying value from the end-use customer's perspective. The QFD process, as deployed by Wiremold, is consistent with the view possessed by Lean leaders that people — suppliers, associates, equipment installers, distributors, and end-use customers — are
valuable resources. As with any Lean process, senior management is responsible for establishing discipline and ensuring that their own participation adds value to the process.[15]

One of the most important benefits of QFD is that it brought all functions
together in a customer-focused product development process. It is another
process, like kaizen, that builds teamwork. It also improves people's understanding of their end-use customers, and saves time and money by avoiding
such common product development pitfalls as developing products that manufacturing can't produce at the required costs or the development of products
that do not meet customer needs.

The QFD process enabled Wiremold to respond quickly to their urgent need to grow the business and utilize newly available resources.
Further, resources were redistributed to product planning and design,
where the impact on customers and business processes was greatest, then
gradually reduced through process planning, production, and product
launch (Figure 6-6). In contrast, batch-and-queue businesses typically do
the opposite:[16] they minimize resources in product planning and design
and are forced to greatly increase the level of resources in production and
product launch to meet delivery schedules, re-design parts, and correct
quality problems.

Figure 6-6 Resource Allocation in New Product Development

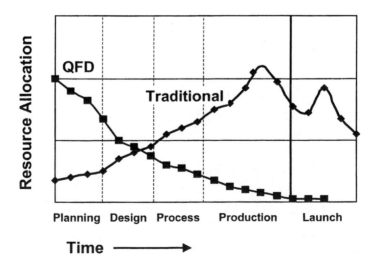

Source: The Wiremold Company

In addition, Wiremold's Product Development System helped eliminate the seven wastes: overproduction, waiting, transportation, processing, inventory, moving, and defects. It would also stop the "blame game," which occurred when designers missed the market's needs or when marketing committed to a launch date that manufacturing could not achieve. Avoiding these errors enabled Wiremold to develop products quickly, release them on time, improve its credibility in the eyes of its customers, and deliver customer satisfaction. Rich Levesque commented on the importance of Wiremold's fast-cycle product development process in achieving market leadership and on its integration with production:

> "We want to be the market leader. In order to do that, we have to generate a lot of new products. We want to get to a position where our competitors can't keep up with us. The minute we come out with a product, and they try copying it, we are off onto the next generation. We've been successful and have had some award winning products. And we are the leader in providing it to the world because we are able to make those parts everyday."

In contrast, batch-and-queue businesses usually operate with the mindset, "we make it and let our customers test it." This results in customer complaints, high warranty costs, reduced cash flow, loss of market share, and blame. Most managers *believe* that 70–90% of the cost of a product (or service) lies in its design, yet they *behave* as if 70–90% of the product cost is in operations. Whenever there's a cost problem, it is operations that typically endures layoffs, plant closing, and squeezing supplier's margins, all of which can erode customer satisfaction.

This behavior is obviously inconsistent because the real problem is the design process itself. Wiremold's Voice of the Customer and QFD processes demonstrates that the management team was consistent in their beliefs and behaviors regarding the sources of product cost and customer satisfaction, which is critical for gaining employee alignment and cross-functional participation in the new product development process. This further demonstrates how the "respect for people" principle was practiced at The Wiremold Company.

Summary

Wiremold senior management recognized that they had no choice but to grow the business in order to return available resources to value adding activities. They did not harvest the productivity gains by laying people off, as is usually the case. Carefully growing the business is an essential part of the Lean management system.

The senior management team put the burden on itself to find ways of increasing sales to customers that were not happy with Wiremold's past performance. Art Byrne, Ed Miller, and Scott Bartosch overcame customers' concerns by meeting with them one-on-one and showing them the results of early kaizen activities, which included better product quality and shorter lead-times. Not surprisingly, they found that Lean sells.

The key strengths of Wiremold's product development system are cross-functional participation throughout the entire development process, direct involvement with the marketplace, concurrent execution of tasks, and closed loop feedback. The management team elevated new product development from the micro-level responsibility of the Engineering department to the macro-level responsibility of the entire organization. In taking the new product development process from a function-specific responsibility to a business-specific responsibility, management demonstrated its belief that every function has a role to play in both cost management and creating value for end-use customers.[17]

Wiremold's product development system is not a static process, but one that is continuously improved over time. It promotes the elimination of waste (muda), unevenness (mura), and unreasonableness (muri) not only in new product development, but in subsequent activities as well. This fast cycle time product development process is the direct result of the emergence of a constellation of unique business practices that permit social and technological capability building to co-evolve.

Key Points for Senior Managers

- Associates whose jobs are eliminated due to productivity improvement should be retained and re-deployed to kaizen teams or new product development teams.
- Businesses embarking on the Lean transformation must have a growth strategy.
- New product development process cycle time must be quickly reduced to enable re-deployment of associates to new value-added activities.
- Selective acquisitions were made to fill gaps in the product line outside of Wiremold's areas of expertise.
- Value can only be defined from the end-use customer's perspective.
- The QFD process builds teamwork and focuses on end-use customer needs.
- Senior management's behaviors must be consistent with its belief that most of the cost of a product is committed in its design.
- Cost management and value creation are enterprise-wide responsibilities.

Notes

1. Most managers will pursue this effortless option to cut costs quickly and improve profitability. Instead, managers should be leading kaizen in non-manufacturing areas so that the rest of the company gains the capability to function with the same speed and flexibility as manufacturing. Simply cutting people and capacity fails to take advantage of one of the primary benefits of Lean and sends the wrong messages to the organization.

2. See, for example, *Quality Function Deployment: Integrating Customer Requirements into Product Design*, Y. Akao, Productivity Press, Portland, OR, 1990, and *Total Quality Development: A Step-By-Step Guide to World-Class Concurrent Engineering*, D. Clausing, American Society of Mechanical Engineers, New York, NY, 1994.

3. The American Supplier Institute is a nonprofit, employee-owned company with the mission of helping organizations meet the needs of customers through research, training, implementation and publications on quality improvement techniques. In 1984, they developed the first United States application of Quality Function Deployment. See http://www.amsup.com.

4. Wiremold would go on to acquire 19 businesses and product lines between 1993 and 1999 in the U.S. and abroad.

5. See *Lean Thinking*, J. Womack and D. Jones, Simon & Schuster, New York, NY, 1996, pp. 15–90. However, note that Toyota has a different view with regards to the fifth principle — perfection: "Toyota's people are famous for being suspicious of the easy answer and the common wisdom. Perfection is not a useful concept to them. Instead, they believe in improvement.... Toyota people don't believe in perfection, only improvement." Source: Toyota Motor Corporation advertorial in *The Japan Times*, 18 and 25 March 2002, http://toyota.irweb.jp/Irweb/invest_rel/advertorial/20020318/part1/page2.html. See Chapter 5, Note 2.

6. Only the end-use, or ultimate customer specifies value. Viewing value from any other perspective introduces waste that end-use customers would not want to (*or should not have to*) pay for. For example, the people in Department A of Widget Company consider the weekly reports they create as value-added in part because their internal customer, Department B, asks for them (often despite the fact that Department B does not really use the reports). Importantly, end-use customers, if asked, will probably not view the reports as value added. The same reasoning can apply to many other types of business activities. See *Lean Thinking*, J. Womack and D. Jones, Simon & Schuster, New York, NY, 1996.

7. The value stream is the information, materials, and processes that add value to a product or service as perceived by the end-use customer. See Chapter 3, Note 18.

8. Ed Miller, the Vice President of Marketing, noted that: "Eight years ago we started an effort to reach the spec influencers; the users, architects, and engineers. Nobody in the electrical industry goes after architects. Well, we do. We have grown to be a very strong force in front of those critical spec influencers."

9. Wiremold product development teams also determined the people that are most influential in the purchasing process and the criteria that influenced their purchasing decisions for each product line. For example, cabling installation and maintenance, perimeter systems, etc.

10. This construct is known as the "Kano Model," after Dr. Noriaki Kano of Tokyo Rika University. See "Attractive Quality and Must-Be Quality," N. Kano, N. Seraku, F Takahashi, and S. Tsuji, *The Journal of the Japanese Society for Quality Control (Hinshitsu)*, Vol. 14, No. 2, 1984, pp. 39–48.

11. The Pugh analysis technique was developed by Stuart Pugh of the University of Strathclyde, Glasgow, Scotland. Pugh charts are a method of evaluating alternative conceptual designs. They analyze the strengths and weaknesses of various conceptual design options compared to a baseline concept in order to identify and select a preferred approach. See *Total Design: Integrated Methods for Successful Product Engineering*, S. Pugh, Addison-Wesley, New York, NY, 1991, and *Creating Innovative Products Using Total Design*, S. Pugh, D. Clausing, and R. Andrade, Eds., Prentice Hall, New York, NY, 1996.

12. The target costing *system* differs from the colloquial term "target cost" used by many companies. The former is a disciplined process that is used to help achieve target profits. Idiomatic usage causes confusion and bears no relation to the target costing method practiced by Lean businesses. See *Cost Reduction Systems: Target Costing and Kaizen Costing*, Y. Monden, Productivity Press, Portland, OR, 1995, and *Toyota Management System*, Y. Monden, Productivity Press, Portland, OR, 1993. The target costing methodology also is applied to purchased materials. It serves as a disciplining mechanism for responding to market conditions and results in improved overall competitiveness of the supply network. For more information on interorganizational cost management, see *Supply Chain Development for the Lean Enterprise*, R. Cooper and R. Slagmulder, Productivity Press, Portland, OR, 1999, and *Strategic Industrial Sourcing*, T. Nishiguchi, Oxford University Press, New York, NY, 1994, Chapter 4.

13. Disputes, non-engagement between individuals or functional groups, or blame is the eighth type of waste, called "behavioral waste." See "Lean Behaviors," M.L. Emiliani, *Management Decision*, Vol. 36, No. 9, 1998, pp. 615–631.

14. This figure excludes acquisitions. Given its high market share, Wiremold would have had difficulty growing faster than the industry average. Every additional point of market share would have been

harder and more costly to gain. The QFD process helped overcome this limitation by creating new products and expanding the existing market.

15. In general, senior management does not just flatly mandate discipline or conformance to Lean principles and practices. They also "show the way" through direct involvement, continuous and thematically consistent communication, and by modeling the desired behaviors over long periods of time (e.g. decades), which, in turn, builds credibility. Management's participation must be perceived by associates as adding value to the process. This helps create a rich social environment for individual and team growth through learning, information sharing, and capability building. See, for example, *The Evolution of a Manufacturing System at Toyota*, T. Fujimoto, Oxford University Press, New York, NY, 1999, Chapter 4.

16. Many companies, steeped in conventional batch-and-queue management practices, will limit resources at the onset of new product development to reduce costs. Managers will often arbitrarily cut development budgets from time-to-time without understanding the process used or what improvements need to be made to the process to better match the development budget. By doing this, senior managers create a situation where they will be forced to expend greater resources as the product launch date approaches if they want to meet customer commitments. This mistake is repeated whenever new products are introduced because management does not understand the root cause of the problem — and may not even know how to do root cause analysis. In contrast, Lean practice devotes more time to planning at the beginning of the process to eliminate wasteful re-work later in the process.

17. The Lean business system is more capable of effectively enabling cross-functional teamwork due to the "Respect for People" principle ("Toyota Way 2001," Toyota Motor Corporation, internal document, April 2001). Thus, responsibility for achieving key objectives such as cost, delivery, quality, product performance, and sales are distributed in varying degrees across all functions, rather than focused within certain functional areas such as engineering, manufacturing, or sales. See *Toyota Management System*, Y. Monden, Productivity Press, Portland, OR, 1993, Chapter 3.

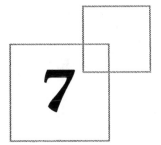

GROWTH THROUGH ACQUISITIONS

Wiremold's Acquisitions

When Art Byrne established Wiremold's strategy of being the leading supplier in the industries it served and one of the top ten time-based competitors globally, he also established two key strategic thrusts to achieve this:

1. Constantly strengthen our base operations
2. Double in size every 3–5 years

Between 1991–1999, Wiremold doubled in size twice. Each doubling took four years, which is right in the middle of the 3–5 year target. About half of that growth came from using the QFD method to introduce new products and from growth of existing markets. The other half came from acquisitions. Wiremold acquired nineteen companies between 1993 and 1999. Orry Fiume described Wiremold's view of the importance of growth:

> "The reality is, in the business world, you can't stand still. If you're not growing, you're going backwards. In addition, if you are going to have double-digit productivity gains and promise that no one will lose their employment as a result of productivity gains, then you don't really have any choice but to grow in order to keep that promise. This helped drive our QFD and acquisition efforts"

The basic approach that Wiremold took towards acquisitions could best be described as a "roll-up" within the wire and cable management market category. It bought product lines as well as whole businesses, some small and some quite large in comparison to Wiremold's size.[1] Where possible, it bought companies that sold products in the same marketplace. Each time it added new products that enhanced Wiremold's overall product offering. Ed Miller described the thought process behind the acquisitions:

> "Over eight years ago, we redefined our business and determined that we needed to think in terms of managing the wire and cable infrastructure of buildings. We bought companies that gave us that capability so that we could provide a solution for every place."

Although Wiremold tried to stay within its basic wire and cable management niche, some acquisitions came with additional product categories such as specialty lighting, which Wiremold then attempted to build upon and grow. Others came with new distribution channels in which existing products could be leveraged (Figure 7-1). Steve Maynard commented on how Wiremold uses its distribution channels and that of its acquisitions:

> "A lot of our acquisitions are synergistic. In other words, we would choose to sell the acquired company's products through the channels that we have, and we may choose to sell some of Wiremold's products through a channel that we acquired."

Figure 7-1 Wiremold's Distribution Channels

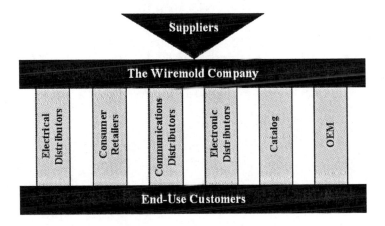

Another key thrust of Wiremold's acquisitions strategy was to grow internationally to make it more difficult for large foreign competitors to enter the U.S. market, as well as to simply take advantage of markets that were growing faster than in the U.S. market. The determination of which areas to target internationally was based upon growth and the absence of large entrenched competitors in the wire management business. Wiremold selected three target markets: the newly emerging Eastern Bloc countries, China/Asia, and Latin and South America. It eventually established operations in all three. Wiremold's presence in Poland and China was created by acquiring businesses that had previously established operations in those countries, while the third was a start-up operation in Mexico combined with an export effort aimed at South America.

Later, Wiremold embarked on a mini roll-up strategy in the United Kingdom due to the unique nature of that market and the fact that the U.K. wire management market[2] was very fragmented among many small companies. Wiremold eventually consolidated five of the most significant companies in the metal segment of the U.K. wire management market and emerged as the leading supplier.

Recall that when Art Byrne arrived in 1991, Wiremold could barely finance its own growth. There was no capability for acquisitions, though the strategy that Art had established anticipated acquisitions. Wiremold first had to raise the needed capital to finance this part of the strategy. This is where the first component of the strategy, "constantly strengthen our base of operations", became critical. Art Byrne explains:

> "I knew when I first came to Wiremold that we had a lot of excess space and excess inventory that could be freed-up to provide us with the capital that we would need to grow. This wasn't 'rocket science;' you could just go out onto the factory floor and trip over it; there was money lying everywhere. Unfortunately, I also knew that it would take us time and a big effort to convert the waste into cash."

Over the next 18 months, Wiremold did exactly that. As shown in Figure 7-2, if Wiremold maintained its inventory turnover at 1990 levels, it would have had $16.7 million of inventory by the end of 1993. By aggressively converting to Lean, Wiremold's actual inventory was only $5.6 million at the end of 1993. This created $11.2 million in cash flow savings.

Figure 7-2 Inventory Reductions Finance Wiremold's Growth

1993 Inventory at 1990 Turnover Rate	$16.7M
Actual 1993 Inventory	$ 5.6M
Cash Flow Savings	$11.2M
Cost of First 5 Acquisitions (1993)	$10.0M

The first four acquisitions were small companies or product lines that Wiremold eventually consolidated into existing facilities. These acquisitions, plus a fifth one also in 1993, added $24 million in new sales for Wiremold — which at the time was a significant amount of added sales. The new products included surge protectors, pre-wired raceway, aluminum raceway and aluminum Plugmold®, and their first steps into the data and communications product category. The latter product category drove Wiremold's overall raceway sales. These new products filled existing gaps and gave Wiremold's sales force many more products to talk about with their customers.

In addition, the $24 million in new sales generated about 10%, or $2.4 million in operating profit. Assume for simplicity that the cost of money is 10%. Wiremold in essence released $11.2 million in cash flow savings, which was costing it $1.1 million in the form of excess inventory and space, and converted it into $24 million in new revenue that was earning approximately $2.4 million in operating income. This represented a total earnings swing of approximately $3.5 million, which was a significant amount for Wiremold at that time. Additional earnings could be generated once kaizen was applied.

The fact that it could generate such earnings from the waste that had always been there, but which no one could see prior to Art Byrne's arrival, was important to Wiremold's growth over the next 6–7 years. Wiremold continued to repeat this approach, aggressively improving operations, both existing and new, to generate the cash necessary to support the quadrupling in size in eight years. What Wiremold achieved is a great lesson in the power of Lean when it is applied to acquisitions. Knowledge of the Lean management system allows companies to look at acquisitions differently, which provides another source of competitive advantage.

The changes that Wiremold made to its operations and balance sheet from September 1991 until the end of 1993 did not go unnoticed by its banks. Lenders were impressed with the changes and willing to help Wiremold grow if the need arose. The confidence that had been built with its bankers proved to be very beneficial to Wiremold when, at the end of 1993, Butler Manufacturing decided to sell its Walker Systems division. Walker was its best performing business at the time, but Butler needed cash. Walker was not highly integrated with the rest of Butler's businesses, so it was a logical candidate for divestiture. Butler hired an investment banker who contacted about eight potential buyers, and then held an auction for Walker.

This turned out to be Wiremold's largest and most important acquisition, though it came at the wrong time from a financial point of view. The Lean transformation had begun just two years earlier, and Walker was quite large in relation to Wiremold. The price was going to be high, requiring Wiremold to become more highly leveraged which increased risk. Art Byrne commented on the Walker acquisition:

> "It was the biggest acquisition that we had done and more expensive than what we could really afford. But we looked at Walker strategically and decided that we couldn't afford not to acquire them because if either of our key competitors bought them, then all of a sudden they've got product lines that go right against ours. The competing buyers were much bigger and much more powerful. It was going to be much harder to grow and to do what we needed to do if we let this opportunity slip away.
>
> One of the reasons we were able to acquire Walker was because we were able to go faster than the other potential buyers. We talked to their investment banker and said, 'Look we can just go faster. If you want, we will pay the same price they are going to pay, and let the management team decide who they would rather work for.' We felt that there wouldn't be any contest in that, as we had some feedback from Walker's management that the other buyers were behaving in a pretty arrogant fashion. We got pre-approval from the board up to the certain price, and then Orry and I could decide. The decision making process was basically, we will or we won't. The other bidders had a complex process that required them to go back and forth, so it took them a long time to do anything. We could decide what to do in three or four minutes and what price to pay. The leading bidder was so bureaucratic and so slow that the investment bankers just swung our way. They realized that they could get a deal going with us more quickly.
>
> We had to borrow money from a bank to buy Walker. But because we had improved our working capital position over the first couple of years, we had a short-term track record that we could show the bank. So we were able to get the money. Walker was the star performer for their parent company at that time, and it was making less than half of the operating income per-

centage that it is making today [July 2001]. It was scary at the time, but by applying Lean aggressively, it worked out well for us. Walker was a perfect fit for Wiremold."

Advantages of Lean for Acquisitions

As The Wiremold Company grew, it continued to improve its ability to evaluate acquisitions and see value where others could not. Wiremold's Lean culture and approach was implemented immediately in every company acquired. The fact that Wiremold could achieve consistent results, no matter what company it bought, allowed it to translate the expected results from a Lean transformation into the financial analysis that it had originally used for the acquisition. Orry Fiume described the advantage:

> "Combining the expected results from a Lean conversion with the type of traditional financial analysis done for an acquisition gave us an advantage when we had to compete to buy a company. Our Lean system and lack of bureaucracy already made us much faster at reacting to opportunities than other companies. We had only three people who were really involved in our acquisition process: Ed Miller, our marketing and strategic thought leader, Art, and myself. When we got down to negotiating and pricing, it was really just Art and I, with pre-approval from the board so that we could move really fast. The advantages of Lean when it comes to acquisitions are that it: 1) reduces the risk of an acquisition, 2) easily frees-up excess assets, inventory and space, 3) lowers the cost of the acquisition through cash back from inventory, and 4) provides a clear integration game plan for everyone."

So how did Wiremold go about assessing the potential of an acquisition from a financial perspective?[3] We'll use a simplified example of a company that is for sale to illustrate the difference in projected performance. Assume that Company "G" has the following profile:

- Sales $160M
- Gross profit $40M (25%)
- Operating profit $6M (4%)
- Inventory $50M
- Space   1,000,000 square feet
- People   2,300
- Sales per employee $70K
- Sales growth   3–5%
- Purchase price $80M

Orry Fiume explained the differences in how a conventional company might look at this opportunity compared to how Wiremold would see it:

"An acquirer that views business traditionally would have to be realistic in a case like this. They would have to look at what the company has done historically and base their projections on that. So here is a company that has not grown very fast, has weak profit margins, low productivity in terms of sales per employee, and a lot of inventory. In traditional companies, improving inventory turns is very difficult to do. Small improvements can result in very bad customer service problems if you are not careful. Putting in a new MRP system will take time, and even then the improvement might not be that great. After all, the company has been in business for 40 years, and inventory turns have never gotten much above 3; and even then, they might drop back to the mid-2's."

A traditional financial analysis is shown in Table 7-1.

Table 7-1 Traditional Financial Analysis — Company G

	Base Year	Year 1	Year 2	Year 3	Year 4	Year 5
Sales ($)	160	166	173	180	187	195
Gross Profit ($M)	40	42	45	48	51	54
Gross Profit (%)	25	25.5	26	26.5	27	27.5
Operating Income ($M)	6	8	10	11	12	14
Operating Income (%)	4	4.5	6	6.3	6.6	7
Inventory ($M)	50	46	43	40	39	40
Inventory Turns	2.4	2.7	3	3.3	3.5	3.5
Sales per Employee* ($)	70,000	75,000	78,000	81,000	84,000	88,000

*Assumes constant number of employees.

Orry Fiume continued his explanation:

"The potential acquirer has been pretty aggressive in their assumptions relative to the company's historical results. But there are a lot of risks. The $80 million purchase price is a high 13.3 times operating income. If they borrow the whole $80 million at 8% interest rate, then they'll add $6.4 million per year to the cost of the business. In the early years, their operating income just barely covers the interest expense. After five years, the difference between operating income less the interest expense incurred to buy the business, plus the reduction in inventory of $10 million, will get them back only about $33 million of the $80 million purchase price. That gives them a lot of risk. If, for example, inventory turns stay at 2.4, in year five they will need an extra $24 million in inventory versus their projection. They will have gotten back only $9 million of the $80 million investment.

But Wiremold is pretty good at reducing costs, and we know that we can do better than the prior management. And because there are strategic reasons why we want the business, we'll be a lot more aggressive in the improvements that we can make. Based upon our experience, we know that certain aspects of the Lean transformation are very repeatable and predictable. So we know that we can build our financial analysis to include the following items without much risk: 1) reduce space by 50% in 1-2 years, 2) double sales per employee in 3-4 years, 3) reduce inventory by 50% in 1-2 years and by 80% in 4-5 years, 4) improving service and quality will increase the rate of sales growth by 100-150%, and 5) the percentage operating profit will double.

One of the more important assumptions is in the area of sales growth. We have always found that just improving service and quality brings some very dramatic increases in sales growth. When we add the QFD method to new product development, we feel that we can sustain this growth. We may not always be 100% correct in all of our assumptions, but we'll be in the ballpark on most of them. And we'll exceed some of them. For example, we have been able to double the inventory turns of nearly every company that we bought within the first twelve months."

Table 7-2 shows the financial projection for Company "G", which undergoes a Lean transformation.[4]

Table 7-2 Lean Financial Analysis — Company G

	Base Year	Year 1	Year 2	Year 3	Year 4	Year 5
Sales ($)	160	166	178	195	215	237
Gross Profit ($M)	40	45	53	62	73	84
Gross Profit (%)	25.0	27	29	32	34	35
Operating Income ($M)	6	10	13	17	22	23
Operating Income (%)	4	6	7.5	8.5	10	12
Inventory ($M)	50	30	18	13	11	10
Inventory Turns	2.4	4	7	10	13	15
Sales per Employee* ($)	70,000	85,000	100,000	122,000	147,000	170,000

* Assumes a 35% reduction in associates through voluntary early retirement, attrition, and plant consolidation over the five-year period (about 820 people).

The difference in projected performance is dramatic, and Wiremold saw these types of results in most of the companies they acquired. At the end of five years, Company "G" would have no debt, versus $47 million in debt in the traditional financial analysis, the sales growth rate would be 10-12% versus 4%, it would have less than half the space, 64% higher operating income, 35% less people, and 75% less inventory.

These advantages reduce Wiremold's risk in any acquisition, and allow it to be very competitive when it enters into an auction process. Part of the advantage is needed because Wiremold includes every acquisition in the profit sharing program on day one, which adds additional cost right away. At the same time, however, it positions everyone to share in the expected gains. Wiremold has never had an acquisition where it could not more than pay for this additional expense quickly through aggressive kaizen activities.

Making a financial projection is one thing, but making it happen is another. The Lean management system is Wiremold's game plan for all acquisitions. Since Wiremold expects to achieve its financial projections, it begins implementing changes immediately after completing the acquisition.

The Integration Process

Recall that part of Wiremold's strategy was to become: "…one of the top ten time-based competitors globally." Does that strategy encompass only Wiremold's core internal operations? No. The senior management team used its deepening understanding of business processes to expand the time-based strategy to its acquisitions processes. Wiremold was actually able to buy two businesses simply because it was quick to secure the terms of the acquisition — going from a handshake to closing in six weeks or less. This had great appeal to the owners, and left other potential buyers wondering what happened. Importantly, Wiremold senior management demonstrated consistency in both words and actions with regards to the time-based competition strategy, and realized how its advantages applied to other business processes.

As expected, every company that Wiremold acquired had operated as batch-and-queue businesses. They all had mountains of waste to be eliminated. So how did Wiremold go about integrating the businesses? Art Byrne commented on the basic process:

> "We don't sit around for six months or a year trying to figure out what to do with the acquisition. We don't wait to assess how the business operates or how the senior management runs the business. We just don't do that. We go right in there on day one and introduce ourselves and start doing kaizen. The kaizen process changes people's way of thinking. You can't simply go in and say, 'OK, I want you to change; here is what I want you to do; here is what your new value system is.' The people will say, 'What the heck are you talking about?' The way that we have always done this is to say, 'Here is what we're going to do; here is the strategy; here is the philosophy, and now we are going to start to teach you and show you how to do kaizen and improve this business.' And the change in culture usually comes along concurrently with kaizen. We don't want people to leave; we want them to change. If people want to resist, then they have to leave. It is not like they

have a choice. Once we buy a company, they can't do anything they want to do. In most of the acquisitions that we have done,[5] we were very up-front in telling them that we'll train you, we'll teach you, and that we don't expect you to know anything about Lean, but you have to support it. And that it will be a really good thing – a very sensible way to run a business."

Art Byrne had established a pattern of the CEO doing the training and leading the first shop and office kaizens starting at the West Hartford plant in 1991. He continued to do this as the company grew. Art did the initial training for each of the new acquisitions and led the initial kaizens on the shop floor and in the office. Art explained his perspective on the importance of CEO involvement:

"There is always resistance to change. Having your company bought by another company is a pretty big change all by itself. To compound this by saying, 'Hi, we're Wiremold, and we are here to introduce you to kaizen and change the way you do just about everything,' is almost too much for people to handle. But if the CEO of the new parent company shows up the first day and puts everyone through a day of training on why Wiremold does kaizen, why it is core to our culture, and why it is going to be good for you, then that helps people understand. If the CEO then proceeds to put thirty people on three kaizen teams and leads them on the shop floor for the rest of the week — well, that's a little unusual. When at the end of the week each team has achieved 30% productivity gains, 60% reductions in space, 70% reductions in inventory, etc., its kind of eye-opening. People start to think, 'Maybe this can help.'

The key is that if the CEO is coming down to do the training and personally lead the kaizen with you, then it's clear that your new parent company, Wiremold, is committed to this approach. You have a clear choice: either get on board with the new approach, or leave. There is no period where the acquired organization spends the first six to twelve months wondering what the new owners will do. You know the first day what we want and why because the new CEO told you in the training session. You also got to experience big gains in the very first kaizens. As a result, Wiremold has been very successful in integrating new companies into its culture and holding on to the key people.[6] They quickly become excited with the big gains being made and the future possibilities."

Tom Goetter joined the company as a consequence of Wiremold's acquisition of Walker Systems in late 1993. He describes his reaction to Art Byrne's arrival at Walker to deliver the training and lead the first kaizens:

"Art came to us within a week after the purchase of Walker Systems, and after the initial kaizen training we had our first kaizen. There were about fifteen people in the training class and maybe a total of 18 people on the three kaizen teams. He started on a Monday and said, 'Here's what I see. It is a great company, but here is how we are going to make it better.' All the senior managers scratched their heads and said, 'We're not sure this is going to work here. We know this business, and he doesn't.' There was an engineering team and two other teams on the shop floor. So right away it was apparent that kaizen was not just for operations. Kaizen is a company-wide practice. It involves operations, engineering, accounting, etc. That first week, all of the Walker executive team was working on the floor, and Art was on the floor with us. We had a wonderful kaizen. It was really eye-opening.

Art often laughs when he recounts the first time he met me. He thought I was a 'concrete-head'[7] — people that are very difficult to change or unwilling to absorb new ideas. Concrete-heads will say, 'We have always done it this way. You can't possibly change it because that's the way it has always been done.' They are not very creative and they will not let themselves think outside the box. They'll participate in the kaizen, but don't expect many good ideas from them. What Art said about me was, 'He seemed too smart to be a concrete-head. I realized by the next kaizen that he wasn't one.' So Art's first impression was that I was very reluctant to change. And initially, all of us were skeptical."

Wiremold acquired Brooks Electronics in 1988. Its President, Gary Brooks, commented on the initial impact Art made on the senior management team:

"Shortly after Art arrived, he came down to Brooks and looked at what we were doing. He didn't beat us up and tell us that what we were doing was wrong. But he did say, 'You're further along than the rest of the company, but you're further along down the wrong path.' We were excited about him becoming the CEO because he was saying that executives have to be the first to learn about Lean, and then we have to go and do it ourselves. You can't implement this at the middle of the organization or delegate it to a department. So here's Art out on the shop floor leading the kaizen, with the broom sweeping, moving the workbenches around, and scrubbing the equipment.

It was a non-threatening, safe transformation, other than the fact that Art made it clear from the beginning that if you were going to resist and get in the way, then you're out the door. Lean was not something that you have the option not to sign up for. You don't necessarily have to participate immediately, but don't try to sabotage it. You can't have the top of the organization sitting around and questioning whether this is the right way to go. You either have to be on board or you've got to get out of the way. You can fight the battles at the lower end of the organization, but you just can't afford to fight the battles at the top of the organization. And that's why companies fail in doing this. If people aren't committed to Lean, they eventually leave on their own. So it was a pretty clear message that this was the way we're going to go."

Steve Maynard described the types of activities that occurred at acquired companies immediately after Wiremold had purchased them:

"The integration process is action-oriented. We clean everything up, get it organized, and throw out the junk that has accumulated over the years. That has a big visual impact. The parts hotels contain slow moving or non-moving inventory and are just sitting there taking up space. So we rip down all those shelves and get rid of them, and either move the inventory back to the cell that made it, to make it visual, or we throw it away. We don't draw all the pretty pictures of what the factory is going to look like, and then do cost estimates and charts and all the rest of those things. We go out in the shop with forklifts and we move everything around, rip everything out, and get it working again. You want to do things that you know are going to work: change-over times, setting up kanbans, cleaning up the factory — very visible things.

It really drives home the point of what our company strategy is and the tools and processes that we use to achieve the strategy. It sends a clear message to all the people in the organization that this is the way we are going to run the business, and that it is not negotiable. I wouldn't say it comes across as autocratic. It is just that we feel that we have a winning business strategy that works. We really try to focus more on educating people as to its benefits first. Probably the most important leadership aspect of the Lean transformation is the boss having a physical presence in the factory, in the office, in all the processes. Leading from the front and being visible all the time lets you communicate face-to-face."

Although many CEO's are characterized as "hands-on" managers, very few actually become engaged at this level in the beginning of the integration process. They instead delegate these activities to a senior executive or consultants. Do CEO's really have more important things to do? What could be more important than rapid and effective integration of newly acquired businesses? The benefits of direct involvement by the CEO are numerous and include:

- The CEO gains first-hand knowledge of how key products are made, non-manufacturing business processes, and customer satisfaction issues.
- Associates get to interact with the CEO in an informal setting, ask questions, and share explicit and tacit knowledge.
- Demonstrates that the CEO is serious about kaizen and the Lean management system.
- Tells people that it's OK to think differently.
- Positive outcomes motivate people to want to share in the success and participate in future kaizens.
- Tells people that if the CEO can make time for improvement, then so can other senior managers, mid-level managers, and associates.
- Establishes expectations for behaviors, processes, and results.
- Allows the CEO to gauge people's reactions and identify future leaders.

Scott Bartosch discussed the benefits of direct CEO involvement with regards to leadership development:

"Promotion and leadership development are among the very first things that the CEO has to think about when interviewing the management of a potential acquisition. That, plus the training and initial kaizens, tell you how many concrete-heads you've got in the organization — and whether they are truly concrete-heads or if they are open-minded enough to change. You always have a combination of the two; it's just human nature. That's a very important process because you can make some big mistakes if you put somebody in a leadership position that stands in the way of change. It's got some risk associated with it; sometimes you may be forced to take the chance, and we've done that.

You get resistance, but the question is, how fast can you make the existing leadership of the new organization see what the big picture is. We've really been quite fortunate. In some cases we have the existing management still in place. Don Beaver runs Walker, and he was there when we acquired it. He happened to be the finance manager at the time, and now he's the general manager. When we have an opening, we look across the organization. Tom Goetter was at Walker in sales, marketing, engineering. When we needed a Vice President of Engineering for Wiremold, the total company, Tom was the choice. Tom was the first person that came from an acquisition that we added to the senior management team here in West Hartford. Sure, we've made some mistakes, but things have worked out quite well overall."

Steve Maynard described additional details of Wiremold's integration process:

"We also integrate the sales force. We interview their sales people, and if they are good they join our sales force and get trained in that sales area. We may have to shuffle some territories around and things like that. If there are duplicate capabilities, then there may also be some downsizing very early in the integration process. In most acquisitions we take their product line and roll it in to ours. We take a look at their systems and start to integrate them.[8] If it is a small company and they make a standard product, then we would get them onto our business system right away. It usually takes three to six months, between the training, the data conversion, and getting them onto our data system.

We integrate the people, move their product into the warehouse, and get their pricing system straightened out concurrently. We find that most of the small businesses that we acquire don't have a standard pricing policy. They are all over the place on price. We get them on our one-price policy and change their terms and conditions as quickly as possible. The reason we focus on these items initially are because that's what the customer sees. Customers hear about an acquisition and they get concerned; they wonder what's going to happen to their supply of materials. That is the point where the acquisition is most at risk of losing market share. So we manage that by communicating closely with the customer base. The sales force doesn't just send them letters. They keep customers informed about the order entry system, the billing system, invoicing, etc.

It takes six months to a year to fully integrate a small entrepreneurial company that we acquire here in the United States. A bigger company like Walker Systems takes 1–2 years. It requires a lot of energy on the part of the parent company to do all these things. It is not just, 'Take two classes, good luck, and let me know how you make out.' I think that's the big difference between Wiremold and how a conventional company views Lean. They don't nurture the new company. They are not there to help. Instead they say, 'Let me tell you about this cool 'manufacturing thing', and then they walk away and say 'Good luck.' And maybe there are one or two people there from the parent company, but it is hard to do a Lean conversion by yourself. We take teams of people from other companies that we acquired and stay with them for a long period of time. There is a real investment in time and energy to get the acquired company converted. We don't walk away from it. The speed at which the transition occurs depends upon on the amount of knowledgeable people available to manage the conversion."

Ed Miller discussed how the acquired company's brands were positioned in the marketplace:

"We end up keeping the company's brand equity in the marketplace where it makes sense to do so, but we put it under Wiremold's umbrella. Some brands fade away quickly if the brand has little or no equity. For example, we never sold aluminum raceway, yet the market always associated us with aluminum raceway. The market viewed Wiremold as raceway in the general sense, not the specific material used. So we bought two aluminum raceway companies, and eliminated their brand name because the market already knew it as Wiremold. Walker is a different case. It had a very strong brand name for in-floor systems. At one time Walker was supreme and Wiremold was the subordinate brand. So we took Walker from a company brand to a product brand. And we had to take Wiremold from a product brand to a company brand. And that's what we've been working on for the last eight years. We've successfully done that with Walker; it's not Walker anymore, it's now Wiremold — but it is Walker in-floor products, Walker floor duct, Walker floor boxes, etc.

Marketing is really about positioning and mobilizing a company. It is a passion that must be instilled in everyone. I believe that everybody needs to do marketing; it's not the sole responsibility of the marketing function. That passion comes across when marketing people talk to salespeople, when they talk to customers, etc. But to do that, you have to be very clear in your message and then you have to be willing to change. We had a lot to change once we defined ourselves as the solution provider for the wire and cable infrastructure, and then added integrated connectivity along with that. It defined strategically whom we bought and it defined how we deployed people in every function, and to me that's what marketing is in a Lean business; deploying people in all functions, focused on strategy, to win market share. It has allowed us to eliminate boundaries, to be able to go across the company to make this happen, and to do it without adding lots of staff.

It doesn't matter whom people report to; it matters what they do. The end market pulls what this company does. It drives deployment of our salespeople, our marketing people, engineering, manufacturing — everything we do."

Performance of Wiremold's Acquisitions

Many of Wiremold's acquisitions were companies whose product lines were later consolidated into other businesses. Therefore, it is not possible to provide a consistent picture of performance gains on a consolidated basis for the period 1991–1999. However, some examples can be presented showing what happened over shorter periods of time, and where there was a consistent basis for comparison. These are representative of the types of gains that can be achieved when transforming a batch-and-queue business to Lean.

The first example is a small, stand-alone company, a union shop, referred to as Acquisition A. This company was later consolidated into one of Wiremold's larger facilities. The kaizen process started immediately, with Art leading the first kaizens on the shop floor. Improvements came rapidly and the business more than doubled in size over the first three years that Wiremold owned it. Table 7-3 shows what was achieved:

Table 7-3 Results for Acquisition A

	1995	1998	% Change
Sales, $M	6	14	133
People*	44	15	−66
Space, ft²	50,000	4,000	−92
Inventory Turns	2.5	12	380

* Reduction in head count is normally the result of voluntary early retirement and attrition.

This was an acquisition in which Wiremold recovered its money in three years. Since then, it has continued to invest in new products, almost doubled again in sales, and gained market share.

The next acquisition, Acquisition B, was a company in which Wiremold consolidated a few early product line acquisitions. In the middle of this time frame, the company's lease expired on its old facility, so it was moved to a new location. Despite this, the dedication to kaizen and Lean principles produced the results shown in Table 7-4:

Table 7-4 Results for Acquisition B

	Year 1	Year 5	% Change
Sales, $M	14.8	23.7	57
Operating Income, $M	−0.7	4.8	−
Sales per Employee, $K	98	167	70
Inventory Turns	4.1	27.9	580

This is a case in which asset utilization improved while sales and operating income soared. Despite mundane product lines and strong competition, this subsidiary held or gained market share and generated considerable cash for Wiremold to invest in future acquisitions.

The next case, Acquisition C, was another example of how the Lean transformation provides a clear game plan to use in an acquisition This was a product line acquisition, purchased from a large publicly traded company. It had lost money for the five years prior to when Wiremold bought it. Art Byrne and Bob Ahlstrom, the president of a Wiremold subsidiary, went to Acquisition C the first morning and brought all 88 employees into the cafeteria. They announced that Wiremold had just purchased their company and explained Wiremold's history and approach to creating Lean businesses. They handed out Wiremold shirts to everyone and told them to take a coffee break. After the break, Art Byrne gave them a two and one-half hour introductory course on Lean and why Wiremold believed in this approach. After lunch, they created two kaizen teams and told everyone else to go back to work. Art led one team, and Bob Ahlstrom led the other. By 4:30 pm that afternoon, Art's team had disassembled a sixty-foot long conveyor belt assembly line, attached it to a forklift, hauled it out into the parking lot, and threw it away. Bob's team had equally dramatic results that first afternoon.

At dinner that evening, the plant manager, whom both Art and Bob were impressed with — although a bit cautious about since he had helped to create what they saw as a mess of a plant — said, "Does this mean I don't have to write the 18 page monthly plant report any more?" Bob and Art looked at each other and said: "Well, you can keep writing it if you want to, but we're not going to read it. We'd rather you spent your time out on the floor doing kaizen." And that's what he did. Table 7-5 shows the results that they achieved:

Table 7-5 Results for Acquisition C

	1997	1998	% Change
Space, %	100	40	−60
Inventory, %	100	50	−50
People*	88	55	−38
Operating Profit, %	loss	14	−

*Reduction in head count in this case was a result of a high attrition rate that was endemic in the geographical area in which the business was located.

The other three or four 60-foot long conveyor belt assembly lines were also scrapped. The floor space needed in the plant was reduced by 60% in one year, and the business became profitable for the first time in five years. The plant manager, Mike Babasick is still with Wiremold and has been promoted to a bigger job. Once Art and Bob got Mike and his team the training and assistance that they needed, they were able to rapidly transform the business. Their prior focus was on controls and reporting, which forced them to spend their time on non-value added work. With these requirements removed, and given the clear goals contained in Wiremold's strategy, they could focus on doing value-added work. Art Byrne summarized Wiremold's approach to acquisitions this way:

> "When we explain our approach as being aggressive and when we say, 'You don't have a choice, you have to learn and do kaizen,' we sometimes get criticized. We hear comments like, 'Gee, that sounds too harsh' or 'Don't you run the risk of losing a lot of good people?' I guess that's why most companies when they make an acquisition wait and see what to do, or take a slow, incremental approach to making any changes.
>
> What we find is just the opposite. People always want to do better and perform at a higher level. When we show them how to do this, it creates tremendous enthusiasm and excitement in the business. The business moves forward, and winning feels good. The only people that we lose are the ones that we want to leave because they won't change and are holding everyone else back. The enthusiasm within a business starting down the Lean journey is infectious. We provide a lot of help and hand-holding, but for the most part each new business makes the transformation themselves. And in doing so, without realizing it, they adopt the Wiremold culture."

Foreign Acquisitions

Part of Wiremold's strategy had been to grow internationally, as well as domestically. Although finding acquisitions overseas was difficult, Wiremold successfully acquired a business that owned a major Chinese factory in 1995; another business that held a leading share of the plastic raceway business in Poland in 1998; and five companies, with a combined share of nearly half of the metal trunking market in the U.K., were acquired between December 1997 and January 2000.

Wiremold used the same approach with these acquisitions as it did with domestic ones. Art Byrne made the first visit, did the training, and conducted the first kaizens. Everyone was added to the profit sharing program and was given Wiremold's one-page strategy statement. The situation in each country was different, with various cultures and historical approaches to doing business. Even so, Wiremold was able to implement the Lean management system using the managers that were in place at the time that they bought the companies and made very good progress. Art Byrne explains:

> "It's interesting when you talk to different people about Lean. Most people say, 'Well, Lean was good for Wiremold and Toyota, but we're different; we're smaller, we're bigger, we make different products, we have different equipment, we have different customers, etc.' It's amazing how many excuses people can come up with to not do something.

When you get to a different country, nearly everyone will say, "Well, you can't do Lean there. The people are different, the laws are different, the labor cost is different, it's too far away, etc." The reality, of course, is very different than this. My experience is that no matter where you go, people are people and will think, respond, and be motivated by similar things. I've led kaizens in Mexico, Brazil, England, Scotland, Poland, and China, and have never seen much difference. The management is different and has varying degrees of concrete-heads, but this too can be overcome. Germany, for example, has a reputation for having some managers who are very set in their ways. Even so, Porsche, who I know very well because they use the same Japanese consultants we use, have done an outstanding job of changing their operations in Stuttgart.

The point is, if you know something that works a lot better than what the company you acquired has been doing, then why wouldn't you try to implement it? Why would you talk yourself out of doing something that you know works just because it's a different country?"

As Wiremold implemented the Lean management system in these foreign acquisitions, it achieved some amazing results. In the U.K., for example, it reduced five factories to two, changed all the products to a common specification, reduced personnel by about 45%, shortened lead times, cut inventories by 70%, eliminated some warehouses, and started to build a strong competitor in a previously fragmented market.

In Poland, the story was much the same, with dramatic reductions in set-up times, over 50% reductions in inventory, increased productivity, and greater market share. In China, Wiremold went from an old batch-and-queue operation in a run-down rented factory to building a new 200,000 square foot plant that is a model of one-piece flow production lines. Inventory turns went from two or three to 14 per year. The plant itself became a major sales tool for the company's OEM customers who were looking to buy product in China. They toured competitors' batch-and-queue factories, and when they saw Wiremold's plant, customers couldn't believe what they saw. Art Byrne commented on the overseas acquisitions:

"I'm proud of all our people and the jobs they have done. In the U.K., we've had a lot of different people contribute to our success. We've had more management turnover there than in most places due to that fact that we consolidated five businesses into two locations. Even so, Joe Marshall at our Scarborough facility, who fought us a little at first, has done an incredible job at changing his plant into a kaizen factory and is hungry to learn more.

In Poland, Celina Radziwon, who is in charge of operations, and Teresa Kaminska, who is in charge of finance and admin-

istration, have done an excellent job of improving their operation. Celina had a hard time at first, and we were a bit worried
that we would never convince her. Greg Stepeck, who leads the
technical part of our plastics business in Connecticut, spent a
lot of time in Poland showing her what we were talking about.
Once Greg showed her, she was unstoppable.

In China, our progress has been as good, if not better than anywhere else in Wiremold. They are certainly the most visual factory
with the best overall discipline. Kelvin Yao, along with his wife
Jor-Ann, Keith Pang, and Joely Wan have continued to improve at
a rapid pace. They have built one of the finest plants in southern
China — if not all of China. They operate with almost no work in
process as a result of their progress on set-up reductions, and their
ability to create one-piece flow. Injection molding presses that
used to take 2 hours and 25 minutes to change over are now
changed over in one minute and 49 seconds by one person and
with virtually no capital investment. Punch presses, including a
coil change that used to take well over one hour, can now be done
in one minute and 29 seconds. In addition, due to one-piece flow,
they have virtually no quality problems and very short lead-times
to their customers. A truly outstanding job in a place where most
conventional thinkers would say, 'Why do kaizen when labor is so
cheap you'll get lower costs anyway?'"

Wiremold's experience shows that Lean can be applied in many cultures
with the same type of results. After all, it's a "people thing," and the same types
of things motivate people around the world.

Summary

Art Byrne recognized that deploying the Lean management system required
Wiremold to grow. But there was another reason why they would have to grow
— and grow quickly: because competition in the industry was intensifying
rapidly. It would be increasingly difficult to compete against larger companies
if Wiremold had relied solely on new product development. Opportunities
that suddenly emerged to acquire businesses would have to be acted upon
quickly, while others would have to be diligently sought out. All senior and
mid-level managers knew where there were gaps in the product lines, and they
acted aggressively seek businesses that would help fill them.

A remarkable aspect of Wiremold's acquisition process is the consistency with
which the time-based competition strategy was applied. The strategy pertained to
more than internal operations or the delivery of products to end-use customers.
It also applied to how businesses were acquired. Wiremold's integration process
is noteworthy with regards to the concurrent, rather than sequential, way in which
various activities are performed. The senior management team in West Hartford,

and the general manager responsible for integrating the acquired company, put forth a sustained effort to place other businesses on the path to Lean.

Wiremold was able to acquire businesses quickly, in part, because the top finance person, Orry Fiume, understood what the phrase "time-based competition" really meant.[9] He learned its true meaning through direct participation in kaizen. Art Byrne set up the conditions that compelled his senior managers to participate in kaizen. Despite initial resistance, the experience changed how people thought. They could see that the concept of waste applied to their area of responsibility. The overall outcome was quite favorable for Wiremold and its key stakeholders.

The acquisition and integration processes are not always perfect. Some stakeholders are negatively impacted, such as associates let go due to redundancies, towns due to plant closings, or suppliers due to the consolidation of purchases. Wiremold management is cognizant of this, and makes a better effort than most companies to help ensure acceptable outcomes.

Key Points for Senior Managers

- The acquisition process should be consistent with Lean principles and practices.
- The value of an acquisition, both strategic and financial, can be more easily discerned when viewed through the lens of Lean management.
- Direct involvement by the CEO in initial training and kaizens have benefits that can not be obtained any other way.
- Kaizen is the method used to integrate acquisitions, quickly improve operating performance, and create a new culture.
- Each acquired business needs sustained support from the parent to convert from batch-and-queue to Lean.
- The Lean management system can be applied to any company, in any country, and in any culture.

Notes

1. The Wiremold Company acquired two more businesses in 2000, bringing the total to 21 business and product lines acquired during Art Byrne's tenure as CEO. Note: Only one true product line acquisition was made. All other acquisitions were companies, which can be viewed as "product lines" from Wiremold's perspective.

2. In the U.K., wire management is called "cable trunking."

3. Obviously, the financial perspective is just one of several perspectives that Wiremold senior management examines.

4. This example assumes that the CEO and CFO understand both parts of Lean management practice: "continuous improvement" and "respect for people."

5. The exception that Art is referring to is the acquisition of Walker Systems, where the specific situation did not permit any discussions about Wiremold's Lean business practices.

6. Indeed, Wiremold has been very successful at integrating new companies. Each of their domestic and international (China, and Poland) Lean transformations went very well. However, the transformation of their five acquisitions in the U.K. was much more challenging, principally due to work rules rooted in labor law that made it very difficult to change people's jobs — which was needed in order to introduce flexible working conditions. Most of the managers that were there when Wiremold acquired them are no longer with the company.

7. The term "concrete-head" is commonly used in Lean practice to describe a person that is hard-headed or unable to "see the light." It is not a complimentary term, though it may be used in a light-hearted way. It does, however, vividly portray the mindset that must be overcome. The term "concrete-head" can be misleading because it implies that a person can't change, when, in fact, they usually can change. The term is not used in Japan. Mr. Iwata or Mr. Nakao, principals of Shingijutsu Consulting Company, Ltd., are believed to have coined the term in 1988 when they began consulting with companies in the United States (see Chapter 2, Note 3). It therefore appears to be a term that originated with the Japanese, but while working with companies in the U.S.

8. Wiremold's many acquisitions resulted in the need for an enterprise-wide information technology system in order to share information and process business transactions such as: consolidate order information, purchase products between internal business units, consolidate the general ledger, standardize the chart of accounts, etc. Nearly every enterprise requirements planning (ERP) software solution that they looked at contained an integrated MRP production control and execution system, which was incompatible with Wiremold's production system. After much searching, Wiremold found an ERP system that had the ability to consolidate the business units and to share information across them, but without having to use the MRP module to drive production. The system was installed in 1999.

9. Most CFO's of conventionally managed business will say (or think) that "time is money." However, the business processes that they own, such as annual budgeting and capital appropriations, are filled with wasteful re-work, delays, and gamesmanship. This obvious inconsistency could be resolved by their direct participation in shop floor kaizens, and then in office kaizens.

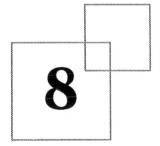

DELIVERING THE BENEFITS
OF LEAN TO CUSTOMERS

Strengthening Links to Customers

Wiremold achieved impressive improvements in nearly all aspects of the business in just the first few years of its Lean transformation: better quality, shorter lead-times, higher inventory turns, and lower product costs. It began to fill gaps in its product line through new product development and selected acquisitions. Wiremold was re-positioned from a supplier of parts to a supplier of wire and cable management solutions for power, data, voice, video, and communication. Though some of the benefits flowed easily and directly to customers, others required a significant amount of additional thought and effort. Wiremold faced two important challenges. They wanted to ensure that:

- More of the benefits of Lean were delivered to customers.
- Its customers understood that Wiremold was different from other suppliers; that nobody can do what they do.

While this may sound simple, responding to these challenges required some major changes in how Wiremold and its customers conducted business together.

Sales orders are signals to Wiremold's distribution center to deliver finished products to a customer. This, in turn, triggers production of goods by manufacturing to replenish the supply of materials in the distribution center. The foundation of the Lean production system is heijunka (Figure 4-6), which helps smooth sales orders as they enter the production system. Manufacturing can efficiently produce the volume and mix of SKU's required by customers even if the sales inputs are non-uniform, provided they are within the range of capacity. However, manufacturing will have greater difficulty if the sales inputs are *extremely* non-uniform. In other words, large orders received several times per year make it difficult for manufacturing to achieve high levels of customer service and also result in higher costs. In addition, large orders are probably inconsistent with how end-use customers will actually consume the products.

Wiremold historically had received large orders periodically from most customers, and they continued to receive such orders well into their Lean transformation. So, Art started asking questions: "What is causing the extreme variability of sales inputs? What is driving this customer behavior? Are we doing things that encourage this behavior? Can our salespeople do anything to smooth the inputs? Does our sales force understand the link between orders, production, distribution, and customer satisfaction?" These questions led to some remarkable changes at Wiremold; changes that would further demonstrate the interconnectedness of the Lean management system. People discovered yet another way in which Lean principles and practices apply to the entire business; that it was not just a "manufacturing thing."

Kaizen and the Sales Force

The sales force, which works with customers daily, was a key communication link between Wiremold and its customers. However, the sales force could not function as effective communication links if they did not understand the changes taking place in the plants. Scott Bartosch[1] explained how the sales force reacted when they first heard that one of the initial outcomes of Lean was a substantial reduction in inventory:

> "When you begin to talk about time-based competition and Lean thinking to a sales force, they look at it and say, 'What do you mean 20 times inventory turns? You're going to cut the inventory? Oh my god, you can't do that! What's going to happen to customer service?' I was nervous too because we weren't going to have as much inventory as we used to have. But I began to realize that this wasn't so bad because I could see what was happening in operations. That's why you have got to get everybody involved in kaizen. Otherwise you're going to have resistance that at times you can't control."

People from both inside sales and field sales participated in kaizen to learn first-hand the benefits to Wiremold and its customers. Scott Bartosch emphasized the importance of having inside and outside sales people participate in kaizen, both in the factory and in the field:

> "Having cross-functional teams participating in kaizen activities did more than anything to explain to the sales force, without a lot of words, that we were going to cut inventory and turn the inventory faster. They would come in here and work for a week, and they'd see tremendous improvement — not only in how we made a product but also in the quality of the product. So, they'd say, 'Well, this can't be all bad.' We don't have a member of our sales force that has not been through at least two kaizens in one of our factories.
>
> I was also pushing our regional sales managers a little bit to figure out a way to get kaizen into the field, to make sure they understand that this affects them. They decided that they really needed to understand what they're carrying with them in their cars, and why they're carrying it. It fit into our efforts to move away from selling parts and pieces of product to selling systems. We knew that our people weren't necessarily carrying with them what they needed to do their job; they were just throwing stuff in the trunk. Part of this was our fault because we kept sending them samples of every darn thing we could think of. Salespeople are notoriously disorganized. They don't clean their trunks; they just throw more stuff into them. Some of them had the back seat full as well. Salespeople would get to a call and find out that they didn't have the piece of literature that they needed.[2] Another

problem was the wear and tear on the vehicles; hauling around steel samples and literature. The first solution that the people thought of was larger vehicles; get bigger cars or vans. But that wasn't the answer.

So we did kaizens on the car trunk of our sales force. That's important because the customer rides in their car; they go to lunch together. We took about eight cars apart within each region. Then we got one person from each region on a central kaizen team, and they compared notes on what they had found. One day I'm talking with one of our salespersons, Kenny Freeman, in Dallas and I said, 'You really did a good job on your trunk; you really got it straightened out.' He said, 'Yeah, you know, if I didn't have something I needed with me and the customer offered to come out to the car and get it, I wouldn't let him come out to the car because the trunk was so messy. I'd tell him to sit right there while I went and got the sample.' The sales force did a really good job. They are proud of their trunks and they can now easily find what they need."

But kaizen, whether in operations or sales or anywhere else, is not a one-time activity, as Scott Bartosch noted:

"Every month they have a kaizen on something at the Memphis distribution center and every month we have a kaizen in inside sales. We do one week long kaizens, as well as two-day kaizens with four people on a specific process. Or maybe three-day or one-day kaizens. In outside sales we'll do maybe six kaizens a year, which is a little more difficult because you've got to get the salespeople together from around the country. For inside sales, we'll do about eight kaizens a year. The Memphis, Tennessee, distribution center, which is the other half of my responsibility, will probably do about 18 kaizens in a twelve-month period. This level of activity helps institutionalize continuous improvement."

The early participation in kaizen helped the sales people become receptive to changes that had to occur in how Wiremold sold its products. Scott Bartosch described one such change:

"Salespeople work on commission, and so they aren't always thinking clearly about what really has to be done. The customer is driving them and sometimes they aren't stopping themselves to say, 'Wait a minute. Can we do this a better way?' For example, let's say we have a contractor who is remodeling a university. That's a big job, maybe half a million dollars worth of raceway; trailer loads of product. In the old days, the contractor would send us a big order and we'd back up all the trailers to the loading dock, fill them up, and send them the material all at once. The contractor would have to figure out where to store the material, and maybe 5 or 10% of it gets damaged in the process. That's the way it worked.

Now, because of our flexibility, when we get a job like that, we go to the contractor and say, 'Okay, what's the construction schedule on this job?' And they say, 'What are you talking about?' We say, 'Well, you just bought 50,000 feet raceway, what are you going to do with it?' They say 'Well, we'll store it.' We say, 'How about if we send you 10,000 feet every 2 weeks. We'll bring it to you on our truck,[3] you unload it and put in the building where you want it so you don't have to store it anywhere. And, you don't have to pay us all at once either. You don't have to have your money tied up with a bunch of product that's sitting in trailers for a year.' Those are the kinds of things that come from Lean that people don't think about. But the salespeople work on commission. So he or she wants to get a big 50,000-foot order, wants it shipped all at once, and wants to get paid for the one big order. So there's a transition that you have to go through in which you teach people that such behavior, in reality, is not good for us or our customers.

That's why we do kaizens in the field, that's why salespeople participate in factory kaizens — to get people to operate to the same set objectives and goals as the rest of the company. You can't be successful if someone in the link just decides that they aren't going to be part of the plan. You can't just tell them that this is the way it is. They have to experience it directly in order to get them to see that it's a good thing and it becomes indelibly etched in their mind. They become aware that the more reliable we get, the more time we have to spend in developing new products instead of fixing old ones, and the more they sell, the more money they make."

Rich Levesque elaborated on how large customer orders are handled:

"We'll get an order for 10,000 floor boxes. They obviously can't install 10,000 at one time. So we ask the question, 'How many do you need to get you started? How many do you need a day? And when do you need a shipment; every day or every week?' If you can consistently show your customers that you can deliver every day, then they see the value and they like doing business with you. It's not just how you manufacture parts; it's the whole way of how you design products, how you make them, how you market them, how you sell them, and how you deliver them. Everybody has to work together."

So an important part of the Lean transformation was learning how to analyze orders and work with customers to smooth their requirements before they were input into manufacturing. As a result, the sales force was trained to contact the customer when they received a large order, and then ask some very important questions. First, they determined whether or not the order represented the actual requirement. In nearly every case, customers batched their orders out of convenience. Determining customers' actual requirements over time, coupled with production leveling, had three benefits: improved service levels, reduced delivery risk, and reduced financial risk for customers. The difficulty was convincing customers to change their buying habits to secure the benefits. The sales force played a critical role in educating customers.

Importantly, the customer's ordering behavior had nothing to do with pricing, as Wiremold had a one-price policy for its products. There was no quantity discount pricing in catalogs or periodic sales promotions. Scott Bartosch explained:

> "We intentionally shielded ourselves from the give and take of the distribution business, where our competitors will sell a product to distributor A at one price and then to distributor B at another price. We've always maintained a 'one price into stock' policy. We also have the advantage of product breadth. We have no competitors that can cross our product lines completely. And in most cases, our products are much easier to install from the contractor's point of view. So sometimes we are able to secure an order for a higher price than our competition. Sometimes we say 'no' to our customers, that we're not doing the deal because the competitive pricing is crazy, but then we get the order anyway at full price. We deliver performance and value that customers recognize."

Ed Miller elaborated on the "one price into stock" policy:

> "We've employed Lean practices in the way we go to market, including how we handle pricing. The one price policy was a very simple, revolutionary idea for the industry. And it unchained the sales force. Think of how much time was spent on negotiating price. With one price, all of that time can be spent on selling."

The leveling of orders and a one-price policy was just the start. The compensation system for the sales force was re-designed to focus on customers, rather than on wasteful competition between salespeople and the protection of individual territories.[4] Scott Bartosch explained:

"We're very tough on our salespeople in that we don't want them taking orders and we don't want them counting inventory. We want them to spend their time selling. We operate on a system that says 60% of your income is salary and 40% of it is commission. We made the compensation system for the sales force as simple as possible because we don't want them worrying about their money. They don't sell if they're worried about their money. So they get paid a commission on every dollar that's sold in their territory, regardless of whether he or she touched it or who the customer was that bought it. They get a commission check once a month and a statement that tells them where the sales came from.

If the salesperson goes to an architect or an engineer who specifies our product, and then it's bought in another territory, then we split the commission so that one person gets half of the money for specifying it and the other person gets half of the money for getting the order. We don't tell them, 'This is your account, but this other one is not.' That creates a bad kind of competition between salespeople, especially when you sell through distributors. Pretty soon you've got them trying to steer the business to certain distributors, and that's all waste. Every bit of it is waste. We have manufacturer's reps, independent businesspeople that will handle distributors and contractors. Then we have a complement of our own people who handle the specifiers in that territory — the architects or engineers. Our people and the reps work together, and they all get paid commission on every dollar sold in that territory. We're unique in the industry in that respect."

Changing Payment Terms

Since Lean is a total management system, all parts of the business must work in harmony to achieve outcomes that benefit customers. In other words, the activities in one function cannot cause problems for other functions. The objective is to improve the entire business system rather than simply optimize the individual parts, and ensure that it operates in a manner consistent with the core principles of eliminating waste and creating value for end-use customers. Don Beaver explained:

"For example, marketing understood that if they made a decision that is good for the customer but was not good for manufacturing, then in the long run it was not going to be good for the customer either."

The electrical products industry uses standard terms for payment that date back to the dawn of electrification in the U.S. over 100 years ago. The terms are "2% 10th prox, net 30th." Wiremold used the same industry-standard terms governing payment, but offered a higher cash discount starting in 1916: "5% 10th prox, net 30th." This means that customers who paid by about the 10th of the month (hence the term "prox"[5]) could deduct 5%, or they could forego the cash discount and pay by the 30th day of the month. To fully understand the meaning of this payment term, one must first recognize that in the late 1800's, the selling month, or billing cycle, was from the 26th of day of one month to the 25th day of the next month.

Assume that Distributor Z, in the days prior to computers, bought products from Wiremold between February 26th and March 25th. Wiremold would have started preparing the monthly statement[6] on the 26th of March. It would have needed a few days to manually collect sales data, prepare the statement, and mail it to the customer. Distributor Z would have received the statement in early April, which gave them five to seven days to review or reconcile the statement, prepare a check, and mail it to Wiremold if they wanted to take advantage of the 5% cash discount. If Distributor Z relinquished the cash discount, then it would have had to remit payment to Wiremold by April 30th.

Distributors recognized quickly that they should place as much of the order as possible on the 25th, 26th, or 27th day to maximize the number of days of "float" they could get, which is the time between order placement and payment. The industry's standard payment terms gave customers 45–65 days of float: five or six days between the 26th and the end of the month, plus the 30 days of the next month, plus up to 30 days for the following month if they did not take the cash discount.

This payment term encouraged customers to place as much of their orders as possible in the last week of the calendar month. Rich Levesque described the problem and how Wiremold responded:

> "One of our principles is to make every part every day. But our business historically has had a lot of spikes in demand. So we started to understand the root cause by asking "why?" five times. We use the "5 Why's" method all the time. Spikes in demand are obviously going to affect customer service. If, in the past, you used your inventory as a way of handling the spikes, and now your inventory is tremendously reduced, what are you going to do? So you have to understand what is creating the problem. We knew early on that our payment terms were causing a lot of the problem. If 40–60% of the month's shipments are being forced into the last week of the month by your own payment terms, then you are your own worst enemy. In order to deliver, you had to be staffed to produce this large volume in the last week. But what about the other three weeks? You'd be over staffed. You would have either a lot of excess capacity during the first three weeks to meet the end-of-month

surge, or you'd have to build inventory during the first three weeks to meet demand in the last week. This, of course, creates another problem: what should you build? The usual solution is to build complicated forecasting tools that increase costs and never really work anyway. This pits manufacturing against marketing and sales. Because no solution is ever possible, you wind up solving the problem — that you created all by yourself to begin with — by building and carrying excess inventory 'just-in-case.'

To make matters worse, you pass the whole production problem on to the distributor. To receive this much product in the last week of the month, the distributors end up being overstaffed for the rest of the month as well. In addition, the distributor is likely to make many more receiving errors, which results in lots of charge-backs, extra paperwork, double shipments from the manufacturer, and overall higher costs — all because your payment terms drive batch-and-queue behavior."

Scott Bartosch explained how the new payment terms were developed and the benefits Wiremold and some of its customers realized:

"The '10th prox' terms means that we got between 40% and 60% of our business during the last week of the month, all in one big clump, because customers would try to take advantage of the terms. So, if you're trying to level production and all your business is coming in the last week of the month, you have a big problem. So, very early on, when we were just beginning Lean, Art said, 'What would happen if we went to 5% 15 days?' In other words, customers would pay us 15 days after shipment. That should help level demand and allow us to give them better service. But I said, 'Oh boy, I'd have to think about that.' We tried that for a while, but it meant that distributors would have to have the ability to write a check on any given day, 15 days after shipment. In the end, we found out that they couldn't do that, so we ended up changing to the 5% if customers paid us twice per month — because we're the only company in the industry that did that, and we were also telling our customers, 'Cut your inventory, don't increase it,' this gave us a unique position in the marketplace. So we changed our terms to 5% 10th and 25th, net 30. As we expected, this also caused some problems. Some of the distributors said, 'We can't pay you twice a month.' It took, with the exception of two distributors, about 18 months before they all really understood that we meant it, and that it made sense for both of us. It really helped level our orders. After a while, some customers would pay us four times a month because they wanted to be sure they did not lose the 5% discount.[7]

We have been very rigid in saying to our customers that you don't get the 5% cash discount if you don't pay us on time. Five percent is well above the industry standard of 2% off of net. We're the only manufacturer giving that big a discount. That's important because it's a heavily discounted marketplace. The distributors go after each other tooth-and-nail on pricing. It's down to a 1% margin business at distribution, partly due to consolidation in the distribution industry. Fifteen years ago it was about a 7% margin business. So the distributor may pass on the 2%, but the other 3%, because it's cash discount, falls right to their bottom line. The distributor doesn't have to give the 3% away in the marketplace. So it's additional profit. Everybody wins."

Changing the payment terms to "5% 10th and 25th" largely eliminated the end-of-month order surge and flattened order input, which helped manufacturing level load production and operate more efficiently. Tom Fairbank noted the difficulty distributors had in changing their ordering practices, despite the new payment terms:

"The way distributors do business tends to be very traditional. So we worked to help them understand that they don't need to order six months worth of material at one time. But a lot of distributors just don't get it. They'll still order large batches even though they know that they're going to get deliveries every week. Their minds just aren't there yet. But the sales force keeps working with the distributors to improve their inventory turns and expand the breadth and depth of the Wiremold products that they carry."

Changing the sales terms for distributors was traumatic. Wiremold was the only supplier going against the industry's traditional sales terms. Distributors had developed their computer systems around the historical sales terms to maximize the float. The noise level from distributor's complaints was deafening throughout the 18 months it took to make the change.

Most managers, especially those who view Lean as a "manufacturing thing" never make the connection between sales terms and efficient manufacturing operations.[8] Further, it is unlikely they would ever challenge their customers on this issue. Wiremold, however, viewed Lean as a comprehensive management system to improve the *entire* value stream, not just the manufacturing portion of the value stream. Wiremold had to make this change to deliver benefits to its customers even if they did not understand it at first. Art Byrne explained this point further:

> "I knew shortly after I came to Wiremold that getting smooth flow in the factory with sales terms that encouraged 40–60% of the month's sales to be in the last week were incompatible. I was preaching to people that we needed to be able to make every product every day, yet our own sales teams were creating an end-of-month batch of orders that not only made this goal impossible to achieve, but it was bad for our distribution partners as well. In order to deliver value to our distributor partners, we had to change the nature of business discussions from price, price, and more price, to the value that Wiremold could provide. We had to solve this problem.
>
> It was painful, but the 5% cash discount that we historically offered versus the traditional 2% for the rest of the industry was more than enough incentive for an industry where the average distributor makes only 1–2% pre-tax margin. All of the distributors complained. It was hard for them to understand that once we could flatten the order inputs, we could return all of their perceived loss of float back to them, and then some, as we started to show them how to improve their inventory turns. We knew that they would not understand this at first, but we were convinced that we could teach them to see value later on. I knew that the basis of our business discussion could change if Wiremold delivered enough value to them: great product solutions combined with high inventory turns and low transaction costs."

Improving the Customer's Business

Wiremold had always shipped its products to distributors using common carriers and parcel services. The common carrier service often resulted in damage to its long raceway products and therefore many disputes with both distributors and the trucking companies. Delivery was unpredictable, as trucking companies would off-load material several times and allow it to sit in queue until there was a full truckload for certain locations.[9]

To avoid this problem, Wiremold developed the "cycle shipping" concept, in which 60–70% of shipments were shifted to its own small fleet of cycle trucks. This enabled Wiremold to make deliveries to larger customers once per week. The trucks returned, backhauling raw materials to its factories across the United States. This started slowly, and had many bumps along the way. Before long, however, Wiremold could tell a distributor they would deliver every week on a specific day within a narrow time window and with 99% certainty that this would occur. It took several years to establish this level of reliability and to get the distributors to trust the on-time performance of the cycle trucks.

The next step was to teach distributors how to use the cycle trucks to their advantage. The problem that Wiremold encountered was that distributors remained committed to re-ordering materials in large batches. They placed orders using MRP software systems that process data using max-min quantity equations. Distributors believed that they must have a lot of inventory on hand because, as the saying goes, "you can't sell from an empty wagon." Fortunately for Wiremold, one of the key performance measurements for distributors is called "gross margin return on investment" (GMROI),[10] or the gross margin that the distributor earns on the sale of their investment in inventory. As might be expected, this measurement is very good for an industry with high inventory and low margins.

The industry target is to have a GMROI in the 1.0 to 1.5 range. Any product that falls below this range is questioned, and strong pricing pressure is placed on the manufacturer to try to help improve the distributor's GMROI. Pricing is the dominant focus because just about everyone believes that improving inventory turns is very difficult, if not impossible. Assume that a distributor's sales are $100,000 per year for a particular SKU, and that its gross profit is $25,000. Table 8-1 shows the relationship between inventory turns on GMROI:

Table 8-1 Inventory Turns and GMROI

Inventory Turns	Gross Profit of Sales Average Inventory Dollars*	GMROI
3	$\dfrac{25,000}{33,000}$	0.75
4	$\dfrac{25,000}{25,000}$	1.0
5	$\dfrac{25,000}{20,000}$	1.2
10	$\dfrac{25,000}{10,000}$	2.5

*At selling price.

The obvious leverage point in the distributor's key measurement is inventory turns. If a manufacturer can get above a 2.0 GMROI, then it is likely that they are among the distributor's top three suppliers. At that point, the discussion changed from price to value and how to work closely together to sell more of the manufacturer's product. Rich Levesque explained:

> "We said to them, 'If we are going to deliver to your distribution company 52 times a year, then why do you need to carry three months worth of inventory?' We told them, 'If we deliver

there once a week, what we want you to do is don't carry as much depth in Wiremold's product lines, but carry more breadth instead.[11] You'll be able to provide more solutions to our customers, but you don't have to tie up your inventory on the depth of product. We will take care of that by delivering product to you every week.' The distributors that came on board are getting 10 or 11 inventory turns. So it is a training process to get them to understand. It is just like holding the people's hands here in the factory to get them to understand Lean principles and what they really mean. It was the same thing with our distributors."

As Wiremold improved its own inventory turns to about 16, its line item fill rate to 92%,[12] and developed the ability to deliver weekly to its key distributors, the discussion began to change. Wiremold started to train its distributors to use its cycle trucks program to improve their inventory turns. This is not easy to do, as a distributor's MRP ordering system drives them to load up on inventory and return them to three inventory turns. So Wiremold made one of the key responsibilities of its sales force to teach distributors not to buy too much of its products so that they can achieve 10 or more inventory turns. This was a very difficult transition for salespeople who are paid commission for selling product. However, Wiremold's salespeople actually delivered more value to distributors than competitors offering a 5% discount if they buy a trailer-load of product. Scott Bartosch explained:

"Our inventory turned about the industry average for electrical manufacturers, 2.5, maybe 3 if we were really good, and that's the industry average in our industry today [summer 2001], between 2.8 and 3.8. So that's nice for us; now we can turn our inventory 16 times — that's wonderful. But you need to be able to migrate that out to the distributors and say to them, 'Look, we're going for 20 turns on our inventory and we think you ought to be getting 10.' If a distributor is getting 3 or 4 inventory turns on a product line but we can show them how to get 10 turns, well now you're talking to them about their pocketbook in a way that no one else can talk to them. So when a competitor walks through their door, the distributor is going to say, 'Yeah, I really like your product, but...' And if you can get the distributor to do 10 turns on your product line, then they won't want to return to a competitors' product line because they would be returning to 3 or 4 turns, which would tie up their cash. The distributor will have to spend a lot of money on inventory that they didn't have to spend with us,[13] so we become their preferred supplier. This is what people don't understand and where Lean education begins to break down. They don't take the time to go from the back door of the factory and understand how this can be leveraged in the marketplace. It makes it really hard for competitors to displace us, and we don't have to spend time talking about discounts either."

Ed Miller saw Wiremold's ability to increase its customer's inventory turns as a source of competitive advantage:

"The only thing a competitor can do if they want to catch us and meet that same performance to the distributor is tie up all their investment in inventory. So they're stuck. And so we tie up the competitor, we delight the distributors, and we outperform anybody in the end market by giving people what they want, when they want it, in the color they like, etc. That's how what goes on in our business gets translated into a win. And we're able to do that with very low investment on our part. It creates a real problem for our competitors, and it will take them years to catch up."

Table 8-2 shows the performance goals and performance levels achieved by the end of 1999.

Table 8-2 Cycle Shipping System

Performance Goals	End of 1999 Performance
Deliver products 52 weeks per year	Deliver products 52 weeks per year
Deliver product same day each week	Deliver product same day each week
100% first time fill rate	92% first time fill rate
1 shipment per order	1.4 shipments per order

The cycle shipping program enabled Wiremold to offer both tangible and intangible benefits that distributors cared about, including fewer phone calls to expedite material and notification by Wiremold of any delays in delivery.[14] Achieving higher inventory turnover required close integration between Wiremold and its suppliers and distributors and retailers. This could only be achieved by engaging these business partners in a long-term mentoring relationship that included joint process improvement.[15] The change in relationship between Wiremold and its distributors led to remarkable results that benefited all parties. Ed Miller commented on the nature of the Wiremold-distributor relationship:

"We don't sell direct to any end markets, except for two small areas: cellular deck, because it has very stringent code requirements, and the other one is our specialty lighting business for large retailers. Over 90% of our business is through distributors. We are distributor-loyal. And that's important because they have to be able to trust you; trust is critical.

When I talk to our distributors, some of our salespeople get very nervous because I tell the distributor, 'You are not a customer of ours, you're a marketing and sales partner. You buy product and put it on a shelf. What is it doing there, looking pretty? If you don't sell it, you're going to want to return it for credit.' We view distribution as a channel and only a channel, not as a market or as a customer, which means we will sell through multiple channels to get our product to the end-use customer market."

Ed Miller and Scott Bartosch noted that the salespeople in their industry, as in many others, rely upon the well-known "loading up" of distributors and retailers to achieve monthly or quarterly sales figures.[16] Ed Miller, describes this common practice:

"Our distributor programs have to be totally based around Lean. In other words, we're not going to reward our salespeople for loading our distributors. Let's say that I am Company X, a publicly owned company that has a very traditional way of going to market. I guarantee you that in the last month of every quarter they'll have a 5% off sale. They'll say, 'Buy this now and have releasable orders in to me by June 30th, and you'll get another 5% or 10% off.' That's a loader. I'm shifting sales that I would have gotten later to the current period because I have to make my numbers. It's not real sales because if the distributor does not sell the product in a down market [which existed in summer 2001], then guess what: you're going to get the product returned to you. So the loader backfires on you. But it allows you to write a quarterly report to the shareholders showing favorable results. Even though we are now a publicly owned company [see the Postscript], we will not do that. I tell distributors when I see them — and so does our whole team — that we don't do loader programs. What we're focusing on is always unloaded; it's a pull rather than a push sales practice."

The long term profitability of Wiremold and its distributors and retailers will be higher without loading up in one quarter, as this practice comes at the expense of sales in the following quarter. Since most sales forces receive commission based upon shipments, it creates great pressure to meet quarterly sales expectations by relying on short-term games.[17] Loading up is inconsistent with the Lean principle of production leveling, and produces surges in demand that are difficult for operations to respond to. Wiremold's quarterly profit sharing provides the correct short-term incentive and is also consistent with Lean business practices.[18] Scott Bartosch recounted how he knew when the Lean transformation was beginning to make an impact on Wiremold's business, and the importance of profit sharing:

"What made me believe that all the work we had done was beginning to pay off was that we could react faster to major jobs as customer service started to improve. We started to see that Lean was taking hold; everybody began to understand what was going on here. We have people running presses who really care about the customer. They'll ask me, 'Are we doing a good job for our customers?' They want to know that.[19] They understand that they are not just making parts that are going on a shelf someplace, but that the customer has to be happy if he's going to buy more product. I also think that as the amount of profit sharing improved, people could see that their efforts were really paying off. In third quarter of 1997, we achieved a profit sharing of 19.5%; half a point off the 20% goal. People responded to that. The whole business system is tied together for the benefit of the end-use customer."

Bartosch commented further on Wiremold's focus on customer satisfaction:

"We are proud that we're a great manufacturer,[20] but we've got a long way to go. Through it all, we never lost sight of the customer. Sometimes it looked like we were out in left field. But the fact of the matter is that the customer has driven us. We were not learning how to become a Lean company just to be a Lean company. Most senior managers want to be able to use their manufacturing system to be more flexible and get a more quality product. After they've achieved that, then what the heck are they going to do with it? To many Lean is just a cost-cutting program, and that's the problem with how it is understood. They miss the biggest opportunities. If you aren't portraying yourself as Lean in the marketplace, if you aren't selling Lean in the marketplace, you're making a big mistake.

The benefit of Lean isn't just less inventory or faster inventory turns. People don't realize that it allows you to get better pricing. We teach our distributors how to sell more and different products, our products are more profitable for them, and they get what they need just about one hundred percent of the time. Lean has a lot more value for the customer than people realize."

Improving Distributors' Inventory Turns

Wiremold had always been interested in getting its customers to 10 inventory turns. To do this, distributors had to be taught a new way to order material. However, that could not be done until distributors made changes to their material requirements planning software. They would have to change the ordering logic that drove the computer system, which would normally trigger an order for 1–3 months of supply of a given SKU when a minimum level of inventory was reached. Alternatively, they could disconnect Wiremold's product line from the

MRP system, and use the sales data to create a report to order only what had been sold the prior week.[21] Unfortunately, most distributors were so committed to their MRP system that this would take time to achieve.

Wiremold developed a six-step process for improving the distributors' ordering process, which would take anywhere from 3–6 months to implement. The six steps were:

1. Clean up the inventory
2. Determine a target inventory 50% lower than before
3. Broaden the inventory offered to customers
4. Cut the inventory another 25%
5. Adjust reorder to weekly
6. Begin to order what was sold in the prior week

Regional sales managers explained the process and reasoning behind each step, then assisted the distributor in implementing the process. The initial resistance exhibited by distributors prompted Wiremold to make another significant change to their business practices. They developed "The Wiremold Insurance Policy" to give distributors further incentive to make the transition.[22] It read:

> Any out of stock position that affects a customer order because of implementation of this program will be rectified by a special shipment at Wiremold's expense to satisfy the customer's requirement.

Importantly, the 10X inventory turns program could only work if key measures were tracked by the distributors and shared with Wiremold.[23] They key measures were:

- Current, 30-day, 60-day, and quarterly inventory value reports
- Current inventory turns, measured as cost of goods sold through stock divided by the average inventory for the measured period
- Quarterly inventory turn measure going forward
- Number of customer orders that cannot be filled on first shipment from distributor
- Distributor customer order fill rate currently and quarterly going forward
- Number of emergency orders that Wiremold services
- Current GMROI and quarterly GMROI measure going forward

Many distributors did not initially embrace the 10X inventory turns program simply because they did not understand it. The common objections raised by distributors, as well as Wiremold's responses, were:

- "This drives more ordering and increases my transaction costs." Wiremold's response: *Not really. Today you're ordering 2 or more times per week. Ordering once per week with a defined cut-off may offer more discipline.*

- "Smaller orders will make me do more work."
  Wiremold's response: *No. Handling in warehouses should be easier with smaller batches to sort and put away.*

- "Less inventory is going to make me have more stock-outs and lose customers."
  Wiremold's response: *No. This should result in increasing your service since you'll be able to stock the breadth and depend upon Wiremold for the depth of product. Wiremold's service is also very consistent.*

Reducing Transaction Costs

As Wiremold's capabilities in Lean progressed — changing the sales terms, flattening order inputs, cycle trucks, and teaching distributors to turn their inventory 10 times or better to achieve higher GMROI — it also kept in mind the need to eliminate the high transaction costs that plague the electrical distribution industry. Electronic data interchange (EDI) is helpful but does not go far enough. Wiremold understood that it needed to do more to reduce transaction costs to deliver greater value to its customers. Wiremold's "one price into stock" policy was as a foundation for achieving this next step.

Most manufacturers in the electrical industry sell products at multiple price levels. They may have six distributors in a large metropolitan area that all get a different price for product A. In addition, they may sell to several national chains and have regional price agreements at different levels for product A. Then they'll create "special" prices at the end of the quarter or include some other special promotion, which only creates confusion. The distributor will have great difficulty trying to determine what they purchased at what price, which generates considerable paperwork for both the distributor and the manufacturer. Add to this the complexities involved in returning goods purchased as a result of a loader program, and the transaction costs increase.

Wiremold's approach was to simplify this situation and deliver value to the distributor customer, and change the nature of the discussion from price to valued business partner. With "one price into stock" and no loader programs, Wiremold already removed some of the barriers. Its cycle truck program will eventually allow distributors to easily return goods ordered by mistake. By the end of 2002, Wiremold is expected to add total electronic bar code control for all orders, shipment, and deliveries. The company already scans all product information into and out of their warehouses, and can put a single order in a repack box and print a bar code label for that box to allow the distributor to scan the bar code and know exactly what is in that box.

Wiremold's inside sales representatives also have a computer display that tells them how many boxes were shipped for each order and when they were shipped. Thus, when a distributor calls and says they did not receive an item, the sales representative can ask how many boxes they received. If the distributor received four boxes, the inside sales representative, who knows that five boxes were shipped, can direct the customer to look for the fifth box on their loading dock. Ninety-nine percent of the time they find it. In the past, Wiremold would have re-shipped the item and thus created additional cost and paperwork.

The next steps are to scan all products onto the cycle trucks and scan it off the cycle trucks at the distributor. This will allow the distributor to simply put away the box upon receipt instead of having to reconcile documents, verify contents, and store it. Once this occurs, then Wiremold can go to simpler statement billing twice per month.[24] This eliminates the paperwork involved with separate invoices attached to every order and every shipment. This will save a considerable amount of money for both Wiremold and its distributors and deliver additional value.

In combination, all of these actions help protect or improve the distributors' profit margins while making it easy to do business with a full-line supplier of high quality products delivered on time. The result is a valuable reciprocal relationship. Wiremold's value proposition is compelling, and helps build commitment to the brand and company-to-company relationships.[25]

Summary

Wiremold used Lean principles and practices to improve its own business condition.[26] Senior management could have been satisfied with that; just about every business performance measure was favorable, so why bother doing anything else? Instead of thinking and behaving that way, Wiremold found ways to improve customers' business performance and deliver greater value. Efforts to improve the value stream over a relatively short period of time transformed Wiremold from a supplier of discrete components to a full-line provider of integrated solutions and service. By improving its processes, Wiremold was able to achieve much higher material velocity. Senior management recognized the opportunity to transfer this benefit to its customers. In doing so, it helped distributors improve their GMROI, which provided Wiremold another way to outperform its competition. It also helped improve material flow throughout the value stream, not just in Wiremold's internal operations, and greatly exceeded the electrical industry's standard material velocity to which distributors were accustomed to getting. Wiremold delivered the benefits of Lean to customers in the form of:

- Better quality
- Shorter lead-times
- Breadth of product line
- One-price policy
- Industry-leading payment terms
- Higher inventory turns
- Lower product costs
- Lower transaction costs

The process for creating change with customers was difficult, carried some initial risk, and took time to accomplish. Nonetheless, Wiremold demonstrated a fundamental characteristic of businesses that truly understand the Lean management system. Senior management was not consumed with selfish optimization of their own position in the value stream, which would be of limited value to customers. Rather, they looked for opportunities to eliminate waste both upstream and downstream.[27] By doing so, they created opportunities to better serve their customers, grow the business, improve profitability, stabilize employment, and increase profit sharing. This behavior provides evidence that Wiremold's true focus was indeed on end-use customers, and that they continued to build upon their foundation of Lean principles and practices.

Key Points for Senior Managers

- Kaizen is for everyone, including the sales force.
- The sales force must work with customers to smooth their requirements before they are input to manufacturing.
- The performance of distributors, retailers, and contractors improves when the benefits of Lean practices are extended to them.
- Developing competitive advantage *with* suppliers and customers requires Lean companies to enter into long-term relationships that include joint process improvement activities.
- People have to develop a different set of behaviors in order to successfully interact with upstream and downstream business partners. Job rotation (Chapter 5) helps achieve this.

Notes

1. For many years, Sales and Marketing were a single function at Wiremold. These two functions were split in 1993, with Sales led by Scott Bartosch and Marketing led by Ed Miller.

2. Wiremold has a long history of providing extensive product information to downstream customers. There is the constant supply of trade literature produced for intermediate and end-use customers. By having a continuous customer presence, Wiremold helps ensure that their brands are the first choice among specifiers (architects and engineers), electrical contractors, installers, and facilities managers.

3. Wiremold established its company-owned trucking service in 1994.

4. This is yet another example of management's recognition of the existence of "behavioral waste." See Chapter 3, Note 9.

5. The word "prox" is an abbreviation for the Latin word "proximus," which means about, around, or roughly.

6. This was before the days where customers received an invoice with each order.

7. Some customers, for whatever reason, to this day, do not take advantage of the 5% cash discount. Wiremold still offers the old payment terms, modified to "3% 10th prox, net 30th," to customers that prefer to maximize the float.

8. There can also be a connection between sales terms and efficient *service* operations.

9. In addition, common carriers would quote their best-case scenario for the "number of days to ship," which did not include weekends, holidays, handoffs to other carriers, weather delays, etc.

10. Gross margin, also called gross profit, is the excess of sales over the cost of sales. Distributors define gross margin return on investment as gross profit of sales of stocked products divided by the average inventory dollars at selling price. Thus, GMROI is a non-dimensional measure of the financial return resulting from the sale of an investment made in a quantity of inventory. It is not an indicator of profitability; use net income instead.

11. Wiremold encourages its distributors to carry "market suitable inventory," which means carrying a wider breadth of Wiremold's products to give customers greater selection and achieve higher inventory turns, while Wiremold provides the depth of products through their fast cycle-time (i.e. high material velocity) production capability. Higher inventory turns frees-up the distributor's capital and helps ensure that they stock a saleable product mix.

12. 92% was the fill rate in 1999. The line item fill rate in summer 2001 was 98%. The fill rate measurement is based upon shipment within 24 hours.

13. For a distributor carrying $100,000 worth of inventory for a particular product line at 10 turns, reverting to 3.5 turns would require an additional cash outlay of $185,000.

14. In contrast, buyers usually have to contact sellers, often many times, to obtain information on the status of their orders.

15. See how Toyota Motor Sales helps auto dealers improve their business in "A New Era of Harmony," a speech by Jim Press, Chief Operating Officer, Toyota Motor Sales USA, at the 2002 National Automobile Dealers Association, New Orleans, LA, 26 January 2002 (http://pressroom.toyota.com/photo_library/display_release.html?id=20020130_press). Also, see Chapter 4, Note 21 for sources that describe how Toyota Motor Corporation, Honda Motor Corporation, and other companies develop their suppliers' capabilities.

16. Also known as "channel stuffing" or "channel loading." To understand the negative impact that loading up can have on a company, its officers, employees, suppliers, investors, customers, and communities, see the SEC form 10-K Annual Reports for Thomas & Betts Corporation (NYSE: TNB; http://www.tnb.com) dated 29 March 2001 and 29 March 2002; the SEC form 10-K Annual Report for Sunbeam Corporation (http://www.sunbeam.com) dated 2 May 2000; and the SEC form 10-Q Quarterly Reports for Bristol-Myers Squibb Co. (NYSE: BMY; http://www.bms.com) dated 15 May 2002 and 14 August 2002.

17. Note that traditional sales commission compensation practice does not necessarily have to change if the sales force is trained to understand why they should not engage in loading up.

18. Stock options are consistent with the Lean management system if management is focused on the long-term. Stock options will be inconsistent with the Lean management system if they focus people solely on increasing short-term share price and drive other forms of short-term thinking that compromise the interests of key stakeholders. Business decisions are better made if the long-term consequences to the company and its end-use customers are considered, which will invariably result in a higher share price whose benefits are realized both short- and long-term (the latter principally through the 401(k) plan). Short-term gains are the outcome and cannot be the principal focus of decision-making.

19. It is very important for management to regularly communicate to associates the feedback obtained from intermediate and end-use customers. This information helps people understand how the dramatic changes in the way work is performed are being perceived in the marketplace. It provides further rationale in support of the Lean transformation and helps gain acceptance.

20. The Wiremold Company won the Shingo Prize Business Award in 1999. The Shingo Prize, named in honor of Dr. Shigeo Shingo, is awarded annually to companies that that achieve superior customer satisfaction and business results. See http://www.shingoprize.org/shingo/index.html.

21. In other words, Wiremold asked its distributors to place smaller orders more frequently, ordering only what they sold each week.

22. The insurance policy was added to the 10X inventory turns program in 2001.

23. The measurements help prevent so-called "free riders" — companies (or people) that enjoy benefits without making the required contributions. See "Homo reciprocans," S. Bowles and H. Gintis, *Nature*, Vol. 415, 10 January 2002, pp. 125–126.

24. Monthly statement billing was common in the electrical industry in the early 1900's. It is interesting to see that this type of billing will return again, albeit twice a month, and is made possible by bar code technology.

25. Wiremold's integrated approach to new product development, production, marketing, and sales delivers value well beyond the unit price of its products. By consistently doing so, its downstream customers have no substantive reason to consider using online reverse auction or other divisive purchasing tools to optimize their own position. In fact, the strength of the incentives and greater value proposition creates powerful disincentives for wasteful gamesmanship that would result in higher costs and therefore reduced margins for both the buyer and seller. See http://www.theclbm.com/publications.html and "The Economics of Fair Play," K. Sigmund, E. Fehr, and M. Nowak, *Scientific American*, January 2002, Vol. 286, No. 1, pp. 82–87.

26. At the same time, Wiremold was also working with their suppliers to improve their business performance. See Chapter 4.

27. Wiremold clearly has many opportunities to use its considerable knowledge of Lean business practices to help its downstream customers further eliminate waste in their own internal business processes. Wiremold's initial Lean transformation, followed by the new payment terms and the 10X inventory turns program, builds substantial credibility with customers and serves as a solid foundation for future improvements in both day-to-day activities and company-to-company human relationships.

Thank you for letting us help you investigate lean initiatives for your organization. We're sure that the enclosed award-winning book by Bob Emiliani will be a great asset in your lean journey.

After you've read *Better Thinking, Better Results,* you'll be ready to put its winning lean principles into action. To that end, Oracle stands ready to help you take your continuous improvement efforts to a new level and sustain the gains you achieve.

Oracle's lean enterprise solutions for automotive can help you:

- **Respond efficiently to fluctuating demand**
- **Support flexible manufacturing environments**
- **Lower IT management costs through outsourcing**
- **Promote shared service environments**

For more information, please call us today at 1.800.633.0936. Or go to: oracle.com/lean

Sincerely,

Oracle Automotive Solutions Team

ORACLE

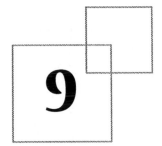

9

PERFORMANCE MEASUREMENT

Measuring Conventional Business Performance

Conventional management practice focuses on optimizing the individual parts of a business and assumes improvements in each functional area will accrue favorably to the business as a whole. It is easy to set function-specific goals and hold department heads accountable for results. This seems like a reasonable thing to do and just about everyone does it.[1] Senior management also will often adhere to the view that "what gets measured gets managed." Most people accept this paradigm as an absolute truth.[2] Typically, it results in the proliferation of business measurements that cause endless management reporting, meetings, and reviews. The question is, does a confusing mix of function-specific and business-level metrics truly help guide effective decision-making and improve competitiveness?

Function-specific business metrics usually pit people at all levels against each other, making real teamwork virtually impossible to achieve. For example, the vice president in charge of quality focuses on improving the quality of goods or services. However, the vice president of purchasing will be charged with reducing the price of goods and services purchased. These two objectives, in conventional management practice, are seen as tradeoffs – i.e. better quality costs more and lower prices result in poor quality. The resulting conflict between these departments wastes time and money. Problems are simply traded between departments and may never be solved. Further, people will game the metrics to avoid negative personal or organizational consequences and attempt to shift blame to other departments or to suppliers. The inability to eliminate systemic problems, partially driven by the view that tradeoffs are necessary, will give customers good reason to want to switch sources.

Business processes and metrics are usually connected and tend to perpetuate one another. If a business process changes, then the metrics should also change. Often though, they do not. In general, experienced senior managers resist changing their function-specific metrics because they understand how to manipulate them. New metrics can be perceived as a threat to one's knowledge and authority. Traditional business measures can be a powerful deterrent to organizational change that must occur to better satisfy end-use customers.

Most people think batch-and-queue processes are limited to manufacturing activities. However, upon closer examination, it is apparent that nearly all business processes are batch-and-queue to a greater or lesser extent, as this is the conventional or intuitive way to perform an activity. The business practices in non-manufacturing functions are termed "hidden" batch-and-queue because they are not perceived as such directly, yet they promote that very practice within a function or impose it upon other functions (Table 9-1). When viewed this way, the total amount of waste (muda), unevenness (mura), and unreasonableness (muri) that exists in conventionally managed businesses is enormous.

Table 9-1 Examples of "Hidden" Batch-and-Queue Business Practices*

Function	Business Practice or Metric**
Finance	Absorption accounting,[3] standard costs[4] & earned hours, scrap, rework, and repair budgets, direct and indirect labor metrics, learning curves,[5] annual budgeting, capital appropriations, ROI, NPV, and IRR calculations.
Purchasing & Materials Management	Order requisition queue, range quoting, economic order quantity calculations, quantity discount analysis, purchase price variance, standard costs, online reverse auctions, financial penalties for non-performance.
Sales & Marketing	Quantity discounts, end-of-month sales push, channel stuffing, rebates, upselling, tying agreements, dumping, forecasts (for driving execution), sales quotas, sales commissions.
Design and Engineering	Design and development, engineering changes, over-specification, sole-source processes, hard-to-manufacture parts, data collection.
Human Resources	Annual employee reviews (all employees at once), "flavor-of-the month" training programs, function-specific incentive compensation, hiring/layoffs, promotion process, direct and indirect labor time cards, piece part incentives.
Management Information Systems	Job order queue, MRP push systems, software change-over, data entry, data processing, code writing and debugging, expensive software solutions
Legal	Complex contract terms and conditions, "one size fits all" contracts, document review, multiple sign-offs, specialist legal skills.
Distribution	Numerous distribution centers, unpack / re-pack, multiple touches, receiving inspection, over-inspections, shortage meetings.

* Defined as practices or metrics that seek to locally optimize performance, promote processing of large batches, create long queue times, distort information or reality, or result in wasteful human behaviors.
** The degrees to which these practices or metrics are batch-and-queue in nature will vary. There may be overlap between two or more functions.

The pervasiveness of batch-and-queue business processes force employees to spend their time optimizing performance within their own functional area, usually without knowledge of the negative impact on the company or its customers. Another way to understand this problem is to recognize that 50% or more of an employee's time is typically spent on activities that do not add value.[6] Management's common refrain is: "we don't have the resources" or "resources are scarce." In reality, waste is abundant.

These hidden batch-and-queue business practices create an even bigger problem: they distort reality and block the flow of information.[7] Management becomes intent on ensuring that the information is precise, but often fails to question its relevance or effect upon the quality or consistency of decision-making.[8] When information is bad, people will be reluctant to tell senior managers what is actually going on. The emphasis is on results and holding people personally accountable, which creates a highly political environment that blames people for problems. The business is left with no choice other than to focus on short-term results. Management gets only the good news, and therefore lots of surprises. Ultimately it must make tradeoffs between key stakeholders – layoffs, plant closings, and squeezing suppliers[9] – to meet financial commitments to shareholders. The ensuing confusion, contradictions, and conflicts create ethical dilemmas and intractable problems. Management is forced to focus inwardly on the company instead of outwardly on its end-use customers.

Most CEO's that embark on the Lean transformation fail to grasp the magnitude of change that must occur, not only in operations, but also within all other service and support functions. Business practices, as well as people's behaviors, must shift from its historical focus on local optimization to learning how to improve the entire system – from a results to a process focus. It is the CEO's responsibility to lead the effort through direct participation and create a safe environment for people, business processes, and metrics to change. Many of the practices or metrics shown in Table 9-1 can be abandoned immediately, while others can be phased-out over time. Some batch-and-queue processes may continue for many years because nobody has yet thought of a better way. However, there will be a general awareness of the limitations of such practices as they affect both people's thinking and the conduct of business processes, and that batch-and-queue metrics should be abandoned because they are a source of conflict. Functional goals will still exist, but they will not be pursued at the expense of the company or its customers. Tradeoffs will be minimized or eliminated.

The Problems with Traditional Cost Accounting

Traditional cost accounting and financial measurement systems have several common characteristics. They both use full absorption standard costs for product costing and inventory valuation. They allocate costs to departments and hold managers accountable for the costs not under their direct control. They make extensive use of variance reports as a primary means of cost control. Differences between actual costs and allowable standard costs are reported and managers are held accountable for the unfavorable variances. Finally, traditional systems emphasize short-term financial results. The focus is almost exclusively on weekly, monthly or quarterly costs and profits compared to budget or standard. These methods are ineffective in promoting Lean business practices because they encourage behaviors that are the opposite of those needed.[10]

Standard costs are usually the result of negotiations or are based on historical data, and thus not a measure of current or near-term optimum practice. Top management generally wants standards to be tight but achievable through efficiency and cost reduction. It also wants some assurance that budgeted profit targets will be achieved. Department and division managers, on the other hand, want standards to be looser to ensure that they can still achieve their targets even when unanticipated problems arise.[11] As the budget process plays out, persuasive department managers may be able to negotiate softer standards. As a result, standards do not represent what can be achieved executing the existing processes at improved efficiency; instead they represent "the plan." Variances from standard mean little beyond the fact that actual results are different than the plan, and do not encourage people to determine the root cause of problems. The plan itself is contrived, as a result of internal negotiations and guesswork. It pits one function against another and senior management against everyone else. Once standards are set, people will do very stupid things to meet the plan, even though it's just a guess made during the prior budget cycle.

Rather than encourage continuous improvement, standard cost control systems emphasize achieving the status quo. If an operations manager discovers a way to produce below standard cost, his or her preference will be to achieve just the standard. This outcome helps ensure that the standard cost will not be reduced in the next budget cycle. The manager will use the ability to produce at a cost below standard as a hedge against future problems.

The standard cost focuses people on making the numbers. This creates a culture much more skilled at manipulating the numbers than improving processes. Many companies completely lose sight of processes because they are fixated on achieving results. The operations manager's goal is to produce standard direct labor hours because the labor hours will absorb the allowable overhead costs. The incentive is to produce the product that has the most labor hours in order to absorb more overhead, even if it is not the product that the customer needs. Orry Fiume described how the traditional factory environment operates:

> "You've got a forecast that drives your production schedule. It's a push type schedule and the push comes from the material requirements planning [MRP] system. MRP software contains a very complicated set of logic that says if you need product A, then it works backwards through the bill of materials and routings, and determines that you've got to start it at location X in the factory and on a given day in order to have the finished product by the forecasted date. The difference between when the part is started and when it is needed is a fairly long time because of delays in batch-and-queue processing. It's totally unworkable because the software assumes that everything is going to go right; that machines aren't going to break down, that material is going to be there, people are going to be there when needed, etc. The reality is business doesn't operate that way. Business is very dynamic and things happen.
>
> So what happens in a typical factory? The first line supervisors don't understand a darn thing about standard cost accounting, but they do understand the concept of direct labor hours. They know that if they don't produce enough direct labor hours, then they will have unfavorable overhead variances, which is bad. So in the last week of the month, the first line supervisors know what the MRP schedule says; it says make item A, and item A needs five sub-components but only two are available. So they can't make

all the required A's. The supervisors scramble around to find other parts that they do have and what products they can produce from them in order to make direct labor hours. So they end up creating hours instead of producing what customers have ordered."

The MRP scheduling and standard cost control systems do not distinguish between products that customers want and products that customers do not want. Importantly, the system equates production for a customer and production for storage in inventory as equally valuable, when in fact they are not. The current period costs of products produced but not sold, including the overhead allocated to them, are pushed off the income statement and onto the balance sheet thereby improving reported income. Overproduction, one of Mr. Ohno's seven wastes, is encouraged.[12] It is a key element in any "make-the-month" batch-and-queue business setting.

For example, assume Department B produces 20 different products in 20 eight-hour shifts per month, and it takes one hour to set-up the machines for each product. Also assume it takes seven hours to produce the average monthly amount demanded for each product. To satisfy this demand, the manager of Department B runs one product per day, taking one hour to set-up and producing one month's worth of product in a seven-hour run. However, since demand for each product isn't perfectly smooth, and each product is produced only once per month, the company keeps a safety stock of finished goods equal to one month's average demand. If production runs smoothly, then the average finished goods inventory will be 1.5 month's worth of each product.

Department B's manager is evaluated based on achieving standard cost. The manager knows that it will be easier to hit budget targets if the machines are kept running on the same job, which means that there will be fewer machine set-ups. Costs will therefore be spread over a larger base of production; direct labor cost will increase and indirect labor cost for set-ups will decrease, thereby making it easier to cover higher costs on other overhead items. The incentive is clearly to produce larger batches of material. If products are produced every other month in a two-day run, then half the number of set-ups and 10 hours of set-up time are eliminated, which creates an additional 10 hours of time for further production. The standard cost system will reward the operations manager, as he or she is able to report higher machine and labor efficiency.

The added 10 hours of production time will be needed because the company will have to build more inventory. The average inventory for each product is one month's average demand plus the safety stock. With the lead-time lengthened to two months, a one-month safety stock is no longer sufficient to avoid stockouts. The company may need two or even three month's worth of inventory to avoid stockouts because the difference between actual demand and anticipated demand will be greater over a two-month period than over a one-month period.

Of course, the added inventory will increase costs. There will be many types of additional costs: transportation, transaction, storage, taxes, insurance, financing cost, and obsolescence, all of which are difficult for a standard cost system to recognize. Most of these costs will occur in periods after the excess production has taken place. Under traditional accounting, most of the costs will be charged to other departments. Department B which is responsible only for production, will seek to optimize its position at the expense of the rest of the company. There will also be delays in discovering defects and greater difficulty in determining the root cause of the defects, as they were produced months before they were discovered.

What happens to the products after they are produced is somebody else's problem. The transaction costs are accounting's problem, the storage and insurance costs are the inventory storekeeper's problem, financing costs are the treasurer's concern, obsolescence is sales and marketing's problem, etc. Traditional accounting and absorption costing allows Department B to overproduce in order to achieve its standard costing numbers, while it creates higher costs and new problems for everyone else in the company.[13] Unit costs appear to be low, but the total costs to the company are high. While Department B looks good, customers will be unhappy and the company may be barely profitable and losing market share. Figuring out what to do about it is very difficult. After all, the standard cost system is showing favorable variances for Department B, and probably the other production departments that are doing the same thing. Productivity looks like it is improving, so where is the problem?

It is not only operations managers that take advantage of traditional accounting to improve their performance numbers while creating innumerable problems elsewhere. Purchasing, sales and marketing, accounting, and other functional managers are tempted to make decisions based upon similar logic. As a result, weekly or monthly meetings to discuss the variance reports frequently become a blame game. Managers blame any failure to make their numbers on the actions of other departments. The emphasis is on making and explaining the numbers, rather than improving the processes.

Assume that Department B had taken a different approach: the manager and associates in Department B improve the process. Set-up times are reduced from one hour to three minutes. Department B can now meet the average demand for all 20 products on a daily basis (See Figure 4-1). Due to the greater production flexibility with the new process, a safety stock equal to a few *days* worth of demand will provide greater protection against stockouts than they had with one month's worth of inventory and hour long setups. Of course, most of the savings will be achieved only if production is more closely matched to the rate of actual customer demand and if the excess inventory is sold. Under the principles of traditional cost accounting, Department B will not be credited with the savings.

While the safety stock is being reduced to the new lower levels, production in Department B will decrease because customer demand is being satisfied out of inventory. The cost of machinery and other fixed costs will be spread over less production and average costs will rise. Direct labor will decline as a proportion of total department labor, and there will be fewer standard direct labor hours to "earn" or "absorb" the manufacturing overhead costs. Under the traditional standard cost system, Department B's reward for improving flexibility and quality, reducing lead-times to better serve the customer, and reducing costs throughout the company, will be unfavorable overhead variances, lower productivity, and lower machine utilization measures.

Transforming the Accounting Function

To be consistent with Lean principles and practices, it was not enough for Wiremold's accounting to provide support for improvement in manufacturing, sales, marketing, and product development. The accounting processes themselves had to be changed. According to Orry Fiume:

> "You have to look at everything you do in the business to see if it is consistent with the Lean philosophy. And if it's not, senior management has to change it."[14]

By analyzing the processes in accounting, it was obvious that the majority of work was devoted to transaction processing, and that transaction processing was waste (Figure 3-1). Orry Fiume elaborated:

> "The accounting processes contain an enormous amount of waste and so one of the things that you need to do when you convert to Lean is focus on the amount of transaction processing that goes on. They are non-value added, and as you get into a Lean environment you can start eliminating a lot of those transactions. For example, as you set up cells and products start going from the first step to the last step all within the cell, you can do away with labor reporting. Labor reporting is a huge drain on resources. You also have the system that determines people's pay – the time card system. This labor reporting system is used to allocate that pay to hundreds or thousands of direct and indirect labor buckets.
>
> One of the requirements in most companies is that you have to balance labor reporting and time cards before payroll can be processed each week. I have yet to see a reconciliation actually balance the first time out of the box. There are always differences, and then people have to scramble and try to figure out why there are differences and put them in the right bucket. But there isn't a company that is going to miss a payday because they can't reconcile labor differences. As a result, the remaining differences get plugged; but if you don't have labor tickets, you

eliminate the reconciliation process. A huge amount of resources are taken up in every accounting process, because all the business processes generally feed the accounting processes in some way. There is a huge amount of waste. The reality is whether a company goes Lean or not, their accounting people ought to be addressing the waste in those things. They need to start changing the focus from traditional accounting-based cost control to cost management.[15]

To move from accounting-based cost control to cost management, the accounting function had to eliminate waste and reduce the time spent on non-value added but necessary work. This would free-up time and resources to devote to value-adding cost management activities. The internal labor reporting described by Orry Fiume is an example of waste. Labor cost that occurs within a production cell is a cost of running the cell, and thus is a cost of the products produced in the cell. Assigning the labor cost to a dozen different direct and indirect labor budget line items does not help the team determine whether activities are adding value or if they are waste. In fact, it distracts the product line team from efforts to uncover and eliminate waste.

Accounting transactions are designed to reflect, support, or control underlying physical business processes. Any accounting transaction process can always be improved, but the necessity of processing accounting transactions and the best means for processing the transactions are a function of the underlying business processes. To have an effective Lean transformation, the accounting processes must change in tandem with the underlying business processes. The change in the production processes at Wiremold eliminated the need to process many internal transactions. The physical reorganization of production into cells allowed Wiremold to eliminate labor tickets and time card reconciliation. Routings were also flattened and move tickets eliminated. The distances inventory traveled while in-process were greatly reduced, and visual controls provided better and more cost effective control of inventory movement than could ever be achieved with routings and move tickets. Similarly, the forecasting and scheduling function of the MRP system was eliminated as kanban systems were installed. As underlying processes were simplified, transaction processing was simplified and replaced by more effective means of supporting production.

Of course, not all accounting transaction processing can be eliminated. Many transactions, especially those between Wiremold and its customers and suppliers, are non-value added but necessary to conduct business. However, the process used to perform the transactions can always be improved through kaizen. Most of the accounting transaction processes were designed as batch activities, either because the underlying business process was a batch activity or because it was assumed that batch processing was the most efficient approach. As with other activities, processing accounting transactions in batches results in lower quality and longer lead times. A kaizen of accounts payable processing in the spring of 1992 allowed Wiremold to process 32 percent greater invoice volume with 50 percent less overall labor and reduce the invoice backlog by 64 percent.

Changes in the underlying business practices allow the required transactions to be greatly reduced or simplified. Wiremold reduced the number of material suppliers serving its West Hartford plant from 320 in 1990 to 43 in 1999. Long-term relationships with fewer suppliers increased the quality and reliability of Wiremold's material supply. It also enabled the use of kanbans to reduce the number of discrete purchase orders and to simplify the receiving and payables transactions.

As transaction processing was reduced or eliminated, Wiremold re-deployed its accounting resources in value-added cost management activities. As Orry Fiume observed, the greatest opportunity for cost improvement was in the product planning stage.

> "Historically, we focused completely on cost control through cost accounting. What I try to do is get people to think in a different way. The first part of cost management is cost reduction, and one of the things you learn is that somewhere between 80% and 90% of the life cycle cost is committed in the design process. So the people that are designing products have to be sensitive to the cost. The traditional design process is one where you design it and give it to the manufacturing people for them to figure out how to make it. Then you figure out what the cost is going to be. And if it's not an acceptable number, then the engineers have to go back and redesign it. And that creates waste. So in cost management, what you want to do is ensure that the target cost is part of the design criteria. You design the product not only for fit, form, and function, but also to the target cost. We integrate target costing with QFD."

Wiremold's accounting staff adds value by joining or assisting product development teams. They help the teams determine target costs and compute the estimated costs of design iterations as value engineering is used to reduce the gap between the target cost and the currently feasible cost. And, they participate in kaizen.

Measuring Lean Business Performance

Once product and process designs are established, further cost reduction can be obtained through kaizen.[16] As Wiremold embarked on its transformation to Lean, its performance measurement system consisted of standard cost measures which focused on cost control. There were no measures to support process improvement or cost reduction efforts. As we have seen, the standard cost measures were ineffective for cost control and actually inhibited process improvement and cost reduction efforts. Wiremold needed a new performance measurement system to support process improvement and cost reduction efforts.

Importantly, senior management did not expect the performance measurement system alone to produce process improvements and cost reduction. Process improvement and cost reduction would only occur through physical change in plant layout and process changes. Kaizen was the method used to achieve process improvement and cost reduction. The role of performance measurement was to encourage these improvement efforts and track their success. Orry Fiume described the interconnectedness of the financial function with production:

> "The second part of cost management is to improve and control costs through kaizen and the use of non-financial measures. One of the most important aspects of the first line supervisor's job is to stand in the middle of the shop floor and observe. By doing so, you will begin to see the waste. How we now think about cost reduction and cost control [in the Lean context] is something that evolved over time. None of us woke up one morning and said, 'Aha, this is the way it should be done and this is the way we should think about it.' By continuing to be involved in the changes that are happening in the business, the people in the financial function don't keep themselves isolated. They keep an open mind, so that their thoughts are about what they need to do to support the business as it continuously evolves. That's how you get from one place to another. But the financial function in most companies is isolated from Lean because financial people think that it is just a manufacturing thing."

Senior management faced the need to eliminate the business practices and metrics that blocked the flow of information and products.[17] Processes and metrics had to change to align the measurement system with the new operating practices. They did not do it all at once. Conventional business measures, rooted in batch-and-queue business practices, would be eliminated one-by-one: some quickly and others more slowly. The emphasis was on eliminating waste (muda), unevenness (mura), and unreasonableness (muri) because they forced unnecessary and destructive tradeoffs between stakeholders. Art Byrne commented on the traditional measures that were in place when he arrived in September 1991:

> "When I first arrived, we had all the conventional systems; move tickets, labor tickets, routings, etc. So to get anything made you had to go through all this paperwork to move it around. We had traditional measurements and traditional kinds of information, so the internal communications were not

that good. We didn't really have good data on a lot of things. When I first came to Wiremold I would ask questions and there were no answers to them because there was no data. But we also made decisions that trying to go get the data would just cause unnecessary delays. We didn't try to go into the level of data and detail that most companies do because we see most of that as waste. We try to just focus on the things that we think are important. Our communication now is very good, and we try to get people understanding what their key priorities are. We never suffered from analysis paralysis because we needed to get moving. We said, 'OK, it looks about like this, so let's make a decision and go.' It is more common for people to want to be sure and study things to death; that is why most companies can't move very fast."

The business processes and performance measures used by a Lean business must be simple, easy to grasp, and provide an accurate reflection of reality. The tools and methods, which can be used for any process, include:

- Kaizen
- Root cause analysis
- Production leveling
- 5C chart
- Total productive maintenance
- Standard work
- Time observation
- Target costing
- Standard work chart
- Kanban
- Percent loading chart
- Mistake proofing
- Set-up reduction
- Takt time
- Spaghetti charts
- Value analysis / value engineering
- Product-quantity analysis
- Visual controls
- One-piece flow

These tools, used in conjunction with a "no-blame" environment, allow people to give management both good and bad news. Management gets the news in real time, rather than delayed by months or years due to fear or intimidation. Art Byrne described the importance of having a "no-blame" environment in helping people feel comfortable delivering bad news:

"People are comfortable coming to me with bad news because we are very realistic and we don't yell at people or beat people up[18] or anything like that. I always try to make decisions as a team because we come out with a much better decision. I come up with lots of ideas and lots of things to do and probably get shot down by my staff at least half the time, for whatever reason. I may not have thought of something, or there is a timing issue, or it doesn't make any sense, or 'Gee Art you are stupid on this one.' But because I listen, anybody in this organization feels free to approach me and ask any questions that they want and discuss any problems that they have."

Scott Bartosch describes how these tools and methods, usually associated with manufacturing processes, were used to improve sales and customer service processes:

"The first time we did kaizen in inside sales and customer service, we began to ask, 'What's the takt time for an order? What's the cycle time for an order? How big is an order, what's the average?' We measure ourselves in sales the same way as if you were in manufacturing. Initially I thought, 'How the heck are we going to do that?' The right measurement is universal in Lean. You just have to understand what it is you want to know; that's the hard part. Early on we started to say, 'This is not a manufacturing thing.' Now we can look at any process that we do and use the same fundamental principles to take it apart and figure out how to make it better.

For example, we wanted to measure how many order entry errors we were making and what kind of errors they were. We had this whole glob of errors stuff shoved into the one category of errors. The reality is that we may have entered the wrong catalog number on a purchase order, it's a keyboard error, or we may have shipped the wrong product because we picked the wrong product out of the warehouse. We may have charged the wrong price. We may have charged freight when it was prepaid. So we segregated the data and could tell what was an order entry error, what was a shipping error, what was a freight problem, what was a pricing problem. What that allowed us to do then was to begin to solving those problems individually at their sources.

We had the same issue for abandoned phone calls from our customers.[19] The customer calls on the phone, wants the information, and then wants to get off the phone. People would say that 10% of abandoned calls is too high. But what's the real number? We want to have zero abandoned calls. But how do you measure that the average customer abandons in 20 seconds or in a minute? And how does that affect your staffing? What's the customer's tolerance level to be on hold? How long is the average call? How long are our salespeople on the phone with us? We found out that the longest calls were coming from our own salespeople. The salespeople would talk for a long time because they wanted to converse with home base every once in a while. We definitely don't want our own salespeople's calls mixed in with calls from the customer, who just wants to do some business and get going. That's why we separated receiving phone calls from our sales people from customer calls. We used kaizen to solve these types of problems."

Ed Miller stressed the importance of being focused on the process:

"I tell my people that I very rarely care about the end result. I'm comfortable that we'll get a good result if the process used to get there is right. If the process is good, it becomes more sustainable and repeatable. Managers in other companies often care only about the end result, and their only focus is beating up people to do that. The most important thing is how you get there."

Lean is a simpler, more direct management system that strives to represent business conditions as they actually exist. The fundamental characteristics of performance measurement in a Lean system are summarized in Table 9-2.[20] Steve Maynard had the following view:

"Why would you measure anything unless you are going to do something about it? The whole point of measurement is to see if you are improving. Are the trends going in the right direction? Is the productivity going up or is it level? It serves as a catalyst to focus in on improvement and do more kaizen."

Gary Brooks described the importance of Wiremold's key performance measures in setting company direction:

"Art brought to us the key measurements that help make a company become a world-class performer. We had a company meeting and he said this is what we're going to do, this is how we are going to do it, this is why we're going to do it, and these are the key measurements that I want you to drive. And there were just a few key measurements [see Table 9-3]. Without them it would be like sailing a ship without a compass. The key measurements allowed us to say, 'If you're going to do something today, your activities need to positively affect those key measurements. If you're not doing that, then don't do it.' And that really drove the organization. Art came along and gave us the direction. This wasn't the program of the month or some crazy thing that the CEO read in a book over the weekend."

Table 9-2 Characteristics of Lean Performance Metrics

Characteristic	Explanation
Must support the strategy	Metrics that do not support the strategy will cause confusion, misunderstanding, and misalignment. Expectations will come ambiguous. People will lose focus on the strategy if metrics appear to be disconnected or contradictory.
Few in number	Too many metrics cause confusion and unnecessary competition among individuals or departments. Most people can only remember a few things.
Mostly non-financial	Most people do not understand financial metrics. Instead, use metrics that people can relate to such as time, distance, number of defects, area (i.e. square footage), number of pieces, number of people, etc.[21]
Motivate the right behaviors	The purpose of the metric is to eliminate waste. Metrics for the sake of metrics is waste. Metrics that do not support the elimination of waste are not helpful. The metrics should focus people's efforts on improvement.
Simple and easy to understand	Most people have many things on their minds. Management has a responsibility to make work easy for people to understand
Measure the process, not the people	Measuring people results in blame, politics, high employee turnover, etc., which is waste.
Measure actuals vs. goals	People can relate more easily to actuals and goals. Standard costs are not real numbers. Measuring variances based upon standards is time-consuming, confusing, and does not help people understand the root cause of problems. Measuring variances against standards is misleading and is slow to respond to changes in the marketplace.
Avoid using ratios	Ratios are confusing and people have difficulty relating to them. Do not use them across the entire business. Management may use ratios in support of the type of work that management does.
Don't combine measures into a single index or create formulas	Indices and formulas are difficult to understand and do not help people eliminate waste. People cannot relate their work to them.
Must be timely: hourly, daily, weekly	Measures must reflect the time-scale in which work actually takes place. Monthly or quarterly measures can be out of step with the marketplace. The lag time between data collection and review often leads to poor decisions.

Table 9-3 Wiremold's Strategy and Key Performance Goals and Measures

Be the leading supplier in the industries we serve and one of the top ten time-based competitors globally		
	Goal	Measure*
1. Constantly strengthening our base operations	• 100% on-time customer service	• First shipment fill rate
	• 50% reduction in defects per year	• Number of defects
	• 20% productivity gain — each year	• Sales per FTE employee
	• 20× inventory turns	• COGS/FIFO inventory value
	• 20% profit sharing	• Actual proft sharing dollars/actual straight time wages
	• Visual conrrol and the 5C's	• 1-5 Likert scale rating
2. Double in size every 3–5 years	• Pursue selective acquisitions	• N/A
	• Use Quality Function Development to introduce new products every month	• New product development cycle time

*FTE = full-time equivalent; COGS = cost of goods sold; FIFO = first in, first out

The goals of strengthening base operations and doubling in size every three to five years were extremely ambitious. Art Byrne deliberately chose stretch goals to send an important message to the organization: Wiremold could not achieve its goals using the existing business processes with everyone simply working ten percent harder. People had to completely change the way work was performed to have any hope of reaching the new goals.

If people believe there is no chance for a positive result, using stretch goals can crush incentive and lower morale rather than stimulate creativity and foster revolutionary change. It is likely this would have happened at Wiremold if management had set the stretch goals, incorporated the goals into standard costs, and instructed Wiremold associates to deliver the desired results.

Art Byrne set stretch goals, but he also provided associates with the means to achieve the goals – kaizen. He led kaizens and showed the associates first-hand that dramatic improvements were possible. In addition, the performance measurement system reported trends in actual non-financial and financial results rather than reporting negative variances from a stretch standard. The reports showed positive trends in actual results rather than a litany of unfavorable variances. The trends in actual performance together with the stretch goals emphasized continuous improvement and reinforced the message that Lean was a never-ending journey, not a destination.

Regardless of the business process, whether it is within a function, between different functions, or across several functions (i.e. value stream), the key measures are generally the same. Wiremold's measurement focus is shown in Table 9-4, along with the corresponding base unit of measure. Notice that the impact of the non-time based measures is, ultimately, time as well. These are the measures that product line teams report on periodically.[22]

Table 9-4 Wiremold's Measurement Focus

Measure	Base Unit
• Customer service	
– Schedule performance (takt time)	Time
– Delivery performance (request vs. promise date)	Time
• Lead time (in days)	Time
• Cycle time (in minutes)	Time
• Defects (number of defects)	Quantity
• Inventory (cell level)	
– Pieces	Quantity
– Turnover	Dollars/Dollars
• Productivity	
– Company level: sales per FTE employee	Dollars/Employee
– Cell level: units produced per hour	Units/Hour
• Worker involvement (number of suggestions and percent of people that make suggestions)	Quantity
• Profit sharing	Dollars
• Degree of 5C's and visual controls (average score)	Quantity

Orry Fiume described the basic principle that guided Wiremold's use of business measurements:

"One of the principles when it comes to performance measurement is that measures have to be expressed in a way that people understand how their job relates to that metric. And if they do something good, it shows up in the metric in a way that they can see it. If you believe that is one of the qualities of a good measure, then you understand that the metrics have to be pretty simple. If they are too complex, then you will lose the link between the job and the metric. A good example of a metric that is too complex is return on investment [ROI].[23] I pick on that one only because it is one that business schools focus on. The ROI metric has many layers to it; the ratio is net income divided by average total assets. If I'm an associate working in the factory or in the office, how do I relate what I do to improving the ROI number? The reality is that he or she can't. We don't use ROI as a metric because we don't want people to focus on it.

We want people to focus on the key measures at the lowest possible level in various activities of the business. You have the same problem with high-level indices. If the index goes up, it means we're doing well and if the index goes down, it means we're not doing well. But how do I relate the job that I am doing to that index? You have to get the measure down to the level so that it changes people's behavior; where people see that they can have some influence and see the impact caused by their work. On a day-to-day basis, people work with the measurements that are relevant to their particular area. In the factory, each of the teams has a visual display that shows performance to takt time, inventory turns, customer service, unfilled shipments, etc. You have to have measurement systems at that local level that track the things that people can affect, and then that all feeds up into higher level metrics."

The reporting system reinforced the kaizen experience because the performance measures directly reflected process improvement at the local level. Associates participating in kaizen saw the improvements quickly and clearly reflected in performance reports. The change is not just a rounding difference in an aggregated higher-level measure. It is not obscured by changes in price levels or absorption levels. The performance reporting supports the transformation to a Lean culture.

The senior management team's focus was on managing the box score, not the scoreboard. For example, the head coach of a football team does not tell the players that they must win the game by a score of 27 to 24. In business terms, this would be like setting a top-level profit, cash flow, or multi-million cost reduction goal. Instead, the coach focuses on basic units of measure that players can relate to such as first downs, time of possession, running yards, passing yards, turnovers, etc. In most cases, a sports fan can look at the box score and figure out who won the game.[24] Orry Fiume recalled how he handled a new product line team leader's request for product cost information:

> "We hired a new product team leader. After a few days on the job, he came to me and asked for a report that showed the selling price and cost of each product that his team was responsible for. I asked him why he thought it was important to know the cost, and told me that he wanted to 'cost reduce' those items that were not making an adequate profit. I ended up telling him that his job was to eliminate waste and not to worry about the cost of any individual item. And by eliminating waste, he would be able to reduce the total cost even further than by focusing on individual part numbers."

In almost every other business, the finance vice president would be happy to tell the manufacturing supervisor the *exact* cost of the product and the amount of cost reduction, right to the penny, that must be achieved in the coming months – without providing any indication of how to do it! The vice president would have taken it as an opportunity to show off how smart he or she was, or the level of detail that the finance department was capable of producing. In contrast, Orry Fiume took this opportunity to get the new product line team leader aligned with Wiremold's philosophy of continuous improvement.

A noteworthy characteristic of Lean leaders is that they do not rely on batch-and-queue tools such as ROI's to determine the merit of doing something. Senior managers don't want people to spend time preparing complex spreadsheets, filled with unrealistic assumptions, just to prove a point. Instead, they prefer simple one-page charts, usually hand drawn, to illustrate the problem. They know waste when they see it, and often even when they don't, and that it costs a lot of money. Scott Bartosch discussed the importance of fixing problems even if the cost can't be measured:

> "It costs a huge amount of money if 15% of our invoices need some kind of rework because we billed the customer wrong or because we made an error.[25] And it's very difficult to measure. In the past, I've tried to figure out what it really costs if we make a mistake. It's really difficult to measure because you've got to take the customer impact into account; such as how many times do we call the customer? It is reasonable to assume that the customer is wasting at least as much time on the problem as we are, probably more. So you've got to at least double what you think it's costing. And we're still only dealing with the distributor. We haven't figured out how much we've cost the end-use customer; the person who is really paying the bill. They are the people that really want the product, and they're still waiting for it, or they have got the wrong product, or not enough of it, or too much of it. It's all waste, every bit of it. And it isn't necessarily a manufacturing problem; it is an information problem. We don't have to know how much it costs to realize that a problem needs to be fixed."

Financial managers in businesses attempting the Lean transformation will typically try to calculate the return on investment for kaizen in the mistaken belief that it accurately captures all benefits. Kaizen teams despise this behavior because they know ROI models are both incomplete and the wrong way to look at improvement. It is an obstacle that kills the kaizen spirit and will ultimately hurt the company and its end-use customers. Don Beaver offered the following comments on how Wiremold senior management views opportunities to reduce waste:

> "When somebody comes up to me and says, 'I need $5,000 because I've got to renovate this piece of equipment, or I have to do this or do that in the office,' I ask 'Why are you doing that?' They say, 'I'm doing it to get flow, or to eliminate cycle-to-cycle variability, or to fix this part of the process.' They've done the work to know that this is a big opportunity. So I take my pen and I sign the paper and off they go. I know that the $5,000 ex-

penditure will have a tremendous payback. I don't even have to ask. The measurement that we look at in terms of improving can be simplistic, but it tells me that people are maintaining the right path – they are focused on achieving flow."

Measuring and Reporting Financial Performance

Wiremold used operational measures both to encourage process improvement and to track its progress. However, it still needed to measure financial performance to see how the process improvements translated into cost reduction and improved profitability. Long before the transformation to Lean, Orry Fiume had become dissatisfied with traditional absorption accounting. He was well aware of the dysfunctional behavior generated by the standard cost system, and was also dissatisfied with the confusing manner in which financial results were being reported. Orry investigated activity-based costing (ABC) as a possible replacement for the standard cost reporting, but decided against it:

"I just decided it was not the right way to go because it was just another method of allocating costs. What ABC said was the old cost driver, direct labor, was outdated so let's go look for new ones. Then you go through this huge exercise of determining what your cost drivers are and allocating cost on that basis.

Then as we started getting into Lean and I was listening to some of the behaviors that ABC was driving in companies that adopted it, I realized it was driving behaviors that were just the opposite of Lean. If the cost driver was set-up time, it didn't drive behavior that said, 'Let's reduce the set-up time.' It drove behavior that said, 'Let's reduce the number of set-ups.' In other words, produce bigger batches of material."

As Orry became convinced that any cost allocation system was undesirable, the transformation on the factory floor was largely eliminating the need for cost allocation. He felt that the operational measures Wiremold was using were more effective, simpler, and less costly to implement. The entire production process for a family of products now took place in small manufacturing cells. Process engineers were assigned directly to the product line team, and the associates working in the cell performed routine maintenance. There were very few manufacturing costs aside from building and occupancy costs that were not direct costs of the product line. The cost performance of a team could be evaluated fairly with very little cost allocation. Administrative costs were no longer allocated to manufacturing cells and instead were controlled in the administrative areas, thereby eliminating the blame game. Orry Fiume recalled how that decision was made:

"We stopped allocating administrative costs because the team leaders of the product lines were beginning to focus on: 'Why did I get so much information technology cost allocated to me? I don't use it.' It was generating non-value added discussion, so we just stopped doing it. We decided to control those costs in a different way."

Wiremold adopted "throughput" accounting to remove the distorted information created by traditional cost accounting. In throughput accounting, only direct material costs are assigned to inventory.[26] Conversion costs, which consist of labor and manufacturing overhead, are treated as period costs. The incentive to overproduce is eliminated because all production costs added in the cell are an expense for the period in which they occur. The incentive to hide costs by deferring them to the balance sheet vanishes. The need to make the earned hours contained in the financial plan in order to "make-the-month" – and thus build inventory even if it was not needed – went away. Throughput accounting has the added benefit of greatly simplifying inventory accounting. Wiremold avoids all of the entries required to continuously apply conversion costs to work-in-process and finished goods. A single end-of-period entry to adjust overall ending inventory to the full absorption value is sufficient to satisfy GAAP and U.S. Internal Revenue Service financial reporting requirements. The precision necessary in this adjustment is low because inventory levels are low. Orry Fiume explained:

> "If I'm turning my inventory 3 times, then I've got four months worth of inventory out there, and valuation becomes a real chore and a concern. If the valuation is wrong plus or minus 10%, it can have a significant impact on my reported results. What happens when you get to Lean, using the Wire Management business as a model, we're turning our inventory 16 times, which says that we've got a little bit more than three weeks worth of inventory on hand. Part of that is raw material, so in terms of work in process and finished goods, we have less than two weeks on hand. I can take my December financial statements and I can tell you right from the financial statements what two weeks worth of processing and occupancy costs are. I capitalize that as the deferred cost element of inventory with a journal entry."

With Lean, Wiremold was able to simplify its financial accounting system and eliminate waste. However, the format for financial reporting remained a concern. Orry Fiume described his dissatisfaction with financial reports based on standard cost, full absorption accounting:

> "If you look at our old financial statements, in standard cost format, you can't tell what the heck is going on in the business. You just can't. If a variance goes from favorable one year to unfavorable the next, you can dig pretty deep and still not find out what caused it."

The financial statements shown in Figures 9-1 and 9-2 illustrate this point. The income statement shown in Figure 9-1 is presented in standard cost format. It actually contains more information than generally found in a standard cost financial statement because the variance is broken down into components, rather than listed as a single aggregate amount. The question is, how informative is this income statement? Orry Fiume explained:

Figure 9-1 Standard Cost Income Statement

	This Year	Last Year
NET SALES	100,000	90,000
Cost of Sales:		
Standard Costs	48,000	45,000
Purchase Price Variance	(3,000)	10,000
Material Usage Variance	(2,000)	5,000
Labor Efficiency Variance	7,000	(8,000)
Labor Rate Variance	(1,000)	8,000
Overhead Volume Variance	2,000	2,000
Overhead Spend Variance	(2,000)	8,000
Overhead Efficiency Variance	16,000	(17,000)
TOTAL COST OF SALES	65,000	55,000
Gross Profit	35,000	35,000
Gross Profit, %	35.0	38.9

Parentheses indicate unfavorable variance.

"Here's a company where sales went up year-to-year but gross profit stayed flat in dollars and was down as a percentage. So if you're the CEO of that business, you want to know why that happened. You start looking at the line items and you see that purchase price variances went from unfavorable to favorable. Well, did that happen because our purchasing department got much more aggressive with suppliers, and if they did, what did that do to quality? On the other hand, did the purchasing department just become much more aggressive with the cost accountants last September in setting new standards, convincing the accountants that the prices were going to go up 10% when they were really going to go up 6%? You can go through every one of those line items, and the reality is, there's nothing that helps you understand what really went on in the business to keep gross profit flat. You can't tell if you had a great year in operations but a bad year in setting the new standards, or vice versa. So not only doesn't the statement tell you anything after the fact, but it encourages dysfunctional behavior during the budget process when standards are being set."

The income statement shown in Figure 9-2 reports the same results as the statement shown in Figure 9-1. Although sales, cost of sales, and gross profit are identical, the supporting details are presented using actual costs. Orry Fiume explained:

Figure 9-2 Alternate Income Statement

	This Year	Last Year	% Change (−)
NET SALES	100,000	90,000	11.1
Cost of Sales:			
Purchases	6,300	55,900	(88.7)
Processing Costs:			
Factory Wages	11,000	11,500	(4.3)
Factory Salaries	2,100	2,000	5
Factory Benefits	7,000	5,000	40
Services & Support	2,200	2,500	(12)
Equipment Depreciation	2,000	1,900	5.3
Scrap	2,000	4,000	(50)
Total	26,300	26,900	(2.2)
Occupancy Costs:			
Building Depreciation	200	200	0
Building Services	2,200	2,000	10
Total Manufacturing Costs	35,000	85,000	142.9
Inventory (Increase) Decrease	30,000	(30,000)	
COST OF SALES	65,000	55,000	18.2
Gross Profit	35,000	35,000	0
Gross Profit, %	35.0	38.9	(10)

Parentheses indicate unfavorable variance.

"Now you can begin to understand what's going on. You can see that in fact factory wages went down, so something good was happening there such as a reduction in overtime. Factory salaries went up, but I know I hired a couple of manufacturing engineers to facilitate kaizen so that makes sense. Benefits are up significantly; that's out of control, so I have to talk to Human Resources. Services and supplies are in control. Depreciation is up, but that's pretty much in line with my capital spending program. Scrap is down a lot, so something good must be happening on the factory floor from a quality standpoint. When I look at processing costs, which is what my first line supervisors are really controlling on a day-to-day basis, good things are happening. Occupancy costs are segregated and I can look at them separately. The reason why gross profit stayed flat is because last year we were building inventory and this year we are liquidating inventory.

The asset on the balance sheet called inventory is really comprised of two things: a real 'asset,' the material content, and deferred costs which are the labor and overhead associated with product made but not sold. If you increase inventory in one year, that year receives the benefit of deferring some of the labor and overhead incurred into a future period. Naturally, when you decrease inventory in another year, that year must bear the burden of those costs actually incurred in a prior year. When a company embarks on the transition from batch-and-queue to Lean, senior management needs to understand at the outset that as it improves its inventory turns from 2.4 times to 20 times, two things will happen. First, the profit and loss statement will incur a charge for all of the deferred labor and overhead of prior years. That will make the company's operating results look ugly. Second, they are going to free-up a lot of cash. Unfortunately, in today's world with all of the emphasis on earnings per share, it is difficult for senior management to do the right thing here because the accounting rules make the results look bad when, in fact, the results are really good."

By 1992, Wiremold had reorganized its financial statements to report actual costs and was segregating processing costs from occupancy costs in manufacturing. The new financial statements were distributed to the supervisors along with the operating performance measures. First line supervisors were told to focus on inventory turns,[27] customer service, and processing costs, and not to worry about the inventory adjustment. If they were doing their job correctly and increasing inventory turns, the inventory adjustment would take care of itself. Orry recalled how the preference for the new format became evident:

"Prior to 1992, when we officially changed to the new format, we used the new format as a spreadsheet supplement. We'd send the regular statements out and a week later we'd send out the supplement with a little note attached saying, 'We're trying something different, would love your feedback.' Occasionally we would get some feedback and we'd make some changes. After a while, we started getting phone calls when we sent out the regular statements asking us, 'Can't I get the new supplement sooner?' It became apparent that people weren't using the old statements and that the new ones were providing some value."

Summary

The transformation to Lean business practices means management must be willing to re-think the usefulness of conventional business performance measurements. They must recognize and accept the limitations of function-specific metrics and see that complexity, gamesmanship, and conflicts between departments create waste. They must also learn how to discern the negative impact of conventional business measures on decision-making, teamwork, and information flow, and be willing to let go of measures that have no effect other than to locally optimize performance at the expense of the company and its end-use customers.

Lean is a completely different way to think, and the CEO must lead the way. He or she cannot delegate it to others. The CEO must personally show the senior management team how traditional performance measures lead to poor decisions and do not support Lean business practices. This is a big challenge for senior managers because it is different from how they understand the practice of business, including what they were taught in business school. The batch-and-queue management system does not prepare senior managers to optimize the entire business system. Instead, they only know how to optimize the individual parts of the business. Almost no aspect of conventional management practice is useful for running a business according to Lean principles and practices. Senior managers that take their responsibilities seriously will want to learn how to better satisfy all stakeholders without having to make destructive tradeoffs.

In nearly every Lean transformation, the vice president of Finance or the chief financial officer becomes one of the biggest obstacles.[28] The Lean management system threatens his or her base of knowledge and skills. There are no learning curves and no economic order quantities. Cost does not decrease significantly with volume,[29] and the company does not exist to maximize shareholder value. There is no absorption accounting, no earned hours, no purchase price variance metric, no labor tickets, and no routings. How can that be? How can I ignore the bedrock of business school teachings? At first, this will seem like a great loss. Over time, however, it will be seen as having been a great waste to manage a business in this way. The loss suffered is insignificant by comparison to the opportunities created when the financial function fully understands and supports the transformation to Lean.

Wiremold successfully moved to a new system of performance measurement because Art Byrne ensured that the senior management team participated in kaizen to see first-hand the many limitations of conventional thinking. Without such participation, it is nearly impossible to achieve the needed changes in each of the service and support functions. The senior management team will be reticent and make excuses to avoid participating. However, most will eventually have a lot of fun, as has been recounted by Wiremold senior managers.

By changing the measurement system, the company will have better quality and more timely information. Importantly, this will help the company respond more quickly to changes in market conditions. Company performance will be strong at the top of the business cycle and suffer less at the bottom of the business cycle compared to peer group companies.[30] This is one of the great benefits of Lean practice – for all stakeholders.

Key Points for Senior Managers

- Conventional business metrics are aimed at local optimization and result in distorted view of reality, poor information flow, and flawed management decisions.
- Lean processes, tools, and metrics, plus a human resource policy that does not blame people, provide an accurate reflection of business conditions and support system-level improvement.
- The accounting function must itself adopt Lean principles and practices, as well as provide information and measures to support the Lean transformation throughout the organization.
- Performance measures should encourage efforts to achieve the strategy and track progress toward achieving the strategy.
- Set stretch goals, but provide the means to achieve the desired results and focus on the necessary process improvements.
- Performance measures should be simple, few in number, mostly operational, and reported on a timely basis.
- Use operational measures to track performance improvement.
- Use financial measures to determine whether operational improvements are being translated into improved financial performance

Notes

1. The principal approach to business school education is to teach students how to manage individual business functions and function-specific goals, including associated tools (See Table 9-1). This infers, either implicitly or explicitly, legitimacy. Students rarely question the merits of these approaches and simply accept conventional thinking as valuable and correct, thereby perpetuating divisive management practices. In some instances, students (principally working professionals that are familiar with Lean principles and practices) may question what they are being taught in MBA programs. However, they will complete the class assignments as requested by the professor, even if they know it is the wrong way to think.

2. The phrase "what gets measured gets managed" (or "what gets measured gets done") is invariably stated as an axiom — a statement that is accepted as true without formal proof. This statement is false when tested using mathematical logic. That is, the phrase "what gets measured gets managed" can be true in some cases but it is not true in all cases. See "The False Promise of 'What Gets Measured Gets Managed'," M.L. Emiliani, *Management Decision*, Vol. 38, No. 9, 2000, pp. 612–615.

3. Absorption accounting leads a business in the opposite direction from Lean — to build inventories, which hides waste.

4. The word "standard" or "standard cost" in a batch-and-queue business system has a different meaning than in the Lean business system. Standards in a batch-and-queue system imply something that never or very rarely changes, while standard costs are "imaginary" numbers because they are usually incorrect — i.e. do not reflect actual conditions or costs. In the Lean management system, standards or standard work refer to actual conditions or costs, which change often as processes improve or market conditions change. The time scale is therefore different: in batch-and-queue, standards and standard costs may remain unchanged for years, while in Lean, standard work is revised every few weeks or months, and there is no such thing as standard cost, only actual cost. Another key difference is that standards and standard costs are forced down from above in batch-and-queue business practice. In the Lean business system, the teams that are responsible for performing the work create and revise standards.

5. Learning curves are graphical representation of the dependence of labor cost (or unit cost) in relationship to production volume. For example, a 90% learning curve means that the unit cost is reduced by 10% each time the volume of units produced doubles. Learning curves are commonly used by batch-and-queue businesses, principally by the finance, engineering, or purchasing organizations, as a means of estimating the future unit cost of products in development or production. The Lean management system does not recognize the use of learning curves for this purpose, and views them as a fatally flawed way to think because: a) the learning curve does nothing to help people understand market prices; b) it implies a diminishing return, after which further efforts to improve are pointless; c) it assumes that learning is continuous; d) it focuses people on direct labor, which may not be the cost driver; e) it encourages people to overproduce as the means for reducing unit costs (but increases total costs); f) it leads to dysfunctional organizational behavior. The Lean management system, however, does not deny the existence of the learning *effect*. The relationship that is recognized is between cost and *time*, not unit cost and volume. The learning effect manifests itself only in pre-production activities. Lean businesses ensure that products enter the market at a cost that the marketplace will accept through QFD, pre-production, target costing, and kaizen costing activities. See *Cost Reduction Systems: Target Costing and Kaizen Costing*, Y. Monden, Productivity Press, Portland, OR, 1995.

6. In a non-scientific poll of MS and MBA students by Emiliani, students with 10–25 years of work experience were asked the question: "What percent of your time is spent on activities that do not add value as perceived by the end-use customer?" (see Figure 3-1). Students, on average, say that they spend 50% of their time on activities that do not add value — which simply increases costs and leads to employee dissatisfaction, and is a waste of people's precious time on earth. In the Lean management system, management recognizes its responsibility to effectively use human resources. Further, it makes no financial sense for a company to pay someone for 2,000 hours of work per year yet receive only 1,000 hours worth of value. Managers often claim that resources are scarce or say that they need to hire more people to get a job done. These are illusions. Instead, waste (muda), unevenness (mura), and unreasonableness (muri) are abundant. Management should eliminate muda, mura, and muri, which then creates opportunities to grow sales without having to increase labor costs.

7. The conventional approach to management is to understand the business principally through elaborate data, analyses, reports, and presentations. It places less importance on direct experience and skillful observation, so that over time senior management loses touch with what is really happening in the few parts of the business where value is actually created. Efforts to improve a distorted view of reality, without understanding the real problem, are senseless. In Lean business practice, managers tend to use simpler data (single-page format, highly visual), and emphasize direct involvement in value creating activities and improving observation skills. In other words, the Lean management system helps people develop an accurate view of reality, which can then be improved upon to deliver greater competitive advantage.

8. Orry Fiume said: "I'd rather be approximately right than precisely wrong." This statement captures an essential difference between conventional and Lean management practice.

9. Dubbed the management "hat trick."

10. Mr. Ohno recognized the severe deficiencies inherent in traditional cost accounting and particularly disliked accountants because of their stubborn adherence to the view that higher volumes result in lower costs. See *Workplace Management*, T. Ohno Productivity Press, Cambridge, MA, 1988, pp. 8–11, 17–19, 30–31, and 38–40, and T. Ohno in *NPS: New Production System*, I. Shinohara, Productivity Press, Cambridge, MA, 1988, pp. 146–149.

11. Notice how the traditional standard cost and budgeting process, from the outset, leads to different objectives and wasteful gamesmanship among people that work for the same entity. In many companies, the budgeting process is months long in duration and filled with re-work – an obvious candidate for kaizen.

12. MRP-driven "push" production systems hide waste, whereas "pull" production systems expose waste.

13. Another reason a manufacturing organization may overproduce is because parts are difficult to make. In most cases, this is because engineers designed parts that are difficult to make. Engineers did not consider the process capability or unrealistic requirements were specified. Managers that allow engineers to throw product designs "over the wall" to manufacturing are irresponsible in the sense that they help create high costs which lead to customer dissatisfaction that may ultimately threaten survival of the business — which precipitates layoffs, plant closings, and squeezing suppliers.

14. This is why Lean is a top-down management system. Only senior management can make the dozens of changes that must be made to company policies and practices.

15. See *Japanese Management Accounting: A World Class Approach to Profit Management*, Y. Monden and M. Sakurai, Editors, Productivity Press, Portland Oregon, 1989; *Cost Management in the New Manufacturing Age*, Y. Monden, Productivity Press, Cambridge, MA, 1992; and *Cost Reduction Systems: Target Costing and Kaizen Costing*, Y. Monden, Productivity Press, Portland, OR, 1995.

16. Because of the tremendous inefficiency inherent in the batch-and-queue processes used at Wiremold prior to the Lean transformation, kaizen yielded large cost reductions even though some existing product designs could not be changed.

17. Technically, products themselves are information (see *The Evolution of a Manufacturing System at Toyota*, T. Fujimoto, Oxford University Press, New York, NY, 1999, Chapter 4), as is kanban (see *Just-In-Time for Today and Tomorrow*, T. Ohno and S. Mito, Productivity Press, Cambridge, MA, 1988, pp. 3–5). Importantly, Lean is a management system, which if operated correctly results in the flow of information. A key enabler for information flow is "respect for people" (see Chapter 3, Notes 9 and 23).

18. The phrase "beat people up" is common jargon in manufacturing and other types of businesses, particularly those dominated by batch-and-queue business practices. It does not imply a physical beating of people, but rather a verbal or mental beating or public humiliation. In almost any context, business managers that "beat people up" are showing disrespect for people. Curiously, managers that beat people up wonder why they do not hear the truth or all the facts from their employees.

19. Abandoned calls are when a customer makes a phone call to Wiremold but hangs up the phone before the call can be answered.

20. See, for example, *Performance Measurement for World Class Manufacturing: A Model for American Companies*, B. Maskell, Productivity Press, Portland, OR, 1991.

21. Financial metrics also combine physical changes and price changes, making it more difficult to determine the reason for changes. For example, are material costs lower because less material is being consumed due to reduced scrap and defects, or because the material costs less?

22. In 1991, the teams reported every week. After about five years, the teams reported twice a month. In 2001, the teams reported monthly.

23. Return on investment (ROI) is a measure of the earning power of a company's assets, in percent. ROI = net income ÷ invested capital = margin x turnover, referred to as the "DuPont Formula." In conventional business practice, ROI is used as a measure for performance evaluation and goal setting. For additional rationale on why Lean businesses tend to avoid using ROI, see "A Japanese Survey of Factory Automation and Its Impact on Management Control Systems," M. Sakurai and P. Young in *Japanese Management Accounting: A World Class Approach to Profit Management*, Y. Monden and M. Sakurai, Editors, Productivity Press, Portland Oregon, 1989, p. 274–276.

24. There are exceptions, of course. A recent example is the New England Patriots' Super Bowl XXXVI victory over the St. Louis Rams on 3 February 2002.

25. See Chapter 3, Note 4.

26. Hewlett Packard adopted substantially the same throughput approach to accounting for manufacturing costs when it converted to Just-In-Time production. See "Direct Labor Cost Not Always Relevant at HP," R. Hunt, L. Garrett, and C. Merz, *Management Accounting*, February, 1985, pp. 58–62. Yasuhiro Monden

observes that: "their [Hewlett Packard's throughput cost based system] new 'simplified system' is none other than a system, commonly used in Japan, of 'integrated cost accounting by machine cost and process'." See "Cost Accounting and Control in the Just-In-Time Production System: The Daihatsu Kogyo Experience," Yasuhiro Monden in *Japanese Management Accounting: A World Class Approach to Profit Management*, Y. Monden and M. Sakurai, Editors, Productivity Press, Portland Oregon, 1989, p. 36.

27. Although only material costs were tracked in inventory, turnover was calculated using the adjusted full absorption, first in first out (FIFO) valuations for inventory.

28. The engineering vice president will also usually have great difficulty with the Lean transformation because he or she will no longer be in the business of creating perfect designs – i.e. local optimization. They will have to listen to the voice of the customer, design to target cost and process capability, and reduce development cycle times in order to keep pace with the rest of the business and the marketplace. In short, they will have to begin behaving in a manner consistent with the reality that 80–90% of the total cost is committed in the design.

29. The relationship between cost and volume is very strong in batch-and-queue and very weak in Lean.

30. In the 2001 U.S. recession, Wiremold experienced at 14% decrease in sales and a 25% decrease in operating income. However, it was able to achieve a 31% reduction in inventory, a 19% reduction in accounts receivable, a 22% increase in cash flow, and an increase in market share compared to year 2000 results. When business conditions are poor, companies that practice Lean well will usually outperform their rivals. For example, Toyota Motor Corporation and Honda Motor Company reported record profits in 2001 ($5.45B and $1.87B, respectively, due in part to favorable exchange rates). Conversely, Ford and DaimlerChrysler's U.S. unit reported multi-billion dollar losses ($5.45B and $1.94B, respectively), while General Motors reported a small profit ($0.6B). Ford, GM, and DaimlerChrysler's U.S. unit announced tens of thousands of layoffs, scores of plant closings, and supplier price cuts at various times in 2000, 2001, and 2002.

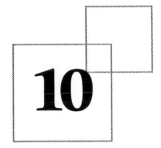

WIREMOLD'S RESULTS

Wiremold's Performance on Key Strategic Goals

Art Byrne had a clear vision for Wiremold and a strategy for achieving that vision from the moment he accepted the job as president and CEO in September 1991. The corporate strategy was revised and clarified, but throughout the revisions two objectives remained constant: strengthening base operations and doubling in size every 3–5 years. Art also had identified performance goals for each of the objectives, and under his guidance, Wiremold developed metrics to track progress toward the stretch goals and assess performance. The stretch goals and measures are summarized in Table 9-3. Table 10-1 compares the performance of Wiremold's core business in 1999 to 1990 in four of the performance dimensions.

Table 10-1 Wiremold's Core Business Results for Key Performance Measures

Measure	1990	1999	Improvement
First Shipment Fill Rate*	60.3%	92%	52%
Sales per Full Time Employee (000's)	92	241	162%
Inventory Turnover**	3.4	15.8	364%
New Product Development Cycle Time***	2–3 years	3–12 months	73%

*   The first shipment fill rate was negatively impacted by the start-up of a new computer system in 1999.
** Inventory turnover is a 12-month moving average based on first-in first-out inventory values (raw material + WIP + finished goods).
***Improvement for new product development was measured median to median.

Strengthening Base Operations

Wiremold had a goal of 100% on-time customer service. While it did not achieve that stretch goal, first shipment fill rates have improved from 60.3% to 92%.[1] In addition, it shortened the allowable time to fill an order from 72 hours in 1990 to 24 hours in 1999. Productivity, measured as sales per full-time employee, improved by 162% over 1990. Although the productivity gains are short of Wiremold's goal of 20% annual improvement, it achieved a compound annual growth rate greater than 11%. As of 1999, it had not yet achieved the stretch goal of 20 inventory turns, but the 15.8 rate achieved in 1999 represented a 364% improvement over 1990, a compound annual rate of improvement greater than 18 percent.[2]

Wiremold's quality improvement goal was to reduce defects by 50% annually. It does not report company wide results on this measure because management does not believe aggregating different types of defects across areas will yield any meaningful results. However, individual defect reduction rates ranged from 40% to 57% per year since Lean management practices were adopted in the fall of 1991.

All production cells and support areas at Wiremold are evaluated on the 5C's and visual controls on a monthly basis. It does not aggregate the scores and report overall company trends over time, so no data were available to assess progress on this dimension between 1991 and 1999. The most recent 5C scores are one of the performance measures displayed on bulletin boards at the cells and in many support areas. A walk through the facilities indicates that Wiremold made significant progress in 5C performance and use of visual controls during the

1990s. Wiremold managers freely admit that ample opportunities for further improvement remain. Visual control and 5C performance continue to be key factors in executing Wiremold's strategy, and periodic assessment of 5C performance is featured prominently in Wiremold's performance evaluation system.

The goal of profit sharing equal to 20% of straight time wages benefits both shareholders and associates. Associates earn a significant bonus over base pay and the shareholders benefit because Wiremold can only achieve the profit sharing target by being a highly profitable company. Wiremold had not yet consistently achieved its 20% profit sharing goal by 1999, though it came close in certain quarterly periods. However, the total amount of annual profit sharing had increased from less than 1.3% in 1990 to over 10% by 1996. After 1996, the total amount of annual profit sharing decreased due to the acquisition of companies that posted losses at the time they were acquired. Since profit sharing is based on consolidated profits, it encourages everyone to cooperate and help improve the performance of new companies joining the group.

Profitably Doubling in Size Every 3–5 Years

The ultimate measure of the sales growth goal is, of course, sales. As the sales index in Table 10-2 shows, Wiremold more than quadrupled its 1990 sales by 1999. The 1999 sales are also nearly four times 1991 sales, so sales have almost quadrupled in the eight full years since the transition to Lean began in the fourth quarter of 1991. Sales more than doubled in the core business (Table 10-3). Some of the core business growth was natural growth in the market and increasing market share, but in 1990 Wiremold was the market share leader in a mature market. Much of the core business growth came from new products, expanding markets, and gaining market share from much larger competitors.

Table 10-2 Wiremold Corporate Results

	1990	1991	1992	1993	1994	1995	1996	1997	1998	1999†
Net Sales Index*	100	106	114	133	208	260	304	331	353	415
Gross Profit Index*	100	103	115	141	213	273	330	378	391	454
Operating Profit Index*	100	156	311	299	490	679	947	1,042	786	1,053
Net Profit Index*	100	192	460	153	693	948	1,253	1,509	973	1,180
Number of Acquisitions	1	–	–	6	–	3	2	2	4	2
Inventory Turnover**	3.8	4.1	6.0	5.1	6.5	8.4	8.9	8.6	9.1	10.5
Working Capital Turnover***	4.5	4.7	6.4	5.7	6.7	8.0	8.4	8.4	9.0	9.8

    * All values are indexed to 1990 = 100.
  ** Sales divided by the average of beginning and end of year inventory values on a first-in, first-out basis to approximate the average inventory held during the year. Wiremold uses a 12-month rolling average in its internal reporting.
 *** Sales divided by the average of beginning and end of year working capital as defined by Wiremold. To focus on the working capital demanded to support production and sales, Wiremold defines working capital as accounts receivable plus FIFO inventory less trade payables.
   † 1999 figures include restructuring costs.

Table 10-3 Wiremold Core Business Results

	1990	1991	1992	1993	1994	1995	1996	1997	1998	1999†
Net Sales Index*	100	99	112	121	142	155	173	203	216	229
Gross Profit Index*	100	102	119	141	164	187	219	261	275	296
Operating Profit Index*	100	237	508	561	711	840	1,145	1,156	1,185	1,343
Net Profit Index*	100	212	484	568	712	850	1,155	1,144	1,191	1,335
Inventory Turnover**	3.4	4.6	8.5	10.0	12.0	14.9	14.3	15.3	16.2	15.8
Sales per Employee (000's)	92	104	130	140	176	188	216	226	238	241

* All values are indexed to 1990 = 100.
** Sales divided by 12 month rolling average inventory values on a first-in, first-out basis.
† 1999 figures include restructuring costs.

Using the Quality Function Deployment process, Wiremold dramatically reduced its new product development time from two or three years to less than a year (Table 10-1), while increasing the number of new products introduced. The rate of new product introduction had grown from two or three per year to two or three per month. In addition, the new product rollouts were more successful because the new product development process was focused on customer needs and desires.

The remaining sales growth was attained through selective acquisitions. From 1993 through 1999, Wiremold acquired 19 companies (Table 10-2). By strengthening the core business, it built a record of profitability. This sound financial base gave Wiremold access to the credit needed for acquisitions. Wiremold was able to free-up cash to partially finance its acquisitions as well. Note the significant improvement in both working capital turnover and inventory turnover from 1990–1992 shown in Table 10-2. Fewer resources tied up funding day-to-day production and sales left more resources available for acquisitions. After 1992, the corporate asset and working capital turnover amounts were negatively affected by the batch-and-queue operations Wiremold acquired.

Working capital turnover amounts were not available separately for the core business, but the inventory turnover numbers reported for the core business in Table 10-3 show continuing improvement from 1993–1998 before a slight downturn in 1999.[3] The new acquisitions headed down similar improvement paths as operations were converted to Lean. In a traditional leveraged buyout, the acquiring management team frequently uses cash, marketable securities, and sales of pieces of the acquired company to pay down the debt used to make the acquisition. Wiremold, instead, leveraged its acquisitions by reducing excess inventory carried by the acquired companies and by consolidating smaller product line acquisitions into existing Wiremold facilities.

Financial Performance and Shareholder Value

So Wiremold achieved its ambitious quality improvement and long-term sales goals, while making considerable progress toward achieving its long-term customer service and efficiency goals. Was it able to translate these gains into increased profitability and shareholder value? As shown in Table 10-2, overall gross profit was more than four times greater in 1999 than in 1990. The gross profit of the core business was almost three times greater in 1999 than in 1990 (Table 10-3). Operating profit and net profit for the corporation in 1999 exceeded the 1990 amounts by more than ten and eleven times, respectively. Both operating profit and net profit for the core business were more than 13 times greater in 1999 than in 1990. Eliminating one-time restructuring costs, 1999 operating profit and net profit were more than 15 times the 1990 amounts for both the core business and Wiremold as a whole.

Wiremold's acquisitions of companies that were marginally profitable or losing money caused overall operating profit and net profit to decline in 1993 and 1998. The acquisitions generally depressed the rates of overall profit performance. When acquisitions are sizeable, this can introduce a wavy trend with profits, as well as with other performance measures, dipping upon acquisition and rising again as the acquired companies are converted to Lean. However, taking the long-term view, rather than worrying about quarter-to-quarter and year-to-year earnings growth, allowed Wiremold to make strategic acquisitions at favorable prices.

The impressive increases in profit percentages that Wiremold achieved are not merely an artifact of minuscule 1990 operating and net profits. The company that had been marginally profitable but in decline in 1990 was by 1999 transformed into a highly profitable, rapidly growing company. Figure 10-1 summarizes the increase in share price between 1990 (base year) and 1999.[4] This represents total appreciation of 552% and a 23.2% compound annual growth rate compared to 345% total appreciation and an 18.0% compound annual growth rate for the S&P 500 index over the same time period.[5]

Figure 10-1 Shareholder Value

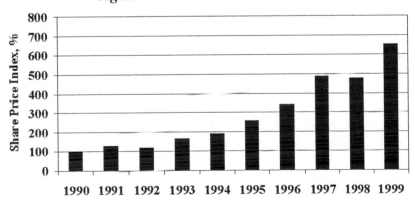

Perhaps the most impressive feature of Wiremold's share price performance was that the management team did not include this as part of the strategy (Table 9-3). There were no stock price appreciation targets. Nor did it exist as a separate, less visible, objective that drove decision-making behind the scenes, as in other companies.[6] There were no pushes to meet quarterly earnings forecasts or to make monthly or quarterly profit budget targets. This remarkable growth in share price was not part of the strategy, but rather the result of a successful Lean transformation.[7]

Summary

Emphasizing financial performance too often leads to managing numbers rather than improving processes. Appearance becomes more important than the underlying reality. Accounting contrivances are encouraged and welcomed as another path to the goal of reporting the right numbers. Accounting tricks may even be favored as the fastest and easiest way to the desired results. Eventually, however, the accounting tricks whither away and the underlying reality pokes through the facade.[8] Businesses can only achieve long-term financial success by creating value for end-use customers, and by producing and marketing products and services at a cost less than or equal to the value received.

For Art Byrne, the key to cost reduction was not imposing budget restrictions, but instead was to continuously improve processes and eliminate waste. The key to increased revenue was better customer service (defect-free products delivered on time) and developing new products that better satisfied end-use customer needs. If products and processes were improved, costs would decline and sales and profits would increase. Though Wiremold management closely monitored revenues and costs, the emphasis was on improving business processes. Even at the highest strategic level, Wiremold's key measures have a process focus rather than a financial focus.

Using the Lean management system, Wiremold was able to dramatically improve its processes, and in some areas it met or even exceeded stretch targets. The process improvements in turn led to superior financial returns and greater shareholder value. The Lean transformation benefited all key stakeholders, not just shareholders.

By emphasizing and reporting on processes, the measurement system provided Wiremold with better quality information and more timely information than is available in traditional, budget-based systems. Importantly, this helped the company respond more quickly to changes in market conditions. Company performance will be strong at the top of the business cycle and suffer less at the bottom of the business cycle compared to peer group companies.[9] This is one of the great benefits of the Lean management system.

Key Points for Senior Managers

- Superior long-term financial performance can only be achieved by eliminating waste in processes and delivering products and services that create value for end-use customers.
- Operational measures and non-financial measures provide a direct and timely assessment of process improvement.
- Trends in actual financial performance over time should reflect the process improvements that have occurred.
- Wiremold's financial and non-financial results were achieved by applying both key principles, "continuous improvement" and "respect for people"simultaneously. Applying only one principal, "continuous improvement," is not sufficient.

Notes

1. Wiremold's first shipment fill rate improved to 98% by the end of 2000. For 2001 and the first half of 2002, the first shipment fill rate remained at 98–99%.

2. Wiremold achieved 17 inventory turns in the first quarter of 2002, and remained optimistic that the 20X inventory turns goal could be achieved in 2002 or 2003.

3. By the first quarter 2002, inventory turns were in excess of 17X.

4. As a privately owned company, Wiremold's share price was determined independently by an external auditor using a discounted cash flow model.

5. See the Postscript for an explanation of the total gain through 2000.

6. Wiremold's senior management team did not focus on maximizing shareholder value in the literal (i.e. purely financial) sense, as this would have required them to make destructive tradeoffs between key stakeholders (see Chapter 3, Note 9 and Chapter 5, Note 4). Yet their share price performance was greater than that achieved by the S&P 500 companies over the same time period. As a privately owned company, Wiremold was able to absorb unfavorable short-term financial problems early in the transformation, which might have been more difficult to do if publicly traded (see Chapter 2, Note 4). The number and types of decisions that must be made early in the Lean transformation obviously favor private ownership, but does not fundamentally exclude the ability of publicly owned businesses to achieve similar levels of performance. For example, Danaher Corporation (NYSE: DHR), where Art Byrne helped initiate the implementation of Lean, achieved the following compound annual growth rates for the period 1990–2000: 13% sales, 17% earnings per share, (excluding costs of pooling of interests transaction), 18% operating cash flow (excluding costs of pooling of interests transaction), and 33% share price. Source: http://www.danaher.com.

7. As with any Lean transformation, the challenge that must be accepted by the senior management team is to remain committed to the process and have the daily discipline to continue forward. Constancy of purpose, long-term commitment, and a deep desire to improve are fundamental characteristics. The two keys are: "continuous improvement" and "respect for people" (see Chapter 3, Notes 22 and 23).

8. Recent examples include Enron, WorldCom, Global Crossing, Qwest, Adelphia Communications, Xerox, Computer Associates, Rite-Aid, Sunbeam, and Waste Management.

9. See Chapter 9, Note 30.

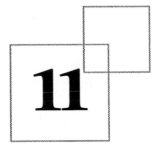

REAL LEAN VS. IMITATION LEAN

Functional vs. Value Stream Improvement

Since Lean is a comprehensive management system, one would expect that the batch-and-queue thinking and processes in existence throughout a business would completely diminish over time. However, in practice there is a dynamic interplay between Lean practices and conventional batch-and-queue business practices. A company can never achieve a completely Lean state because batch-and-queue thinking is the normal way most people go about solving problems. The job of becoming Lean is *never* done because there is no such thing as being Lean, which implies a definable end-point. Instead, people will work hard every day to expand Lean principles and practices across the entire value stream. This level of commitment, which the entire senior management must tangibly demonstrate on an ongoing basis, is referred to as "Real Lean."

The Lean management system requires ongoing maintenance by people to eliminate batch-and-queue practices and to improve Lean practices. The batch-and-queue practices will grow and shrink over time, depending upon management's knowledge of Lean and their commitment and capabilities. However, batch-and-queue practices will never disappear entirely. There may be system constraints or people may be unable to identify Lean solutions to certain business problems. People will recognize these problems as batch-and-queue in nature and will seek improvement opportunities even if the solutions are temporary. While impressive gains can be achieved rather quickly, becoming Lean is a process that evolves as people's knowledge of Lean increases over time. While one objective is to strive for perfection,[1] people recognize that this is a goal and not an attainable end-point for either a process or for the entire business system. In other words, perfection, such as zero defects, may be attained for certain periods of time, but not for all time.

In contrast to Wiremold, most companies operate a static hybrid conventional-Lean management system, referred to as "Imitation Lean." They apply Lean principles and practices in operations,[2] but remain batch-and-queue everywhere else in the company, including their relationships with suppliers and customers. It is both ineffective and impractical to operate this way because it will result in serious conflicts. Conflict is wasteful, and results in confusion, re-work, and sub-optimization. In some cases, after a period of time, typically three to five years, management may recognize the limitations of the hybrid conventional-Lean approach and seek to apply Lean principles or practices to other functions. There will, however, be strong resistance because people have been trained to think that Lean is a "manufacturing thing." The CEO's incomplete understanding of the Lean management system, from the outset, will make future changes more difficult, but not impossible, to achieve. For most companies, Lean will just die out and become viewed as another "flavor-of-the-month."

Wiremold is a very important example of a "widespread fast" Lean transformation, which contrasts to the "local incremental" transformation favored by most CEO's. The latter is common because it is consistent with how CEO's are trained, how they tend to think, and how they perceive risk. There is a very strong preference for local optimization and sequential, function-based, trans-formations.[3] As a result, the vast majority of managers will prefer to start the Lean transformation in operations, and then a few years later move on to the next biggest "bang for the buck," say in engineering. This is the wrong way to think about the Lean transformation. As the Wiremold case shows, there are many different business policies and practices that must change concurrently. It is the simple recognition of the reality that business processes, or, more cor-rectly, value streams, are connected. The currency exchanged across the value streams is *information*. If information flows in one function, but not in all oth-ers, then end-use customers experience little or no benefit. End-use customers buy more than a single optimized functional capability such as world-class manufacturing.[4] They also purchase other business processes that may or may not deliver value, and hence satisfaction. Figure 11-1 illustrates the futility of locally optimizing a single business function, such as production, while waste remains abundant in other related business processes.[5]

Figure 11-1 Functional vs. Value Stream Improvement

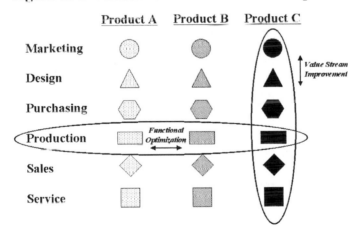

The risks associated with "local incremental" or sequential Lean transforma-tion makes this a far less desirable approach, though it may be a necessary first step in most cases.[6] Art Byrne had ten years of experience with Lean in two orga-nizations, General Electric and Danaher Corporation, before he could implement the "widespread fast" Lean transformation throughout Wiremold. The practical reality is that CEO's with no experience in Lean may feel that they have no choice but to proceed in a "local incremental" or sequential manner, as it is their first ex-perience with the transformation process.[7] However, the CEO and the entire man-agement team must clearly understand and behave in a manner which demon-strates that Lean is a management system that applies to all functions, not just another "flavor-of-the-month." In other words, a commitment to Lean requires acceptance of certain new types of responsibilities that CEO's must thoroughly understand. To be successful, an organization must adopt Lean as complete management system and work towards linking all processes together. Becoming Lean only in manufacturing will not do much for business results or for end-use customers if the rest of the company's business processes are not connected.

Given the sub-optimal nature of the "local incremental" approach, there is a systemic logic that says it is both necessary and reasonable for Lean to be an all-or-nothing commitment. Whether or not the CEO accepts Lean for the entire company, and for its suppliers and customers, the basic logic must be understood. Lean principles and practices must either grow and spread or shrivel and die within and between businesses. Conventional management systems respect boundaries, either implicitly or explicitly. The emphasis is on local or functional optimization, not on value streams. As a result, managers closely guard their turf, performance measures and rewards reflect narrow functional objectives, employees become trapped in wasteful internal competitions and organizational politics, and the company likely will have poor relationships with suppliers and downstream customers. That is why real teamwork is so difficult to achieve in such environments despite well-intentioned efforts. In contrast, the Lean management system does not respect boundaries.[8] The system is operated in a manner that promotes real teamwork by using processes, tools, and policies such as QFD, kaizen, root cause analysis, and a no-blame environment. Indeed, the Lean management system will not be able to reach its full potential within a company unless it begins to transform relations outside that company — with all of its key business partners.[9]

Wiremold's senior management team set out to improve downstream relations with its customers: distributors, retailers, architects, builders, contractors, and installers. It also worked to develop upstream relations with suppliers, banks, and logistics companies. It had to develop upstream and downstream relationships with business partners in order to deliver value to end-use customers that could be clearly differentiated from the competition. In addition, the comparatively low level of performance of upstream and downstream business partners at the start would limit Wiremold's performance. These efforts were actually prompted by necessity, rather than simple altruism. However, Lean leaders understand that "respect for people," which manifests itself as unselfishness or sharing, is a necessary component for good business because it is recognized as a socio-economic activity. Business is viewed as a non-zero sum activity, where all stakeholders share in the gains and the opportunities are enlarged, versus a zero sum activity where opportunities are narrowed and all benefits must accrue to the company at the expense of upstream and downstream business partners.[10]

Managers often rationalize the benefits of Lean activities in terms of their "return on investment" (ROI).[11] This tool is used principally in the domain of conventional business practice. Lean leaders tend not to think in such terms because their interest is in eliminating waste and delivering value to end-use customers, not calculating ROI's. In addition, ROI thinking focuses managers on short-term profitability, which limits innovation and leads to incorrect decisions.[12] Orry Fiume explained why ROI is not used in Lean practice:

> "We do not think of Lean in terms of ROI at all. The problem with ROI is that it is not actionable. ROI is a mathematical expression of many complex inter-relationships, so it is impossible for associates to relate their actions to it. Metrics that focus on lower level activities will ultimately improve ROI."

It is clear that CEOs must make an all-or-nothing commitment to Lean principles and practices. There will be many times where the CEO must take a "leap of faith," believing that adherence to fundamental Lean principles and practices will yield outcomes that create value for end-use customers.[13] This is very difficult for CEO's leading conventional businesses to do because they want guaranteed outcomes. Art Byrne and other senior managers had to take a leap of faith on numerous occasions. The all-or-nothing commitment is both necessary and reasonable when viewed from the joint perspective of needing to improve value streams and creating distinctive competitive advantages in business. CEO's that are unwilling or unable to do so increase risk for all stakeholders.

A Day and Night Difference

Many CEO's across a wide variety of industries have taken an interest in Lean over the last fifteen years — principally manufacturing businesses, but more recently service businesses, non-profits, and government organizations. A fundamental question is: "Why is the CEO interested in Lean?" The dominant perception is that Lean is simply a way to reduce costs. Taking that perspective, and assuming that all CEO's think alike,[14] the "5 Why's" method is used to determine the root cause of why a typical CEO of a for-profit business would be interested in Lean:

1. Why is the CEO interested in Lean?
   To reduce costs
2. Why does the CEO want to reduce costs?
   To improve competitiveness
3. Why does the CEO want to improve competitiveness?
   To increase profits
4. Why does the CEO want to increase profits?
   To increase earnings per share
5. Why does the CEO want to increase earnings per share?
   To increase stock price
6. Why does the CEO want to increase the stock price?
   To increase shareholder value
7. Why does the CEO want to increase shareholder value?
   Because his or her compensation is based on stock price

The root cause is that Lean will help senior management achieve higher personal wealth, as a large portion of their compensation is usually obtained through stock options.[15] Thus, the driver for adopting Lean, in most cases, has nothing to do with end-use customers. This line of reasoning is characteristic of senior managers that do not understand value streams.[16] Profits, earnings per share, and share price are all very important, but they are the outcome of Lean management practices (Figure 10-1), not the reason for embarking on the Lean journey.

Let's examine Toyota's rationale for creating a coherent system of Lean business practices.[17] The first question to ask is: "Why did Toyoda Automatic Loom Works, Ltd., create the Toyota Motor Corporation, Ltd. to begin with?"[18] Was it to increase personal wealth? No, Toyoda's initial motivation was to create an indigenous Japanese automobile industry and increase the *national* wealth.[19] Why did Toyota Motor Corporation initially develop the Toyota Production System?[20] It was simply to enable them to compete against much larger automobile companies such as General Motors and Ford. Toyota did not have the resources to create the massive scale of vertically integrated operations that U.S. automobile companies had. Further, the U.S. style of automobile production was not right for Japan, whose markets were characterized by low volume and high product variety. The Toyota Production System was a way for them to survive as fledgling automakers against the imports. As Toyota's management system developed in the late 1940's through the early 1970's, it became increasingly focused on cost reduction through the elimination of waste and creating value for end-use customers. The byproduct of those efforts has been stable long-term growth, and a current market capitalization greater than Ford, General Motors, and DaimlerChrysler combined.[21]

Wiremold's Lean transformation focused on eliminating waste and creating value for end-use customers. The increase in share price that was achieved, 60% higher than the total appreciation of the S&P 500 for the period 1990 to 1999, was the outcome and not the focus. CEO's that focus primarily on share price are forced to make destructive trade-offs between key stakeholders, which will in turn create many other problems.[22]

Returning to the "typical CEO" example, it is normal to think that a quick way to reduce costs is to implement Lean in operations, using it as tool-based approach for localized improvement.[23] In doing this, the CEO negates six critical factors:

- That Lean is a *comprehensive* management system
- The existence of waste in non-manufacturing business processes
- The existence of end-use customers and other key stakeholders
- The existence of value streams
- That all parts of the company must work together to create value for end-use customers
- The importance of people in making the Lean management system work

In addition, competitiveness cannot be achieved by improving a single business function such as operations. In a partial Lean transformation, only a small fraction of the total business processes is improved. Few changes will have been made in other areas to support the improvements that have been achieved in operations because management sent the signal early on that Lean is just a "manufacturing thing." Presenting Lean as an *initiative* or *program* results in "Imitation Lean." People's well-intentioned efforts will eventually succumb to the heavy weight of the batch-and-queue business practices that surround them.[24]

Hundreds of companies have been practicing various elements of Lean over the last 15–20 years. However, the achievements of most are less than spectacular. Why is that? Could it be because Toyota has been at it for many more years? Wiremold's experience shows that a remarkable amount of positive change can be accomplished in a relatively short period of time. What is clear is that many CEO's adopt Lean for the wrong reason, and they don't implement Lean correctly because they don't understand it. While many CEO's understand the importance of the first principle, "continuous improvement," most do not yet recognize the "respect for people" principle.[25] Both principles must be practiced simultaneously in order to realize "Real Lean." In order to make progress, the Lean transformation must advance at a pace that exceeds the rate at which people install batch-and-queue solutions to everyday problems.[26]

People that have experienced "Real Lean" first-hand know that there is a "day-and-night" difference between it and batch-and-queue business practices or even "Imitation Lean." Figure 11-2 illustrates the differences as they pertain to fear of failure, information flow, politics, and management ability to recognize reality, on a 1–10 scale.[27] These diagrams depict a striking difference in how batch-and-queue and Lean businesses operate in terms of daily human interaction. They are very important because efforts to become Lean in the absence of significant changes in beliefs and behaviors by senior management will not be successful.[28] The explanation is as follows:

- Fear of failure means people will not be willing to tell management what is really going on. People get blamed and lose their jobs when something goes wrong. The root cause of problems are not understood, and so important problems go uncorrected for several years or even decades.

- Information that is plugged, blocked, or filtered means that management and other key stakeholders will not receive information on a timely basis, which results in lots of surprises. Information from end-use customers is not acted upon.

- Fear of failure and plugged information contribute to create a highly political business environment. Important issues will not be discussed or acted upon. The focus is on who looks good or bad. Blame is shifted between people, functional groups, or other key stakeholders.

- Fear of failure, plugged information, and politics make it virtually impossible for management to have an accurate grasp of reality, as it pertains to both internal and external business conditions. Instead, management focuses inwardly on the company's problems and ignores its end-use customers.

Figure 11-2 Batch-and-Queue vs. "Real Lean"

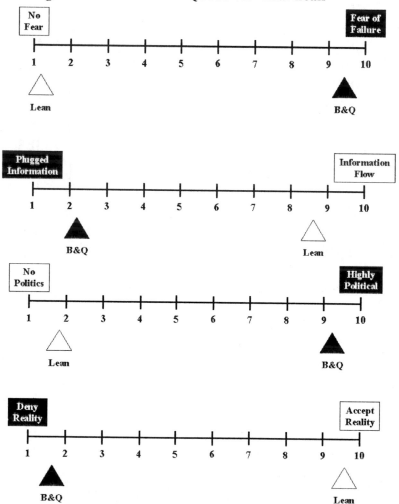

Figure 11-2 also shows why businesses that practice "Real Lean" are such formidable competitors. The "respect for people" principle creates an environment in which wasteful behaviors are minimized. As a result, creativity inherent within people can be accessed and used to continuously improve the business at very low cost — which benefits all stakeholders. In contrast, batch-and-queue management practice lacks a coherent system for gaining a higher level of employee participation and specific methods for translating this participation into increased competitiveness.[29] So, instead, they spend large sums of money on expensive equipment or high-tech solutions, which increases the cost of goods sold.

Many people mistakenly view Lean as a management practice whose success depends, to a large degree, upon national culture or other extant factors.[30] While it is true that Japanese culture values harmony, it is doubtful that any culture truly values wasteful conflict. The fact is that most people want to do a good job and will try to continuously improve themselves and their area of responsibility.[31] Importantly, who wouldn't want to be treated with respect? What the Lean management system does is create an environment responsive to fundamental human needs. The challenge for senior managers is to recognize that business is not a machine-like entity designed solely to create cash. Cash is certainly important, but competitiveness depends upon people: their commitment, desire to improve, and ideas. Art Byrne described the relationship between people and business competitive capabilities:

> "How do you get someone who has been doing it one way to change when they are resistant to change? If I walked into your living room and said, 'Gee, this is a nice living room, but I think we can improve it. We're going to do kaizen and move all the furniture around,' you'd have a fit! Lean has a big impact on people. If the CEO does not understand the people aspect, then it's really hard to make the change to Lean. That is where most CEO's fall down. You can read all the business books you want, but the reality is that business is one collection of people competing against another collection of people to satisfy the same customer. If I hire better people, if I train them to be better, if I empower them better so that I get all the people thinking about how to improve, if I do all those things well, then we will beat the competition."

Gary Brooks commented on the key differentiator, management behaviors:

> "You can't be the type of executive that reads a book, and just because you've read the book, you think you are now an expert in Lean. I've met a lot of executives that understand the words but when you ask them how to do it, they can't tell you. So in terms of behaviors, the leader has to be able to show that he or she can change. The leaders need to create and lead the constancy of purpose. The good news is that he or she can start today. The bad news is that it never ends."

Again, Art Byrne:

> "Everything has to change. Are you willing to do that?"

A New Change-Over Model

Senior managers typically seek a highly prescriptive approach to transform a business from batch-and-queue to Lean.[32] They are looking for a detailed series of steps, or a recipe, that they or their delegates can use to facilitate implementation. As the Wiremold case shows, its transformation was not accomplished using a step-by-step approach. It simply did not have time for sequential conversion of various business processes to Lean. Instead, it improved many business processes concurrently because end-use customers do not buy a single functional capability; they buy value streams.

The Lean transformation can appear complex, but the fundamental principles and practices are relatively easy to grasp. While the overall intent of the Lean management system is to eliminate waste and create value for end-use customers, the outcome is simplified business processes that people can perform more easily and with fewer errors. In keeping with the notion that simpler is better, the Lean transformation process can be viewed as nothing more than a change-over problem, going from batch-and-queue to Lean.

One of the first things done in the Lean transformation is to substantially reduce the time it takes to set-up a machine, or change-over, from one type of part to another. The process consists of four steps, which are repeated whenever it becomes necessary to further reduce set-up time. Figure 11-3 illustrates the four-step process.[33]

1. Identify and separate internal and external set-up[34]
2. Convert internal to external
3. Decrease internal set-up
4. Combine and eliminate tasks to decrease internal and external set-up

Figure 11-3 Machine Change-Over Method

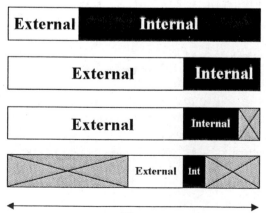

Time

Now let's extend this process to the more general case of what kaizen is designed to do with the valuable knowledge that is contained inside people's brains (Figure 11-4).[35] People possess two types of knowledge: explicit and tacit. Explicit, or external knowledge is knowledge documented in the form of patents, work instructions, procedures, or formulas — the "science". Tacit, or internal knowledge is knowledge that is unspoken, implied, assumed, or learned through experience — known commonly as the "tricks of the trade" or the "art." In a batch-and-queue business, people are loath to share tacit knowledge — how the work *really* gets done — because knowledge is power. People cling to their tacit knowledge thinking that it will help them hold onto their jobs, especially in business environments that have persistent threats of layoffs to improve financial performance. The kaizen method is related to the four-step machine change-over method in the following way:

1. Identify and separate explicit and tacit knowledge
2. Convert tacit (internal) process knowledge to explicit (external)
3. Simplify tacit (internal) process knowledge
4. Combine and eliminate tasks to simplify internal (tacit) and external (explicit) process knowledge

Figure 11-4 Change-Over Model for Kaizen Method

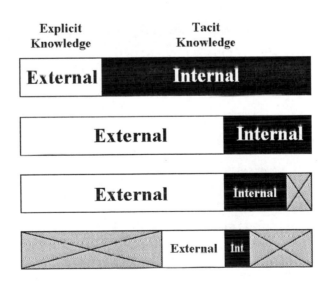

Kaizen requires people to participate in the process of changing-over of their personal knowledge from internal to external, or tacit to explicit. That's a threat, and Art Byrne knew it. That's why he gave associates the qualified job guarantee. People's natural reaction when threatened in a business setting is to hoard information,[36] just as people hoard material items in times of shortages.[37] External knowledge is created by documenting processes using such tools as spaghetti charts, product-quantity analyses, time observation forms, set-up observation analysis worksheets, percent loading charts, standard work charts, standard work combination sheets, process-at-a-glance, and visual controls.

So what should the CEO do in the first years of the Lean transformation? The leader must respond to people's concerns. The CEO cannot simply adopt Lean and expect people to automatically buy into a dramatically different way of doing business, especially if different types of threats remain in place. The CEO has to create a less threatening business environment. The four-step change-over model can also be used to describe the leader's role in the Lean transformation in the following way (Figure 11-5):

1. Recognize tacit (internal) concerns
2. Convert tacit (internal) concerns to explicit (external)
3. Reduce tacit (internal) concerns
4. Decrease tacit (internal) and explicit (external) concerns

Figure 11-5 Change-Over Model for the Lean Transformation

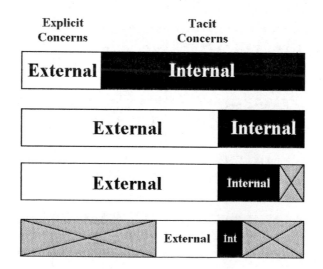

When the CEO announces the adoption of Lean principles and practices, people will have many concerns, including:

- Will the CEO walk the talk?
- Will I lose my job?
- Is this a flavor-of-the-month?
- Does higher productivity mean I have to work harder?
- What's in it for me?

- Are we broken? Do we really need to be fixed?
- What's the real reason for doing this?

Some of these concerns will be voiced in employee meetings, while many other concerns will remain unspoken. It is not likely that the CEO will be able to address these concerns if Lean is presented as a "program" or "initiative" whose fundamental driver is share price. Uncertainties will consume valuable mental energy, and the associates that actually add value to products and services will not be fully committed to change. They will hesitate to contribute ideas and creativity, and there will be many concrete-heads that get in the way. The CEO has unintentionally created a situation that results in additional wasteful behaviors. Some improvement will certainly be made, but it will be a great struggle. Orry Fiume had this to say about employee concerns:

> "Everything you read about change says that people are afraid of change. I've gotten to the point where I don't really believe that anymore. When I hear people say that, I ask, 'Have you ever gone on vacation to a new place, one that you have never gone before?' Invariably, the answer is, 'Yes.' So I ask, 'Why did you do that? Why did you spend your hard-earned money and limited vacation time to take a chance on going to a new place? Why did you make that change, instead of going back to a place that you were already happy with?' And the answer to those questions is generally that someone, a friend, a relative, an article, or a television show convinced them that they would like it there, that it would be good for them.
>
> So people aren't really afraid of change. What they have is anxiety about the unknown. When most managers start to change things — re-organize, re-engineer, etc. — they don't do a good job of helping people understand the positive outcomes. They don't paint a believable picture that shows that the employee will benefit from the change."

Art Byrne anticipated these fundamental human reactions by informing people that Lean was the new way of doing business, not a "program," and more than the way in which they would manufacture parts. Art recognized that people had tacit concerns (step 1), which most CEO's simply ignore. He converted internal concerns to external (step 2) by listening to employees and discussing their concerns in both small group and all-employee meetings. He reduced internal concerns (step 3) by personally training associates and leading them in kaizen. He created a setting where people would be more comfortable talking to senior managers one-on-one. That plus a no-blame environment enabled people to discuss their tacit concerns. The qualified job guarantee, profit sharing, the "five lines of defense," and unplugging processes built for batch-and-queue in

other functional areas, all helped reduce internal concerns. Art and the entire senior management team decreased internal and external concerns (step 4) by
growing sales, developing new products, and acquiring new businesses.

These four steps were instrumental in overcoming resistance and creating a
management system that was better for all stakeholders.[38] With explicit and
tacit concerns effectively addressed,[39] people could instead focus on learning
new Lean principles and practices. Art wanted people to think of ways to eliminate waste and create value for end-use customers. They would not be able to
do that if they were wasting mental resources thinking about other things, or
were focused on increasing the share price. The two principles, "continuous
improvement" and "respect for people," are reflected in Figures 11-4 and 11-5,
respectively. Art Byrne commented on the behaviors that he saw in people that
demonstrate a change in mindset:

> "You see people that are enthusiastic. People walk up to me
> and say, 'Wow, this is so much better.' One of the more plea-
> surable things for me over the years has been to see people
> change. When people start out as aggressive concrete-heads say-
> ing, 'This will never work; this is stupid, it can't be done,' and
> then when I visit them a couple of months later, they are telling
> me, 'Why didn't we do this 20 years ago? This is the best stuff
> I've ever seen; this works so much better and my job is so much
> easier.' Now that's fun.
>
> When you convert somebody from batch-and-queue mentality
> to the Lean mentality — it doesn't matter whether it's manufac-
> turing or marketing or whatever — when they flip to this men-
> tality, they will never go back the other way. They can't be happy
> in an organization that does it the old way. All of the old prob-
> lems, the structure, the extra people, and the difficulty in deci-
> sion-making, come back. So they say, 'I've seen a different way,
> and I know a better way to do this. Why are we doing it like this?
> Why are we wasting our time? Why are we dealing with titles
> and structure and different things that mean nothing?' The
> hardest thing is to change the people who have been here for 30
> or 40 years. One of the most fun aspects of kaizen is to watch
> the change occur in them. About 95 to 98 percent of the time
> you can change people. Once you help them see a different way,
> they become a tremendous resource for the company."

Most of the time people can change, including the CEO. As Art Byrne said,
"Everything has to change. Are you willing to do that?" An important part of the
Lean transformation is the development of new leadership skills. This, again, is
a change-over problem. The four-step change-over model can also be used for
the development of Lean leadership skills in the following way (Figure 11-6):

1. Recognize tacit (internal) batch-and-queue beliefs and assumptions
2. Convert tacit (internal) batch-and-queue beliefs and assumptions to explicit (external)
3. Reduce tacit (internal) batch-and-queue beliefs and assumptions
4. Decrease tacit (internal) and explicit (external) batch-and-queue beliefs and assumptions

Figure 11-6 Change-Over Model for Leadership Development

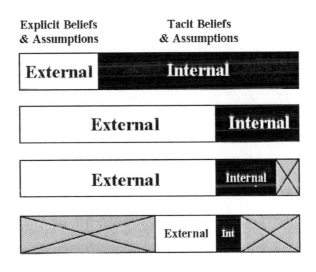

People who have made it to the top of an organization generally will see no need to change their leadership method, thinking, or behaviors. They are obviously successful, at the peak of their earning power, and perhaps just a few years away from voluntary retirement. Why risk trying to establish a new management system? Wouldn't it be easier to stick to the conventional management playbook as their successful peers do? Although most CEO's will not want to take on a new challenge, some will. So what should they do?

The first step is to critically analyze the effectiveness of conventional management practices. These are rooted in internal beliefs and assumptions such as "companies exist to maximize shareholder value"[40] or "volume lowers cost."[41] They must also question the effectiveness of such common business tools as learning curves, economic order quantities, absorption accounting, return on investment calculations, and business metrics such as purchase price variance, standard costs, or earned hours. They must ask themselves if these beliefs, tools, and business measures result in local optimization. Do they cause uneven business perfor- mance, poor process understanding, and conflicts in human and company-to- company relationships? The CEO must ask whether or not their formal education, training programs, and work experience, lead to consistently positive outcomes for key stakeholders. Ultimately, the CEO should ask, "Is this the *least-waste way* to do the work?"[42] or "Is this the *least-waste way* to create value for end-use customers?"

Step two would be to convert these internal beliefs and assumptions to ex- ternal. In other words, the CEO must confront them directly. Most CEO's can arrive at only one conclusion: that there is great opportunity to improve lead- ership thinking and practice. In step 3, the CEO must decrease his or her inter- nal beliefs and assumptions related to batch-and-queue management practices. The final step, decreasing internal and external batch-and-queue beliefs and as- sumptions, requires the CEO to learn more about Lean principles and practices. The most effective way to do that is by participating in or leading kaizens.

Successfully accomplishing this transformation will enable the CEO to put into practice the two key principles: "continuous improvement" and "respect for people." Scott Bartosch described the characteristics of an effective Lean leader:

> "First of all, you have to be committed. And that does not mean that you've read a book and you agree with it. You have got to get your hands dirty and learn what it's all about. I think that the sin- gle most important thing is the ability to listen. That has been paramount from the beginning, because you're asking people to make a tremendous change. You're also asking them to be part of the team that helps the company grow. If you aren't willing to lis- ten to them, or if people don't believe that you're listening to them, then you're never going to get there. So I think that part of our success is the fact that we'll listen. The other thing is, how much questioning is done? If you're not listening, you can't ask questions. You may be taking in information, but the more ques- tioning you do the better off you are because sometimes the nugget of the idea isn't in the first answer; it's buried somewhere else in there. I can't emphasize enough the need to listen, because people will tell you things. It's amazing; once people understand that there's no blame and that it's all right to fail, then you start to find things out. A lot of companies say, 'It's OK to fail,' but it's not true; it's not okay to fail. At Wiremold, it's okay to fail. You can't learn or experiment without failing. We want people to learn and experiment and to find new ways of improving the business."

Rich Levesque described his view of what it takes to lead a Lean transformation:

> "One of the other challenges you have when you get into Lean

is education. People resist change, so you need to spend time being a real teacher and make them understand why you want Lean. How can you lead an organization into Lean unless you understand it yourself? So you have a lot of managers that sit in mahogany offices, that make decisions on behalf of the business, say in manufacturing, but they never spend any time in the factory. So the skill is to understand Lean, to believe in it, and then to have a passion for teaching people about Lean."

Ed Miller commented on other important leadership characteristics:

"A key part of being successful in Lean is communication. It can't be an event; it has to be a way of working everyday. You have to be able to talk and communicate, not write. The leader also has to get away from wanting to control everything. That's the wrong focus; it's totally inward. The leader has to focus on learning new things, not only for themselves, but to teach the people that they lead."

The Discipline of Lean

Table 9-1 and Figures 3-1, 11-1, and 11-2 reveal some remarkable differences between conventional batch-and-queue practices and the Lean management system. The quality of the information in batch-and-queue is poor because it is incomplete or highly distorted, and everyday activities and business measures create conflicts between stakeholders that cannot be effectively resolved. The business is unable to respond quickly to changes in market conditions and experiences wide variations in performance every 3–5 years.[43] As a result, senior managers find it very difficult to manage the business in a systematic manner. Instead, they must rely on ad hoc methods, which do not often yield favorable results that can be easily repeated. Under such circumstances, CEO's will prefer to exert control over people[44] because they believe it shortens the response time when unexpected problems arise.

Few CEO's truly grasp the significant differences between conventional management practices and the Lean management system.[45] One of the key differences is the much higher level of discipline that is required to operate the Lean management system, including the discipline to:

- Understand what is actually happening
- Follow structured processes
- Simplify activities
- Eliminate waste
- Listen
- Learn
- Teach
- Be patient

- Follow-up
- Continuously improve
- Respect people

People have difficulty grasping the significance of having discipline in day-to-day activities.[46] Further, most are not accustomed to thinking about processes. This is especially difficult for CEO's, as they are used to thinking in terms of results, not processes. The only way to truly understand processes is to participate in kaizen, which is learned on-the-job.

Take, for example, the discipline that must be in place to manage the size of the workforce. The initial part of the Lean transformation often results in a reduction of the workforce. In Wiremold's case, this occurred principally through attrition and voluntary early retirement. Once the business nears the correct headcount, management must have the discipline to maintain it. When business issues arise, such as an increase in customer demand, the tendency is to hire more people. The Lean business instead works to find ways of reducing waste and expanding capacity to satisfy customer demand without increasing the number of people. That discipline positions the organization to fare much better when business conditions inevitably decline a few years later.

Some CEO's may not like the Lean management system because they believe that it means having to give up control. That perception is incorrect. In a Lean organization, the CEO controls those things that need to be controlled by the CEO, while others control things that do not need to be controlled by the CEO. In other words, careful thought is given to those activities or practices that must be mandated and those that are the domain of empowerment. People are not empowered to say, "We will not work to takt time." However, people are empowered to determine how to improve their work to be better able to respond to the takt time. For some activities, the CEO has to give up some control. For example, Orry Fiume described the hiring and firing process at Wiremold:

> "We try to make it hard to be hired and hard to be fired. Nobody at Wiremold, including Art, is empowered to unilaterally hire anybody. In terms of the hard to be hired, there's an expectation that the candidate does not even get past the initial screening process unless they have got the technical skills required for the job. It doesn't matter whether it is an engineering job or an accounting job or an assembly job. If we are trying to hire a company controller, for example, we will narrow it down to two candidates, either one of which I must be able to accept. Then I go to the team and I say, 'These are the two candidates I want you to interview them, and it's your choice in terms of which one we hire.' That greatly increases the probability that the candidate will be successful in their new job, since the team has a vested interest in the choice.

And nobody at Wiremold, including Art, is empowered to uni-laterally fire anybody. In order to fire someone, we go through a peer review process. During the peer review, you have to demonstrate that the person was made aware of their short-comings and that there was a written improvement plan with specific targets and milestones. And throughout that process, the person has to be informed that they are not making it. If you've done all that, then you can fire the person. If you haven't, then you have to start the process. So it's hard to be fired."

Other CEO's believe that becoming Lean means that employees will be "turned loose," and thus might make costly mistakes or cause other types of problems. That perception, which focuses on negative outcomes, is also incor-rect. A culture that "asks why" (Figure 5-2) avoids much of the organizational politics that cause the types of problems that concern the CEO. Secondly, in a "Real Lean" environment, there are structured processes for doing activities, within which people can be very creative and contribute their ideas. So, peo-ple *are* "turned loose" on the right things — improving the business and cre-ating value for end-use customers — and bounded by sensible processes that help ensure consistently positive outcomes.

The CEO can't do it all. He or she must give up control of some things, share control of other things, and retain control of yet other things. In other words, the Lean management system gives careful consideration to the ques-tion of which person or team should control a process. It does not presume that senior managers can understand the details of all activities and therefore make correct decisions all the time. The transformation from conventional to Lean management practices is thus a shift in control from senior managers to a wider base of capable, well-trained people.[47] The benefits are innumerable compared to the alternative of batch-and-queue management practices. Don Beaver commented on the tools that were used to help ensure discipline:

"At a certain point, the key focus becomes standard work be-cause if the operator or office person does not do the same thing each and every cycle, then you can't measure it and you can't begin to understand where the improvement opportuni-ties are. When you get to that level, the skills required of man-agement are different. You need to be able to educate people as to why they need to do standard work. You need to be able to see when standard work is not being done or not being fol-lowed. The challenge is trying to get people to do the same thing the same way, each and every time. In America, we have the 'John Wayne' mentality: 'I'm going to do my own thing.' A lot of education has to happen to get past that mentality, and then there has to be tremendous follow-up every minute, every hour of every day, to maintain the discipline to do that. It is a big challenge for an organization to continue down the Lean path. Most organizations will drop out at that point. They won't have the discipline. They won't have the support or the knowledge that it takes to move forward.

After the big improvements are behind you, the opportunities become much more focused. You have to look more intensely at the elements within a process and variation within a process, and removing waste from those elements. To do that requires a different management style, different management skills, and different management tools. We adopted Policy Deployment[48] because we were at a point in our evolution where we needed to be much more focused in our application of resources: capital, people, and time. It is a very visual tool, it's specific, and it's focused. We deploy it throughout our organization, so now employees can actually look and see how their contribution works upward to support the upper level goals or the organization."

Gary Brooks commented on importance of discipline:

"Lean is a robust management system if done correctly and with the proper discipline. It is a system that can take some hits without getting dented. Yet it's flexible enough for continuous improvement."

Art Byrne commented on the much higher level of discipline that is required to run a Lean business:

"You need a much, much higher level of discipline to do Lean. That is why it's harder for people to do.[49] Think of it from a very simple point of view. In most batch-and-queue operations, it is difficult to get people to do actual value-added work for much more than about 30–40 percent of the day. The people are just there at the workstation. What we would define as value-added and just being there are different things. In a Lean environment, people are working 80–90% of the day on value-added activities. It's a huge difference. The difference between those two things is pretty much how you organize the work and with the discipline you need to follow-up and make that happen.

Let's say that in a batch-and-queue organization, you are going to make a product that has to go through ten machines to get made. If one of those ten machines is broken, the batch-and-queue environment will be quite happy that nine out of the ten machines are running. Therefore, nine out of the ten people are working and busy and active. The one machine that is broken will get fixed, but in the meantime one person will be moved over to do something else. The mentality is to keep people busy, not to add value. You have to ask yourself, if it takes ten machines to make something, but only nine machines are running, then are you really making anything? The answer, of course, is no, because you are not making anything that you can sell. If you can't sell it, then in our opinion you're making waste. What you are doing is employing nine people to make waste; piling up stuff that you may or may not use later on.

Now if you switch to a Lean environment and one machine goes down, then all ten people are not doing anything. You've got a big problem. The discipline at that point is, we better fix that really fast. So Lean makes problems much more visible, and it gives you the opportunity and tools to solve them. In a batch-and-queue environment, this problem is not even visible. Management does not even notice it."

What happened to the people who cannot adjust to a more flexible and disciplined work environment? Art Byrne explained:

"Some of the people that are aggressive concrete-heads will never change; they are so stuck on what they learned 20 or 30 years ago; that it was right and they can't accept something different. They become a poison in the system if you don't get rid of them. The good thing is that most of them run for the exit screaming all by themselves because they can't stand it. The change is too dramatic for them. They want out because it's not the environment they want to be in. Occasionally, we have to fire somebody because they are fighting us to death. You have to get them out because they won't leave on their own, and if they stay they'll drag you backwards. That's not fair to everyone else."

Real Lean Yields Superior Results

The people of Wiremold accomplished an amazing amount in a relatively short time. The first few years were critical because they laid the foundation for what was to come. Their "widespread fast" Lean transformation stands in sharp contrast to the "local incremental" transformation preferred by most business leaders. Wiremold's focus on processes yielded results that any CEO would love to achieve — human resource development, speed and flexibility, market expansion, higher profits, greater end-use customer value, and increased shareholder value. The key was Art Byrne's understanding that Lean was not just about "continuous improvement." To be successful, the "respect for people" principle had to operate simultaneously. Both principles had to become part of Wiremold's culture.

When asked what accomplishments they were most proud of, members of the senior management team said:

Gary Brooks:

> "I'm very proud that the organization has given people who really want to advance the opportunity to advance, and that we have raised the standard of living for a lot of people within the organization. People have been able to put their kids through college, go on nice family vacations, and enjoy some of the better things in life.

> I am proud to have been a part of the executive group that created that culture. I don't have to watch my back because the senior management team does not play political games. It's very exciting to go to work and learn new things; the last ten years have been an education that is second to none in many different principles that apply to both business and life.

> It is my belief that it's a crime to use human effort and materials on waste. By eliminating waste we have been able to refocus our efforts on useful things. I'm proud that we have been good contributors to society, and that we've been able to keep jobs here in the United States. We've also been able to help other companies do the same thing."

Ed Miller:

> "There are basically two parts. One involves people development; being able to see people change and see them grow to heights they didn't think they could has been a wonderful experience. The other part, and probably as significant as the people internally, is the total repositioning of the company; from changing the logo, to forward-looking direction, to our whole go-to-market and mobilization of the company. That was very exciting; it involved the total company."

Judy Seyler:

> "To me, changing relationships was a big accomplishment. Things like negotiating the union contract in a win-win mode; teaching and counseling management to lead instead of being 'the boss'; changing from a hierarchical structure to a participative one; opening job and career opportunities through a dual career ladder and broad band compensation; reducing work related injuries; surveying the total work force annually for job satisfaction; sharing company financial information; creating

teams and then teaching them how to function effectively; and implementing a universal Code of Conduct. We worked to improve every aspect of the people part of the business using their own feedback to implement and assess the results. I loved working there!"

Orry Fiume:

"Survival. I don't think that we would have survived in a way that would be recognizable if we did not change. If we had continued down the old path for just another year, I'm convinced that the shareholders would have sold the company to some larger company who would have absorbed it. We would have been history. I'm proud of the fact that we survived that period and that we grew.

I'm also proud of having developed accounting processes to deal with this environment, which you're not going find in a textbook. The early years were important in terms of introducing some of the concepts and successful implementation of the concepts. Credit for that, of course, goes to a large group of people. It's great that I had the opportunity to do it, but I also had the encouragement to do it. In spite of my functional title, I've been able to be involved in every part of this business in one way or another."

Art Byrne:

"To me business is just people. So the part that I'm most proud of is the people. I am proud of the changes that they were able to make. I'm proud of the fact that we were able to protect and enrich all of our people as a result of the fact that they were willing to make all of those changes; because we told them that probably would happen and it did. The gain that everybody got in their 401(k) plan when the company was sold [July 2000; see the Postscript] was very big. But in addition they are still here, they still have their jobs. It is a bad economy right now [summer 2001], but we are still sort of OK. To me it is the people part.

The reality, from my point of view, is that if you are responsible for running the company, you have a tremendous obligation to people: to try to protect them, and to try to enhance their skills and enhance their value. That is the thing that I always feel the proudest of. I think that we have done a good job of cross training people so they have lots of different skills. Sometimes you have to force people to do things that you know are good for them, even though they inherently want to protect and stay within their little niche; convincing people that they should let go of their security blanket of just doing one job. You have to push a little bit, but I think that they all feel pretty proud that we have been able to protect the people, enhance their skills, and enrich them in their pockets better then we could have done without Lean. After all, Art Byrne didn't make the change to Lean — they did."

While there is much to be proud of, Wiremold's senior management team also knows the job is never done. Business conditions will change, competitors' capabilities will strengthen, and the leaders will retire or move on to other opportunities. Obviously, Wiremold cannot rely on past successes to generate future prosperity. Every manager and associate has the challenge to continue to press forward along the path that Art Byrne started. If, for some reason, they are unable, then they will surely succumb to the massive force of conventional business thinking and practice,[50] and end-use customers will have great difficulty obtaining the value that they seek.

Summary

There is a profound difference between the Lean management system and conventional business practices, rooted in batch-and-queue thinking. Many managers realize this is true, at least to some extent, but the driving force for becoming Lean is often to increase share price. This misguided approach will limit greatly what can actually be achieved. Many CEO's believe it unreasonable to expect more of them. Others, though, will surely expect more, especially end-use customers.

Fundamentally, it makes no sense to operate a management system that creates mountains of waste instead of creating value for end-use customers. It is both inefficient and ineffective. The cost to key stakeholders over time is enormous and will ultimately threaten the viability of the business. The need to change should be evident, but few will have the energy or interest to do so. Perhaps they fear the unknown, or failure, or are anchored in biases that make them believe the conventional way is better. However, since failure may be imminent, why not give Lean a try?

It is true that most businesses embark on the Lean journey only when troubles, created by decades of batch-and-queue business practices, threaten their very existence. This was the case for The Wiremold Company. Why wait for a crisis? The many benefits of the Lean management system are now well known. Why not instead be proactive and make the change-over, both personal and in management practice, before the crisis strikes? After all, leading a Lean business turns out to be more fun than work. It is simply a better life experience — for all stakeholders — compared to the alternative.

Key Points for Senior Managers

- "Real Lean" focuses on improving value streams, while "Imitation Lean" focuses on optimizing individual business functions.
- The driving force for the Lean transformation should be to create value for end-use customers, not to increase share price.
- There is a "day and night" difference between batch-and-queue and Lean as it pertains to human interactions, operational effectiveness, and end-use customer satisfaction.
- The machine change-over method is a useful model for understanding how to approach other important change-over problems in the Lean transformation.
- Wiremold was successful, in part, because it mastered the change-over problem.
- Lean is a much more highly disciplined management system than conventional management practice.
- Everything has to change; are you willing to do that for your end-use customers?

Notes

1. The principle of "perfection" encourages people to continuously improve; i.e. re-analyze the value stream for opportunities to eliminate waste. See *Lean Thinking*, J. Womack and D. Jones, Simon & Schuster, New York, NY, 1996, pp. 90–98. See Chapter 6, Note 5.

2. Often, even that is not done well because management will pick certain tools to implement and disregard others, which demonstrates a lack of knowledge and commitment to Lean principles and practices.

3. The CEO's strong preference for local optimization and sequential, function-specific transformations is partly rooted in structure of undergraduate and graduate business school education. Coursework is function-specific, and students are not taught to integrate the learning across the entire business system. For example, organizational behavior and finance and managerial accounting courses are usually disconnected, despite the fact that the principles and tools used by the latter contributes to dysfunctional organizational behavior and high employee turnover. Also, CEO's get to where they are by being skilled at conventional management practices. The path to success was achieved without having to understand how to improve the entire business system. Personal success is a powerful deterrent to change, even if it risks the future of the business though long-term customer dissatisfaction.

4. Functional optimization focuses managers and employees only on the part of the business they see and not what customers see. Often, when companies run into trouble, they reorganize themselves. In most cases, the new organization chart is a re-affirmation of long-standing efforts to locally optimize performance. Managers that fail to "specify value" and "identify the value stream" (see *Lean Thinking*, J. Womack and D. Jones, Simon & Schuster, New York, NY, 1996, pp. 29–49), and organize business processes accordingly, demonstrate a lack of respect for people and increase risk for all stakeholders.

5. Recognize that Figure 11-1 illustrates only a portion of the value stream. Also, Products A, B, and C can be viewed as Services A, B, and C as well.

6. To an extent, this is also true for Toyota Motor Corporation. While Toyota had long worked with suppliers to achieve Just-In-Time material deliveries, it was not until the 1973 oil crisis, which resulted in a zero growth period and high costs, that Toyota expanded its unique production methods to its suppliers. Toyota taught its suppliers how to improve their performance, which created the foundation for the network of competitive capability that we have seen over the last 30 years (see Chapter 4, Note 21). Efforts to transform relations with automobile dealers predate Toyota Motor Corporation's efforts with suppliers. See *My Life With Toyota*, S. Kamiya, Toyota Motor Sales Company, Ltd., Nagoya (Toyota City), Japan, 1976.

7. Part of the purpose of this book is to show senior managers how to achieve a "widespread fast" Lean transformation and illustrate the limitations of "local incremental" transformations.

8. Not respecting boundaries is itself a barrier for many people, which can make it difficult for them to accept the Lean management system.

9. For an excellent example of rapid and boundary-less response to a disaster, see "Case Study: The Toyota Group and the Aisin Fire," T. Nishiguchi and A. Beaudet, *Sloan Management Review*, Vol. 40, No. 1, 1998, pp. 49–59.

10. A current example of a new business tool that is designed to deliver most, if not all of the benefits to buyers is business-to-business (B2B) e-commerce, specifically online reverse auctions (see Chapter 5, Note 2). Suppliers are reluctant to participate in reverse auctions because buyers, as well as the companies that provide online reverse auction services, have failed to demonstrate the benefits of participating to suppliers. See http://www.theclbm.com/research.html.

11. See Chapter 9, Note 23.

12. Managers unfamiliar with Lean principles and practices will often try to apply ROI calculations or other measure of economic value added to determine which kaizen projects to work on or to justify the outcome of a kaizen activity. ROI calculations should not be applied to kaizen. Instead, managers should eliminate waste from value streams. Managers must learn to closely examine conventional performance measures and recognize their ineffectiveness when used in the Lean management system. In other words, applying conventional thinking to the Lean management system creates wasteful confusion and conflict. Be very careful to ensure that performance measurements and incentives are consistent with Lean principles and practices.

13. Most senior managers prefer to avoid taking leaps of faith because they do not like uncertainty, while many will use this as a reason, either implicitly or explicitly, to avoid making important decisions. However, this rationale is not credible, as the leaders of conventionally managed businesses take big leaps of faith *every day*. For example: they assume that the information used to run the business is accurate (see Table 9-1), or that companies exist to maximize shareholder value (see Chapter 5, Note 4). In fact, managers whose capabilities are rooted in batch-and-queue thinking require formidable "leap of faith" skills. The trouble is that most managers are not aware of this. In contrast, taking a leap of faith in the Lean management system is less frequent, but perhaps more dramatic when the linkage between elim-

inating waste and creating customer value is difficult or impossible to measure. In most cases, a Lean leader will not permit the lack of precise data to stop them from making decisions that are consistent with Lean principles and practices.

14. Assuming all CEO's think like the CEO's of large, publicly owned businesses. The CEO's of privately owned businesses (or non-profits or government organizations) often see business quite differently compared to CEO's of publicly owned businesses. The former tend to view business as a socio-economic, rather than a pure economic, activity. This is just one of many differences.

15. The financial scandals of 2001 and 2002 have revealed flaws in stock option based compensation for senior executives. Dozens of large publicly owned companies voluntarily announced in July and August 2002 they will begin to expense stock options as one measure intended to curb abuse.

16. The concept of value streams and the value stream mapping tool are not yet widely taught in business schools.

17. The Toyota Production System was based in part upon the work of Henry Ford and Charles Sorenson. See *Today and Tomorrow: An Autobiography*, H. Ford, Special Reprint Edition, Productivity Press, Portland, OR, 1988, and *My Forty Years With Ford*, C. Sorenson (with S. Williamson), W.W. Norton Company, Inc., New York, NY, 1956.

18. That was quite a leap to take — going from the loom business to automobiles business. It is a great story of entrepreneurship. See *My Life with Toyota*, S. Kamiya, Toyota Motor Sales Co., Ltd., Toyota City, Japan, 1976; *My Years with Toyota*, S. Kato, Toyota Motor Sales Co., Ltd., Toyota City, Japan, 1981; *Toyota: 50 Years in Motion*, E. Toyoda, Kodansha International, Tokyo, Japan, 1987; *Toyota: A History of the First 50 Years*, Toyota Motor Corporation, Toyota City, Japan, 1988; *Against All Odds*, Y. Togo and W. Wartman, St. Martin's Press, New York, NY, 1993; *The Origin of Competitive Strength*, A. Kawahara, Springer-Verlag, New York, NY, 1998; *Toyota: People, Ideas and the Challenge of the New*, E. Reingold, Penguin Books, London, England, 1999.

19. *Toyota Production System*, T. Ohno, Productivity Press, Portland, OR, 1988, pp. 88–89.

20. Toyota Motor Corporation, Ltd., was established on 28 August 1937. Some of its current practices, such as autonomation, are rooted in loom designs dating back to the early 1900's. Thus, Toyota's management system has been under development over an eight-decade period. Many people see Toyota as it is today and incorrectly assume that this is the way it has always been. The fact is that current management practices are the result of a steady, purposeful evolution in thinking. See Chapter 3, Note 23.

21. Market capitalizations on 21 November 2002: Toyota, $93.4B; Ford, $18.9B; General Motors, $21.6B; DaimlerChrysler, $35.1B. Total of Ford, GM, and DaimlerChrysler = $75.6B

22. See "Cracking the Code of Business," M.L. Emiliani, *Management Decision*, Vol. 38, No. 2, 2000, pp. 60–79, and "Redefining the Focus of Investment Analysts," M.L. Emiliani, *The TQM Magazine*, Vol. 13, No. 1, 2001, pp. 34–50.

23. Almost always accompanied by layoffs as productivity improves — a common mistake.

24. Many managers look forward to the day that Lean will begin to "stick" in their company. That is, they believe that there is a point at which they will make enough progress for Lean to become a self-sustaining management system. This is the wrong way to think. The Lean management system will never really "stick" because it requires ongoing maintenance and improvement; hence the concept of "continuous improvement." Lean is a never-ending journey.

25. It is simple to understand the words "respect for people," but its true meaning is much more difficult to grasp. To broaden your understanding of this term, make two lists containing all the ways that you can think of that show: a) respect for people, and b) disrespect for people. Start with everyday business principles and practices as source material for your analysis. These lists should take you several months, or even years, to complete. Only then can you begin to understand the true meaning of "respect for people." Also, see the Caux Round Table *Principles for Business*, http://www.cauxroundtable.org/ENGLISH.HTM.

26. Batch-and-queue is the intuitive way for people to solve problems. See Chapter 5, Note 1.

27. Based on a conversation with Kevin Fahey, Vice President of Human Resources (16 August 2001), as well as Emiliani's experience working in both the batch-and-queue and "Real Lean" part of an otherwise "Imitation Lean" business.

28. See "Lean Behaviors," M.L. Emiliani, *Management Decision*, Vol. 36, No. 9, 1998, pp. 615–631; "Continuous Personal Improvement," M.L. Emiliani, *J. Workplace Learning*, Vol. 10, No. 1, 1998, pp. 29-39; and "Cracking the Code of Business," M.L. Emiliani, *Management Decision*, Vol. 38, No. 2, 2000, pp. 60–79.

29. As a result, senior management works to gain increased competitiveness through artificial means such as financial engineering, or by forced means such as layoffs, plant closings, squeezing suppliers, outsourcing, mergers, divestitures, etc. — and not by creating value for end-use customers.

30. Note that most Japanese companies do not practice the Lean management system.

31. Notwithstanding the fact that solutions to problems tend to be batch-and-queue in nature.

32. In part, because most senior managers typically have difficulty translating robust management principles into everyday thinking and practice.

33. *A Revolution in Manufacturing: The SMED System*, S. Shingo, Productivity Press, Portland, OR, 1985, pp. 26–31.

34. Internal set-up is activities that must be performed when the machine is shut down. External set-up is activities that can be performed when the machine is running. See *A Revolution in Manufacturing: The SMED System*, S. Shingo, Productivity Press, Portland, OR, 1985, Ch. 3.

35. The models presented in Figures 11-4, 11-5, and 11-6 are based upon the machine change-over method. Wiremold did not use the models shown in these Figures during its Lean transformation. Rather, they are new constructs developed independently by Emiliani between 1999–2001. However, they do effectively explain what Wiremold did.

36. Threats can be well articulated or implied. In either case, people will limit information sharing and participation, and instead favor self-preservation. One prominent fear many people have, particularly hourly associates, is that they will no longer fit in. A superstar in a batch-and-queue business may no longer be a superstar in a Lean business. The threat of losing power or individual identity, whether real or perceived, can be a powerful deterrent to accepting Lean principles and practices. Management must recognize this important issue and respond to it in a manner that demonstrates "respect for people."

37. *Toyota Production System*, T. Ohno, Productivity Press, Portland, OR, 1988, pp. 14–15.

38. Between 1988 and August 1991, Wiremold's management had engaged the company in Total Quality Management, and later "Total Quality Process." That, plus the values of a family-owned business, may have helped prepare the organization for the changes that Art Byrne would begin to make upon his arrival. According to Art: "Despite the fact that the management team hadn't been successful with Total Quality Management, the people really bought into its basic principles. So the things that I was talking about when I was being interviewed were different, but the basic principles were the same. The basic beliefs and values were also the same, and I had the knowledge that they were looking for, so they hired me. I changed almost everything that Wiremold was doing, but I didn't change the fundamental beliefs because they were pretty much the same."

39. Effectively, but not completely addressed, as explicit and tacit concerns can only be decreased over time.

40. See Chapter 5, Notes 4 and 9.

41. See Chapter 9, Note 29.

42. "Least-waste way" is a term used by Wiremold to describe a way of performing an activity that has the least known amount waste at a given point in time. In other words, it is the best way known at the current time to perform an activity, which could be different a week from now or a year from now due to new ideas, new process, or new equipment. The "least-waste way" is therefore not the absolute minimum waste associated with doing an activity. The term was introduced to Wiremold's Walker Systems subsidiary in 1999 by Bob Pentland, a partner in Moffitt associates and former Vice President of Operations (1988–1991) and President of Jacobs Vehicle Systems (one of the companies that Art Byrne was responsible for when he was at Danaher Corporation). Its original use was in the context of standard work, but it has more recently applied to the "Lean Compass" (Wiremold's roadmap for getting to the "least-waste way" in any activity) and Policy Deployment (i.e. hoshin kanri). For standard work, it refers to the least amount of time it takes to perform an activity of the range of times observed. The "Least-waste way" is an interesting term because it can compel people to start asking: "What is the least-waste way of doing an activity?" By asking this question, people continuously refer back to the basis of the Toyota Production System, which is "the absolute elimination of waste." This helps ensure that activities and decision-making do not stray from one of the primary objectives of Lean.

43. Management usually has no other choice but to lay people off, close plants, and squeeze supplier's profit margins. This type of workplace is very taxing on key stakeholders, including investors. Surprisingly, key stakeholders do not yet exhibit a sufficient level of dissatisfaction to demand a change in management practices from batch-and-queue or "Imitation Lean" to "Real Lean."

44. Predictably, under such circumstances, "empowerment" is elusive.

45. The following sports imagery can help provide a sense of the difference with regards to discipline (but not speed). For example, think of the difference between: ice hockey and synchronized swimming. The former is less organized and opportunistic (batch-and-queue), while the latter is orderly, deliberate, and repeatable (Lean).

46. This includes personal (behavioral) discipline as well as task discipline. See "Lean Behaviors," M.L. Emiliani, *Management Decision*, Vol. 36, No. 9, 1998, pp. 615–631.

47. The shift in control can be thought of as similar to going from a dictatorship to a democracy.

48. Wiremold began using Policy Deployment (called "Hoshin Kanri" in Japanese; the literal translation is "policy management") in 1995. Policy deployment is a focused planning, or direction setting, process

derived from the strategic plan that links key objectives to resources. Many companies take a disorganized approach to kaizen, particularly early in the Lean transformation, which in some cases can result in improvements that have no real benefit for end-use customers. The disciplined use of policy deployment to set direction helps avoid such outcomes. Therefore, it is preferable if management begins using policy deployment at the onset of the Lean transformation. Its use also demonstrates "respect for people" in that managers and associates efforts are focused on activities that eliminate waste and create value for end-use customers. Importantly, people at all levels can easily see how their activities contribute to the organization's strategic objectives. See *Hoshin Kanri: Policy Deployment for Successful TQM*, Y. Akao, Ed., Productivity Press, Portland, OR, 1991, and *A Field Guide to Focused Planning: Hoshin Kanri-American Style*, J. Colletti, The Woodledge Group, Inc., E. Granby, CT, 1996, hoshin1@aol.com.

49. "Real Lean" is harder to do because it requires large-scale coordination of activities among people. In batch-and-queue, people perform their activities in isolation; hence the system is disorganized, it takes a long time to satisfy customer requests, and large amounts of resources are consumed. An interesting metaphor based upon phase transformations in metals can be used to illustrate this point. The most common route to phase transformations (changes in structure or composition) is heterogeneous nucleation and growth by diffusion because the free energy of formation is lower than that required for heterogeneous nucleation. Diffusion is a disorganized (i.e. random) and time-consuming process because other atoms stand in the way. In contrast, diffusionless shear transformations such as martensitic reactions are less common because they require the simultaneous movement of large numbers of atoms. Another example is twinning, a deformation reaction, which is also relatively rare because it requires the coordinated movement of many atoms at the same time.

50. Toyota Motor Corporation has avoided this fate so far, principally because generations of managers that embody "The Toyota Way" have always filled top management positions and kept it going. While the principal stakeholders — associates, suppliers, customers, investors, and community — are also the principal beneficiaries of the Lean management system, they seem to have had little direct influence in helping Toyota maintain its long-term commitment to "The Toyota Way." If in the future Toyota begins to lose its way, then perhaps these stakeholders should play an active role in ensuring that Toyota maintains its unique management system. The same could be true for Wiremold or any other company that has had success with the Lean management system.

Postscript
Solving the Liquidity Problem

On July 17, 2000, the French company Legrand S.A.,[1] a manufacturer of low voltage electrical equipment, announced that it was acquiring The Wiremold Company on July 31, 2000. In its press release,[2] Legrand characterized the acquisition as follows:

> Legrand announces today the acquisition of U.S.-based The Wiremold Company. Wiremold is the U.S. undisputed leader for raceways and floor boxes used to channel power as well as voice, data and image (V.D.I.) cables throughout commercial and industrial buildings ("wire management").
>
> Legrand reinforces its world leadership in low voltage fittings and accessories and becomes a top tier actor in the US market which is the world's largest market. The transaction amounts to 770 M$ [sic].
>
> - Legrand doubles in size in the U.S. which now represent 25% of its total sales as compared to 13% before the transaction.
>
> - Legrand 2000 proforma [sic] sales will grow by more than 30%, exceeding 3 billion Euros.
>
> This strategic acquisition provides Legrand with a unique competitive position in North America with a complementary and original association between its 4 product families: wiring devices with Pass & Seymour, V.D.I. products with Ortronics, lighting control with The Watt Stopper and now wire management products with Wiremold.
>
> Wiremold operates in high-growth segments and holds both a remarkable brand image and market share (more than 80% of its sales are made with products being in a leadership or n°2 position). This is accomplished with its extensive offering of 35,000 items, monthly innovative product launches and quality service levels.
>
> Wiremold is projected to achieve sales of $460 million with an operating margin exceeding 12%. More than 80% of Wiremold's sales are in the U.S. and Canada.
>
> François Grappotte, Chairman and C.E.O. of Legrand, said: "This strategic acquisition shows our commitment to tackle major opportunities in our market at conditions strictly consistent with the interest of our shareholders".

Art Byrne, Chairman and C.E.O. of Wiremold, said: "This association between 2 [sic] leading companies will give birth to a major player in the American market. Complementary growth, service-oriented spirit and innovation are keys to success in the power and VDI markets."

Wiremold will be consolidated from August 1, 2000. The transaction is relutive [sic] before depreciation of goodwill; after depreciation of goodwill and excluding synergies, it will have a limited dilution of about 5% in 2001 (first full year of consolidation). It will be relutive [sic] in 2003.

The transaction is subject to the approval of the relevant administrative authorities which should be granted shortly.

Legrand is a world leader in low voltage fittings and accessories and is active in 54 countries. 1999 sales amounted to 2.3 billion euros of which 2/3 are derived from sales outside France. Legrand products are [sold] to specialist wholesalers and installed by professional electricians. They cater for the residential market as well as for offices and factories.

Legrand shares are traded on the French stock exchange. (Italics original)

The question is, why did The Wiremold Company put itself up for sale? Business had improved dramatically since Art Byrne arrived in the fall of 1991. Was something amiss? Did it have anything to do with the Lean transformation? Was the Lean transformation faltering?

The Problem

In the late 1990's, Wiremold senior management knew that they had two growing problems to confront: industry consolidation and an impending liquidity crisis. The four surviving children of D. Hayes Murphy, his sons John Davis Murphy and Robert H. Murphy, and his daughters Rosalie Murphy Massey and Marjorie Murphy Morrisey, were all nearing 90 years of age. Wiremold's annual financial plans had included contingencies to buy out each of these four large shareholders, assumed to be at a rate of about one every other year, as they passed away. They did not pass away, however, having been blessed with longevity. It was becoming increasingly likely that these four major shareholders could all pass away within the next few years.[3]

As their children, grandchildren, great-grandchildren, and related family members were not actively involved in managing The Wiremold Company,[4] the passing of the four senior Murphy's — John Davis Murphy and Robert H. Murphy, and their sisters Rosalie Murphy Massey and Marjorie Murphy Morrisey — would likely result in the rapid liquidation of their shares upon settlement of their estates. Liquidating a large percentage of the shares in a short span of time would have consumed all available cash and impeded the company's ability to continue to grow. Wiremold would have had to divert cash from reinvestment in the business to share repurchases, and likely miss important business opportunities because it couldn't afford to invest in them. If Wiremold were forced to buy out the principal family shareholders, then some of the smaller family shareholders would likely want to sell their shares as well. Wiremold would have found itself in a severe liquidity bind.

The Solution

In early 2000, Wiremold received an unsolicited offer from a potential acquirer. At that point, Art Byrne and Orry Fiume had decided that it was time to begin looking for companies that might be interested in buying Wiremold. If successful, the buyer could provide liquidity to all the shareholders and Wiremold could continue to grow the business using internally generated cash. Art and Orry knew that the late 1990's were a period of unprecedented economic expansion. So, the timing for selling Wiremold was good; the stock market was strong and the valuation of Wiremold would be very high, in part due to its outstanding performance over the preceding nine years. Shareholders would realize substantial gains if the right buyer could be found. Art Byrne and Orry Fiume knew five or six companies that might be interested in buying The Wiremold Company. They, along with the Board of Directors, hired an investment banker to determine Wiremold's valuation compared to peer group companies and go about the task of finding a buyer.

Art and Orry took the various proposals that they had received from candidate buyers to the Board of Directors. The board selected Legrand S.A., a publicly owned French electrical equipment manufacturer. Figure P-1 shows the growth in enterprise value[5] of Wiremold from 1990 through the sale of the company to Legrand. The Wiremold senior management team selected Legrand for the following reasons (not in order of importance):

- Purchase price
- Similarity in corporate culture
- Global reach
- Expanded U.S. presence
- Local management

The sale to Legrand had a very good outcome for Wiremold, the Murphy family, and most importantly Wiremold's employees, who through the 401(k) plan were the single biggest shareholders at the time of the sale. The enterprise value had risen over 1600% from its level in 1990 to the date of the sale to Legrand in 2000. The compound average annual growth rate of the stock over the period 1990–2000 was therefore 32.3% per year.

It is certain that none of this would have been possible had Wiremold not transformed itself into a Lean business. Wiremold would have remained as a much smaller batch-and-queue manufacturer without the ability to finance much growth. Its employees would therefore have been put at risk if the company eventually had to be sold at some distressed valuation.

The Lean transformation, however, allowed Wiremold to grow, gain market share, and improve its results to the point where it was attractive when it became the logical time to sell. Neither Art nor Orry expected to sell the company based simply upon its Lean capabilities. They always expected that Wiremold would be valued based upon its market positions and track record, which were the result of the Lean transformation. This is indeed the way it turned out.

Figure P-1 Enterprise Value

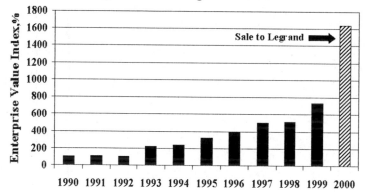

Local Reaction

The Hartford Courant newspaper ran two stories on the sale of Wiremold to Legrand. The first story[6] contained the following quotes by Orry Fiume:

> "The industry has been consolidating, and we certainly have been following that trend. As that continues, it makes it more difficult for an independent company to continue to stay independent. You have to become a global player because, as your customers become global players, they're looking for global partners.
>
> They [Legrand] operate in 56 countries around the world, and their track record is, it's run by local management."

A commentary in the editorial page of *The Hartford Courant* had this to say about the acquisition:[7]

> "Wiremold, a century-old family-owned business, represents the good.[8] This maker of wire products has sales exceeding $400 million a year and has a national payroll of 3,600. It is known for its fair treatment of employees and its efficient manufacturing methods. It was one of the first American companies to adopt Toyota's 'kaizen' teamwork practices. Executives from

throughout the United States visited Wiremold to study its management organization systems.

Despite its success Wiremold was too small to compete globally. Facing reality, it agreed to sell itself to a French conglomerate, Legrand, for an estimated $770 million. Employees, whose 401(k) savings will triple in value as a result of the sale, will share in the bounty. Moreover, Wiremold will keep its name and operate as it has for many years. But it will have a global reach because Legrand owns businesses in 56 countries and had a track record of letting local managers run its operations.

Legrand's trust in local autonomy has been amply rewarded on the bottom line. The expectation is that Wiremold will continue to grow, which can only be good for the Hartford region."

Analysis

The reasons Wiremold decided to seek a buyer are clear:

- The liquidity problem
- Industry consolidation
- Lack of global reach

It had nothing to do with the Lean transformation, which proceeded very well. Why, then, did Legrand purchase Wiremold? According to its press release, Legrand was clearly interested in achieving the following business objectives:

- Complementary product families
- Expand U.S. market share
- Increase U.S. sales
- Earnings growth
- Wiremold brand name
- Wiremold's speed to market

The price that Legrand paid was related to the high valuations placed upon most businesses near the peak of the business cycle. It was a seller's market, and Wiremold certainly got a good price. Did Legrand buy Wiremold because of its nine-year efforts to transform itself into a Lean business? Did Legrand recognize or have any *direct* interest in Wiremold's capabilities in Lean? The answer is "No," but they had an *indirect* interest as it related to earnings growth, the Wiremold brand name, which was developed over a period of nearly 80 years in the U.S. market, and Wiremold's speed to market with regards to new product development. Legrand also realized Wiremold's superior quality and customer service levels.

Legrand, like most manufacturers, operates their business according to batch-and-queue principles and practices.[9] Therefore, it is unrealistic to expect

Legrand's senior management to recognize the value of Wiremold's Lean management system directly. Instead, they would see the benefits of an enterprise-wide Lean transformation indirectly. However, the benefits did stand out.

Would Legrand have viewed Wiremold as an attractive acquisition if Art Byrne had not arrived on September 23, 1991 and transformed the business? That, of course, is impossible to say. It is clear, however, that Wiremold was headed towards financial distress, and it is likely that they would not have survived as an independent business for more than just a few years after 1991. The Total Quality Process program, which had been initiated prior to Art Byrne's arrival, was an attempt to get out from under the weight of decades of batch-and-queue practice, which caused tremendous problems as competition intensified in the late 1980's. The TQP program, however, would probably not have been successful in the long-term because it was not actionable.

Art Byrne's leadership, and that of the entire senior management team, came at a critical time. The Lean transformation ensured the integrity of the Wiremold brand name, which had value to Legrand. The Lean transformation helped Wiremold expand its product lines, achieve speed to market, and expand market share, which had value to Legrand. The Lean transformation resulted in both sales and earnings growth, which had value to Legrand. The Lean transformation enabled Wiremold to deliver both tangible and intangible benefits to its distributors and retailers, which had value to Legrand. The Lean transformation delivered value to end-use customers, which had value to Legrand.

What CEO's must understand is that Lean is a comprehensive management system, and that the two key principles are "continuous improvement" *and* "respect for people." Done correctly, Lean creates value for all stakeholders, not just shareholders. So, as Art Byrne said, "Why wouldn't you do this?"

Notes

1. See http://www.legrandelectric.com and http://www.legrand.fr

2. "Legrand acquires Wiremold and doubles in size in the U.S.," Legrand press release, 17 July 2000

3. Robert H. Murphy died on 26 July 2002 at the age of 87.

4. None of the Murphy family members had been involved in day-to-day management of the company for over 20 years.

5. Figure 10-1 shows the increase in shareholder value between 1990 and 1999, while Figure P-1 shows the increase in enterprise value between 1990 and 2000. Enterprise value is a total value without regard to the source of financing (i.e. debt or equity). Shareholder value is the residual amount of enterprise value that would accrue to the shareholders after satisfying all debt (enterprise value – funded debt = shareholder value). The discounted cash flow approach to valuation employed in the shareholder value calculations was designed to obtain a per share valuation of a minority interest. Legrand's computation of enterprise value includes the benefits of having a controlling interest and the synergies with their existing business, sources of considerable value not relevant to a passive holder of a minority interest.

6. "Wiremold Selling Itself To Grow — French Buyer Will Make Company a Global Player," Dan Haar and Christopher Keating, *The Hartford Courant*, page E1, 18 July 2000. Copyright © 2000 by the Hartford Courant. Reprinted with permission.

7. "Aetna, Dexter, And Wiremold," Editorial, *The Hartford Courant*, 23 July 2000. Copyright © 2000 by the Hartford Courant. Reprinted with permission.

8. The editorial discusses other contemporaneous changes in ownership of businesses that "symbolize Connecticut's identity." Specifically, the "continuing dismemberment" of Aetna — the purchase of its financial services and international units by ING — which the editorial refers to as a "not-so-good" transformation, and the piecemeal sale of Dexter Corporation's businesses to companies based in Germany, Finland, and California, which the editorial refers to as the "ugly."

9. It will be very interesting to see how The Wiremold Company fares in the years to come under a parent company whose management practices are rooted in wasteful batch-and-queue thinking and practices. Will autonomous local management be able to keep the Lean management system alive, or will it succumb to the strong forces of conventional business practice? Only time will tell.

Afterword

The Lean management system is not a "silver bullet" that will make all business problems go away. It is not the perfect management system either, but is significantly better than the alternative of conventional batch-and-queue business practices. It is hard work, both physical and mental, to transform a business from batch-and-queue to "Real Lean," but it is fun and rewarding work, as Wiremold managers have attested. The Lean organization has numerous social and economic advantages, which The Wiremold Company has amply demonstrated. Significantly, the financial performance of Lean businesses is better than batch-and-queue, and comes without the need to make large capital investments, destructive tradeoffs between key stakeholders, or engage in deceptive or fraudulent accounting practices. Most managers will have great difficulty comprehending the fact that focusing on creating value for end-use customers, rather than increasing share price, can achieve better overall business performance, including share price. After all, that's not what business schools teach.

The plain fact is that Lean businesses are formidable competitors. When market conditions are favorable, most businesses do quite well. When market conditions deteriorate, Lean businesses do much better than their peer group companies. A well-executed time-based competition strategy that focuses on end-use customers will put a business at the top its industry.[1] But it won't stay there forever. Lean businesses require ongoing maintenance and improvement, which is achieved only through broad-based participation by all associates and managers. If senior management does not completely understand what "respect for people" means,[2] then it will be impossible to succeed. While most senior managers recognize quickly the benefits of shop floor kaizen consulting, they have yet to recognize the value of the new leadership behaviors needed to correctly practice the Lean management system. The simple message is: don't be a "concrete head" when it comes to changing leadership behaviors.[3]

Wiremold's Lean transformation contains dozens of useful ideas and practices that CEO's can apply to their businesses. However, CEO's must recognize that picking only the best practices could cause some unwanted problems.[4] The specific things that Wiremold did are part of their larger system of Lean management principles and practices. They may not work for another company if it does not possess the other important parts of the management system. The entire senior management team must therefore give careful consideration to the new policies and practices they wish to adopt. Indeed, Lean done correctly is an all-or-nothing proposition. Therefore, it would also be important to determine the root cause of why commitment is lacking. Lean is an advanced management system, and, as Art Byrne says, "Everything has to change. Are you willing to do that?"

Notwithstanding the important issues related to "cherry-picking" best practices, some of Wiremold's practices clearly stand out as things that CEO's should want to do early in their Lean transformation, while others could be adopted over time. For example, Wiremold's strategy is generic and almost timeless in its applicability. Why wouldn't you use this as your strategy? Is there anything so different about your business that you couldn't use Wiremold's strategy as-is, or with very slight modification? What about Wiremold's Code of Conduct? Why wouldn't you adopt it as-is? And shouldn't you be using simple surveys to better understand your key stakeholders, take action, and then assess the results of your efforts? What about changing the accounting system so that everyone can understand what is really going on? What about profit sharing and the "five lines of defense?" Why can't your company adopt these key practices right away?

A question that many readers will likely ask is: "Our CEO isn't like Art Byrne, so what should we do?" First, recognize that Mr. Taiichi Ohno, creator of the Toyota Production System, did not have an Art Byrne-type CEO either, yet he was able to make enormous progress. Mr. Eiji Toyoda was a great and insightful CEO whom Mr. Ohno credits for having developed the Toyota Production System. One of the reasons Mr. Ohno gives him credit is because Mr. Toyoda supported Mr. Ohno's efforts by "absorb[ing] all the discontent and grumbling directed at Mr. Ohno from the factory and never mentioned it to him."[5] So there are thousands of improvements that you can make even if your CEO is not exactly like Art Byrne.[6] While it may appear as if Wiremold's Lean transformation was all due to Art's efforts, it was not. Senior managers, product line managers, sales people, cell leaders, associates, and others all helped make it happen.

Also, remember that Art Byrne was not a ready-made Lean CEO. He learned and applied Lean principles and practices over a ten-year period until the opportunity arose in which he could become the CEO and transform an entire business. So if you don't have an Art Byrne-type CEO, one can either be made or found. This book will help companies ask the right questions in interviews.[7] Perhaps a member of your Board of Directors will read this book and become interested in finding a CEO who understands both "continuous improvement" and "respect for people."

A second question that readers may ask is: "We're completely devoted to Wall Street's short-term interests. How can we change that?" The challenge is not necessarily to change the primary interests of investors.[8] Instead, it could be to teach them how the Lean management system yields better results for them, as well as other key stakeholders. Or, you can seek out the segment of the investment community that is interested in achieving stable long-term equity growth. Alternatively, you can change the balance of ownership by buying back shares to reduce percentage of your business that is owned by short-term investors. Or, you can return to private ownership through a management buy-out or by seeking one or more private-equity investment partners. However, from a practical standpoint, the CEO — and CFO — would have to educate investors on the benefits of Lean under almost any circumstance.

It is interesting to note that most successful Lean transformations had a company culture that retained the core beliefs and values of a family-owned business.[9] Public ownership, including mindless singular devotion to investors, can rapidly sever these ties, which may be difficult to restore. This is not to say that Lean won't work in publicly owned companies — quite the contrary.[10] Rather, it simply highlights an additional challenge that senior managers will have to recognize and to which they must respond.

A third question that readers might ask is: "Can we succeed with Lean given that we have high turnover among managers?" The answer is "No." Don't forget that the cause of high management turnover is batch-and-queue business practices, whose ad-hoc problem solving style, plugged information flow, politics, blame, and intense focus on results places unreasonable pressure on managers to succeed. In every case where Lean is implemented correctly, there is stability in management and the workforce at-large. Leadership is cultivated internally, rather than by recruiting large numbers of people from other companies. Managers recruited from external sources often have difficulty understanding the Lean management system and may favor the use of business philosophies or tools that conflict with Lean principles and practices. For many companies, this had led to a loss of momentum or even abandonment of the Lean management system.

A fourth question readers might ask is: "This book made it sound so easy. Is the Lean transformation really that easy?" The answer, again, is "No". The Lean transformation requires a dedicated effort by the entire senior management team to thoroughly understand and apply Lean principles and practices as a management system, not as a group of tools for simply improving operating performance. It also takes the dedicated efforts of all associates, as well as suppliers. While Wiremold made many small mistakes, it managed to avoid making big mistakes that could have set back their efforts. The Wiremold Company did not make big mistakes because Art Byrne had prior experiences with Lean principles and practices at General Electric and especially at Danaher Corporation. So Art had an advantage that few other CEO's had at the time, which can make Wiremold's Lean transformation appear effortless. The truth is that it was far from effortless, as the many excerpts from interviews with the senior management team illustrate. However, they also had a lot of fun doing what they did and can be rightfully proud of their accomplishments.

Importantly, Art did not delegate the Lean transformation to his direct reports. Instead, Art led the transformation, and he clearly understood the two key principles: "continuous improvement" and "respect for people." As Orry said, "Art lives, eats, sleeps, and breathes this stuff. And people know that." The Lean transformation is not easy because it challenges the fundamental business beliefs, behaviors, and competencies of business leaders. But it can be done and is worth doing because it results in improved competitiveness and much better outcomes.

In general, the CEO's of conventionally managed businesses are very tough on other people. That's easy to do. In contrast, Art Byrne was very tough on himself, which is much harder to do. He was also tough on Lean principles,

business processes, and process discipline. To be sure, some business principles and practices were not negotiable. But the "no blame" environment at
Wiremold enabled people to learn the new Lean management system so that
the entire company could practice it. The role of post-modern management
can be viewed, in part, as a supplier of labor to implement changes in response
to changing market conditions. Employees won't change in the ways that they
need to change if they are unduly threatened. Anyone can learn the tools of
continuous improvement, but to make Lean really work requires a deep understanding of how people respond to changes that dramatically affect their
daily lives. CEO's that can't or won't acknowledge this fact will simply let go
to waste both human potential and competitive advantage.

A fifth question readers might ask is: "I'm the CEO, and the Lean transformation looks awfully hard to do.[11] Our company needs to become Lean, but I
don't have the practical experience to lead the transformation the way Art did.
What should I do?" One approach that a CEO could take is as follows:

- Hire a few key senior managers with significant prior experi-
  ence in one or more Lean transformations
- Hire the right consultants to assist in the transformation
- Participate in kaizen, CEO on down
- Make the policy changes across all functions that are neces-
  sary to support Lean
- Use the change-over models presented in Figures 11-5 and 11-6
- Commit to a higher level of discipline, including the regular
  use of root cause analysis to understand and solve manage-
  ment problems
- Start to practice the "respect for people" principle

Many CEO's espouse the importance of life-long learning. However, they
often behave in ways that are inconsistent with those words. Adopting the Lean
management system gives CEO's a platform to show that they actually believe
in what they say. It will require them to think differently about everyday business activities, and sometimes have to take a "leap of faith". As Mr. Ohno said:[12]

> "As the Toyota production system evolved, I frequently applied
> reverse common sense or inverse thinking. I urge all managers,
> intermediate supervisors, foremen, and workers… to be more
> flexible in their thinking as they go about their work."

Lean is an evolutionary management system. You won't get there in two years,
or ten years, or twenty years because there is no end to improvement, and it takes
time to understand the true intent and proper practice of the Lean management system. But you have to start somewhere and believe that future social and economic
conditions can and should be improved for all key stakeholders.[13] The place to start
is with yourself and then work from there, even if you are not the CEO.[14]

Notes

1. For example, compare the year 2000 and 2001 financial and non-financial results of time-based competitors such as Dell Computer versus Hewlett Packard, Compaq, and Gateway; Southwest Airlines versus Delta, United Airlines, American Airlines, and U.S. Air; Toyota and Honda versus General Motors, Ford, and DaimlerChrysler.

2. See Chapter 11, Note 24.

3. See Chapter 3, Note 9.

4. Many organizations that implement a few stand-alone tools will call themselves "Lean." For example, companies will implement Just-In-Time in isolation of Autonomation or production leveling. Or, they will move machines into U-shaped manufacturing cells and declare themselves "Lean." Others will have developed some skill in set-up reduction, 5S, and total productive maintenance, for example, but not do much else. Or they may think that they are Lean because they have established a "kaizen office" or "office of continuous improvement." These are examples of "Imitation Lean."

5. *Just-In-Time for Today and Tomorrow*, T. Ohno and S. Mito, Productivity Press, Cambridge, MA, 1988, pp. 74–75.

6. Indeed, large business recipients of the Shingo Prize were principally awarded to divisions of large companies whose CEOs, in most cases, do not fully understand the Lean management system. The CEO's of small businesses that have received the Shingo Prize may also not fully understand the Lean management system. Importantly, a significant amount of improvement can be achieved despite this limitation. See http://www.shingoprize.org.

7. Obviously, candidates may have read this book as well and thus have ready answers for things that they may not have really done. Being able to discern the difference between talking about Lean and doing Lean is key. See Chapter 1, "A Change in Leadership."

8. The following would be worth reading if one were to try changing investors' principal outlook: "Redefining the Focus of Investment Analysts," M.L. Emiliani, *The TQM Magazine*, Vol. 13, No. 1, 2001, pp. 34–50. Also, see Chapter 5, Note 4. For various proposals designed to correct the key extrinsic structural financial and legal constructs that compel boards of directors and senior managers to focus literally on maximizing shareholder value — which typically results in exactly the opposite outcome — see *The Divine Right of Capital*, M. Kelly, Berrett-Koehler Publishers Inc., San Francisco, CA, 2001, and *Corporate Irresponsibility: America's Newest Export*, L. Mitchell, Yale University Press, New Haven, CT, 2001. Also see the Caux Round Table *Principles for Business*, http://www.cauxroundtable.org/ENGLISH.HTM.

9. See Chapter 2, Note 19.

10. For example, Toyota Motor Corporation, Honda Motor Company, Denso Corporation, Danaher Corporation (see Chapter 10, Note 6) are publicly owned businesses. Many others have been recipients of the Shingo Prize (see http://www.shingoprize.org). The fact that there are not scores of publicly owned companies, across a wide range of manufacturing and service industries, recognized as "Real Lean" illustrates the fact that Lean is not understood by CEO's as a management system, it is hard to do, and its benefits are not well-known. Also note that some companies prefer not to be identified because they fear losing competitive advantage or losing their key people to competitors. Finally, while they can not be considered "Lean" as described in this book, some publicly owned companies exhibit selected Lean-like characteristics that contribute to strong long-term competitive advantage, including: Dell Computer Corporation, Southwest Airlines Co., Wal-Mart, Progressive Casualty Insurance Company, and Johnson & Johnson.

11. When senior executives understand what "Real Lean" means, most find the Lean transformation to be overwhelming and use this as a handy reason for not doing anything or proceeding very slowly. Senior managers, with responsibility to many stakeholders, must look at this another way: which is better, the Lean transformation or a slow, steady erosion of competitiveness (possibility resulting in bankruptcy or liquidation)? The Lean transformation should be viewed as an inspiring opportunity, not as an overwhelming obstacle.

12. *Toyota Production System*, T. Ohno, Productivity Press, Portland, OR, 1988, p. 115. Copyright © 1988 by Productivity Inc., http://www.productivityinc.com. Reprinted with permission.

13. If you don't manage your business with the interests of key stakeholders in mind every day, then you will one day likely find that some stakeholders, through various direct and even indirect means, will begin managing your business for you. Think about that. Inevitably, CEO's that ignore key stakeholders will find their business in trouble (e.g. WorldCom, Ford Motor Corporation, Enron, Sunbeam, Warnaco, etc.), only to later admit that they need the support of their key stakeholders (suppliers, employees, customers, investors, and community) in order to recover. It should not have to take a period of severe corporate distress to recognize the importance of key stakeholders and the wide-ranging benefits of the Lean management system.

14. But especially if you *are* the CEO!

Wiremold Management Team

Robert "Bob" Ahlstrom is President of Airey-Thompson Company. He has been President of the subsidiary since 1994. Prior to that he was National Sales Manager of the Wiremold Canada subsidiary and became its President in 1989. Before joining Wiremold, he was National Sales Manager of Prescolite Lighting in Ontario, Canada. Ahlstrom attended the University of Minnesota and Pennsylvania State University.

Scott Bartosch† is Vice President of Sales. He joined Wiremold in 1983 as a sales representative in Washington, D.C. Since then, he has held positions of Regional Sales Manager, Marketing Manager and National Sales Manager. Previously, Bartosch was a partner in Haacke Associates, a manufacturers' representative firm in Washington, D.C. Bartosch holds a B.A. degree from Marquette University. He retired from The Wiremold Company in July 2002.

Donald Beaver† is General Manager of Walker Systems in Williamstown, West Virginia. He has been with Wiremold since 1993. His prior positions at Walker includes Manager of Finance, Manager of Human Resources and Information Systems. He has a B.S. in accounting from Lebanon Valley College and an M.B.A. from University of West Virginia. Beaver left Wiremold in May 2002 to become Vice President of Operations for American Safety Razor Company.

Gary Brooks† is responsible for day-to-day operations at Brooks Electronics, a Wiremold subsidiary since its acquisition in 1988. In 1999, he was given responsibility for day-to-day operations at Interlink Technologies. He co-founded Brooks Electronics in 1974 and was instrumental in selling it to Wiremold. Brooks has an Associate degree in Business Administration from Bucks County Community College. He became the President and CEO of The Wiremold Company in July 2002.

†Denotes managers interviewed.

Arthur "Art" Byrne† is Chairman, President, and Chief Executive Officer. He joined Wiremold in 1991 as President and CEO, and was appointed Chairman of the Board in 1994. Previously, Byrne was group executive of the Danaher Corporation, a diversified public company, where he was responsible for eight operating companies. He also has served with the General Electric Company in general management and planning positions including General Manager of its Nickel Cadmium battery operations and its High Intensity and Quartz Lamp Division. Byrne earned a Bachelor's degree in Economics from Boston College and an M.B.A. from Babson College. He retired from The Wiremold Company in July 2002.

Kevin Fahey† is Vice President of Human Resources, Wire Management Group. Fahey joined Wiremold in March 1999. Prior to that, he was Vice President Human Resources, Corbin Russwin, a division of Williams Holdings, PLC from 1994 to 1999. Earlier, Fahey was Director of Total Quality for Corbin Russwin. He has also held HR positions at American Can Company, Terry Steam Turbine, and Milford Corrugated Container. Fahey holds a B.A. degree in Economics from the University of Connecticut.

Thomas Fairbank† is General Manager of the West Hartford plant. He has been with Wiremold since 1989. He has worked in sales and also has experience as a draftsman/designer, tool and die maker, and manufacturing engineer. He has a BS in Manufacturing Engineering Technology and an M.S. in Operations Management from Central Connecticut State University.

Orest "Orry" Fiume† is Vice President of Finance and Administration and a Director. He joined Wiremold in 1978 and is responsible for the Company's controller and treasury functions. Previously, Fiume was an Audit Manager with Coopers & Lybrand in their New York and Hartford offices. Earlier, he was a U.S. Navy Officer. Fiume holds a B.B.A. from Fairfield University in Accounting, with minors in Economics and Philosophy, and an M.S. in Management from Rensselaer Polytechnic Institute. He also is a Certified Public Accountant. Fiume retired from The Wiremold Company in July 2002.

Frank Giannattasio† is Vice President of Operations, Wire Management Group. He is responsible for manufacturing, materials management, and manufacturing engineering. He has been with Wiremold since 1992. Previously, he worked with General Motors Corporation and Subaru-Isuzu Automotive in the areas of metal forming and painting. Giannattasio holds a B.S. in Mechanical Engineering and an M.S. in Mechanical Engineering from the General Motors Institute of Technology.

Thomas Goetter† is Vice President of Engineering. He leads the engineering team and the product development efforts at Wiremold. He has been with the company since 1993. Previously, Goetter was Vice President of Project Sales and Engineering Services at Walker Systems Inc., a Wiremold subsidiary. Goetter earned a B.S. in Structural Engineering from the University of Wisconsin and an M.B.A. from the University of West Virginia. Goetter is registered in three states as a Professional Engineer.

Andrew Gress is President of Wiremold, Canada. Gress joined Wiremold in 1992. Previously, he was Plant Manager. Prior to joining Wiremold, Gress was Area Manager with A.G. Simpson and Production Manager with Armstrong World Industries. He earned a B.S. degree in Industrial Engineering from the University of Toronto.

Richard "Rich" Levesque† is Vice President of Marketing and Engineering at Walker Systems. Previously, he was Product Marketing Manager and has worked as the facilities manager for the West Hartford plant, designer of electrical products, and manufacturing engineering for Wiremold. He has been with Wiremold since 1980. Levesque has a B.S. degree in Electronics Technology from Central Connecticut State University. He became the General Manager of Walker Systems in May 2002.

Steven Maynard† is Vice President of Information Technology and Chief Information Officer. He was promoted to this position in 1996 after seven years as Vice President of Engineering for Wiremold, which he joined 1989. Prior to Wiremold, he was involved in concrete pipe fabrication, solar heating and alternate technologies, aerospace, advanced composites, communications, plastic fabrication and metal fabrication industries. Maynard holds a B.S. in Engineering from Worcester Polytechnic Institute and an M.B.A. from Rensselaer Polytechnic Institute.

Edward Miller† is Vice President of Marketing. He joined Wiremold in 1993 as Vice President of Marketing. He is involved in the strategy and business development and market positioning of the company's various business segments integrating go-to-market and product development plans. Previously, Miller served as Vice President of Engineering at GS Edwards Co., a unit of General Signal, Manager of Product Marketing at GE Electrical Distribution & Control, and Manager of all Engineering functions for GE Wiring Devices. Miller holds a B.S. in Electrical Engineering from City College of New York and an M.S. in Electrical Engineering from Union College. He assumed the dual role of Vice President of Sales and Marketing in July 2002.

Richard "Dick" Ryan joined Wiremold in 1986 as Vice President of Marketing and Sales for the Electrical Group. In 1992, he was appointed President of Shape Electronics, a Wiremold subsidiary. Earlier he served in executive positions at GEC-Automation Projects Inc. and Klockner-Moeller. Ryan earned a B.S. in Mechanical Engineering from Marquette University and an M.B.A. from Loyola University.

Judy Seyler† is former Vice President of Human Resources. She started at Wiremold in 1989 as Manager of Human Resources and was promoted to Vice President in 1990. She has a B.A. in Economics from Cornell University and an M.A. in Business and Public Administration from George Washington University. She was elected to "Who's Who in American Women" in 1970-71. Her work in Human Resources included the Executive Office of the Secretary of the Navy, Bank Street College of New York City, various banks, and the Caterpillar Corporation. Seyler retired from The Wiremold Company in January 1999.

Recommended Reading

The titles listed below encompass the premier books on Lean business management. Some of these books do not explicitly or consistently portray the importance of people in Lean organizations, or how the design of this management system enables successful interactions between key stakeholders. Therefore, readers are advised to carefully discern the extremely important interplay between "Continuous Improvement" and "Respect for People."

In-Print

Productivity Press titles can be obtained from Productivity, Inc. (www.productivityinc.com). Titles published by the Lean Enterprise Institute, Inc. can be obtained from www.lean.org. All titles can be obtained from Amazon (www.amazon.com) or Barnes & Noble (www.bn.com).

- S. Ansari, J. Bell, T. Klammer, and C. Lawrence, *Management Accounting in the Age of Lean Production*, Irwin/McGraw Hill, Chicago, Il, 1999
- S. Basu, *Corporate Purpose: Why It Matters More than Strategy*, Garland Publishing, Inc. New York, NY, 1999
- R. Cooper and R. Slagmulder, *Supply Chain Development for the Lean Enterprise*, Productivity Press, Portland, OR, 1999
- H. Ford, *Today and Tomorrow: An Autobiography*, Special Reprint Edition, Productivity Press, Portland, OR, 1988
- T. Fujimoto, *The Evolution of a Manufacturing System at Toyota*, Oxford University Press, New York, NY, 1999
- W. Fruin and T. Nishiguchi, "Supplying the Toyota Production System: Intercorporate Organizational Evolution and Supplier Subsystems," in *Country Competitiveness*, B. Kogut, Ed., Oxford University Press, New York, NY, 1993, pp. 225–246
- M. Imai, *Kaizen: The Key to Japan's Competitive Success*, McGraw-Hill, New York, NY, 1986
- M. Imai, *Gemba Kaizen*, McGraw-Hill, New York, NY, 1997
- H. Johnson and A. Bröms, *Profit Beyond Measure*, The Free Press, New York, NY, 2000
- D. Jones and J. Womack, *Seeing the Whole*, Lean Enterprise Institute, Brookline, MA, 2002
- O. Katayama, *Japanese Business into the 21st Century: Strategies for Success*, The Athlone Press, Atlantic Heights, NJ, 1996
- A. Kawahara, *The Origin of Competitive Strength*, Springer Verlag, New York, NY, 1998
- Y. Kondo, Ed., *Human Motivation*, 3A Corporation, Tokyo, Japan, 1991
- J. Liker, Ed., *Becoming Lean*, Productivity Press, Portland, OR, 1998
- D. Lu, *Kanban: Just-In-Time at Toyota*, Productivity Press, Portland, OR, 1985

- B. Maskell, *Performance Measurement for World Class Manufacturing: A Model for American Companies*, Productivity Press, Portland, OR, 1991
- B. Maskell, *Making the Numbers Count*, Productivity Press, Portland, OR, 1996
- S. Mito, *The Honda Book of Management*, The Athlone Press, Atlantic Heights, NJ, 1990
- Y. Monden, *Toyota Management System*, Productivity Press, Portland, OR, 1993
- Y. Monden, *Toyota Production System*, Engineering and Management Press, Norcross, GA, 1998
- Y. Monden, *Cost Reduction Systems: Target Costing & Kaizen Costing*, Productivity Press, Portland, OR, 1995
- T. Nishiguchi, *Strategic Industrial Sourcing*, Oxford University Press, New York, NY, 1994
- T. Ohno, *The Toyota Production System*, Productivity Press, Portland, OR, 1988
- A. Robinson, *Modern Approaches to Manufacturing Improvement*, Productivity Press, Portland, OR, 1990
- M. Rother and J. Shook, *Learning to See*, Lean Enterprise Institute, Brookline, MA, 1999
- M. Rother and R. Harris, *Creating Continuous Flow*, Lean Enterprise Institute, Brookline, MA, 2001
- R. Schonberger, *Japanese Manufacturing Techniques: Nine Hidden Lessons in Simplicity*, The Free Press, New York, NY, 1983
- R. Schonberger, *World Class Manufacturing: The Lessons of Simplicity Applied*, The Free Press, New York, NY, 1986
- S. Shingo, *A Revolution in Manufacturing: The SMED System*, Productivity Press, Portland, OR, 1985
- S. Shingo, *A Study of the Toyota Production System*, Productivity Press, Portland, OR, 1989
- J. Womack, D. Jones, and D. Roos, *The Machine that Changed the World*, Harper-Collins, New York, NY, 1990
- J. Womack and D. Jones, *Lean Thinking*, Simon & Schuster, New York, NY, 1996

Out-of-Print

You may be able to find these books at your local public or university library. To purchase a copy, try online used booksellers Alibris (www.alibris.com) or Barnes & Noble (www.bn.com).

- M. Cusumano, *The Japanese Automobile Industry: Technology and Management at Nissan and Toyota*, The Council on East Asian Studies, The Harvard University Press, Cambridge, MA, 1985
- C. Dyer, *The Canon Production System*, Productivity Press, Cambridge, MA, 1987
- H. Ford, *My Life and Work*, with S. Crowther, Garden City Publishing Co., Inc., Garden City, NY, 1922

- Y. Hatakeyama, *Manager Revolution!*, Productivity Press, Cambridge, MA, 1985
- S. Kamiya, *My Life with Toyota*, Toyota Motor Sales Co., Ltd., Nagoya (Toyota City), Japan, 1976
- S. Kato, *My Years with Toyota*, Toyota Motor Sales Co., Ltd., Nagoya (Toyota City), Japan, 1981
- S. Kimoto, *Quest for the Dawn*, The Dougherty Co., Milwaukee, WI, 1991
- T. Mikami, *Management and Productivity Improvement*, Japan Management Associates Consultants Inc., Tokyo, Japan, 1982
- Y. Monden, R. Shibakawa, S. Takayanagi, and T. Nagao, *Innovations in Management: The Japanese Corporation*, Industrial Engineering and Management Press, Norcross, GA, 1985
- M. Nemoto, *Total Quality Control for Management*, translated by D. Lu, Prentice Hall, Inc. Englewood Cliffs, NJ, 1987
- T. Ohno, *Workplace Management*, Productivity Press, Portland, OR, 1988
- T. Ohno and S. Mito, *Just-In-Time for Today and Tomorrow*, Productivity Press, Portland, OR, 1988
- I. Shinohara, *NPS: New Production System, JIT Crossing Industry Boundaries*, Productivity Press, Cambridge, MA, 1988
- C. Sorenson, *My Forty Years With Ford*, with S. Williamson, W.W. Norton Company, Inc., New York, NY, 1956
- Y. Togo and W. Wartman, *Against All Odds*, St. Martin's Press, New York, NY, 1993
- E. Toyoda, *Toyota: Fifty Years in Motion*, Kodansha International, New York, NY, 1987
- Toyota Motor Corporation, *Toyota: A History of the First 50 Years*, Toyota Motor Corporation, Toyota City, Japan, 1988
- Y. Yasuda, *40 Years, 20 Million Ideas*, Productivity Press, Cambridge, MA, 1991

Important Related Books

- M. Kelly, *The Divine Right of Capital*, Berrett-Koehler Publishers Inc., San Francisco, CA, 2001
- L. Mitchell, *Corporate Irresponsibility: America's Newest Export*, Yale University Press, New Haven, CT, 2001

Index

About the Authors

M.L. "Bob" Emiliani

Bob Emiliani is President of The Center for Lean Business Management, LLC and Clinical Professor[1] in the Lally School of Management and Technology at Rensselaer Polytechnic Institute (Hartford, CT department). His teaching responsibilities include graduate courses in leadership and supply chain management. He has 15 years of business experience in engineering, manufacturing, and supply chain management in the aerospace and consumer products industries. Bob was educated in gemba-kaizen by sensei from the world-famous Shingijutsu Company, Ltd., and has had responsibility for implementing Lean management practices in both the manufacturing shop and in supply networks at a Fortune 60 company.

Bob is the leading authority on leadership for Lean businesses. He has authored or co-authored over 45 management and technical publications. Bob has written several ground-breaking papers including "Lean Behaviors," "Continuous Personal Improvement," and "Cracking the Code of Business," that show how Lean principles and practices can be applied to develop leadership and organizational behaviors. He identified and defined the Eighth Waste[SM] — Behavioral Waste[®] — and developed a breakthrough model that aligns and fully integrates leadership and operating practices, called Lean Behaviors[®]. His papers "Lean Behaviors," "Cracking the Code of Business," and "Redefining the Focus of Investment Analysts" have received Citation of Excellence awards from Emerald Publishing. His work has been cited in national and international publications including: *Sloan Management Review, Automotive News, Purchasing Magazine, Industry Week, Entrepreneur Magazine, The Hartford Courant, Darwin Magazine, Line56 Magazine, Pharmaceutical Technology, The Japan Times,* and *Manufacturing News.*

Bob received a B.S. in Mechanical Engineering from the University of Miami, an M.S. in Chemical Engineering from the University of Rhode Island, and a Ph.D. in Engineering from Brown University. He is a member of the American Society of Mechanical Engineers and the Academy of Management, and is a member of the editorial board of *Management Decision, Supply Chain Management,* and *Industrial Marketing Management.*

David J. Stec

David Stec is Vice President of The Center for Lean Business Management, LLC. David's professional career includes over 12 years experience in the aerospace industry. He has worked for Boeing, Wyman-Gordon Company, and Pratt & Whitney. David has experience in design and manufacturing, and has held management positions in operations and supply management. David was trained in Lean business practices in the early 1990's by Pratt & Whitney's Office of Continuous Improvement and the sensei from Shingijutsu Company, Ltd. Lean implementation projects included work cell design and scheduling, performance measurement, and supply management.

David is an expert facilitator of shop and office kaizen and executive education workshops. He is also the co-author of several papers that show how online reverse auctions are inconsistent with the Lean management system. David is also an Adjunct Assistant Professor in the Lally School of Management and Technology at Rensselaer Polytechnic Institute (Hartford, CT department), where he teaches graduate courses in business statistics and supply chain management.

David received his B.S. in Mechanical Engineering from Worcester Polytechnic Institute, an M.S. in Management from Rensselaer Polytechnic Institute, and graduated from the Leaders for Manufacturing program at the Massachusetts Institute of Technology with a M.B.A. from the Sloan School of Management and a M.S. in Mechanical Engineering (production system design).

Lawrence Grasso

Larry Grasso is a Clinical Associate Professor in the Lally School of Management and Technology at Rensselaer Polytechnic Institute (Hartford, CT department). Prior to beginning his academic career, Larry worked in public accounting for seven years, holding a CPA certificate in the State of Connecticut. He was a member of the faculty at the School of Accounting and Information Management at Arizona State University before joining the faculty at Rensselaer in January 2000.

Larry teaches a manufacturing accounting and control systems course that focuses on modern accounting methods and measures, and their roles in supporting integrated Lean business strategies. The course also highlights the limitations of traditional accounting controls and the ways traditional controls may act as an obstacle to progress in a Lean business environment. Larry also regularly teaches the introductory graduate courses in financial and managerial accounting and has taught other courses in accounting and financial management. Larry's research interests are in the areas of performance measurement, performance evaluation, and incentives. He is particularly interested in the development and use of financial and non-financial measures to support Lean business practices.

Larry received a B.S. in Accounting from Utica College of Syracuse University, an M.B.A. in Management from the Rensselaer Polytechnic Institute, and a D.B.A. in Accounting from Boston University. He is a member of the American Accounting Association and the Institute of Management Accountants.

James Stodder

Jim Stodder is a Clinical Assistant Professor in the Lally School of Management and Technology at Rensselaer Polytechnic Institute (Hartford, CT department), where he teaches graduate courses in business economics and international economics. Jim spent nine years as a seaman, oil-field worker, and marine mechanic before getting his B.A. in Economics from Harvard University. He went on to earn a Master's degree from the University of Essex (UK), and a Ph.D. from Yale University, both in Economics.

Economic systems often hide their most costly forms of waste — they do not come with price tags. Jim teaches how economic analysis can help detect these unexamined constraints and spillovers. Systemic change occurs when those forces must be accommodated. A basic message is that technology requires changes that are both "hard" (i.e. redefining property rights) and "soft" (i.e. changing business culture). Jim's published work is on post-communist transitions, development and corruption, money-less electronic exchange, and the economics of education.

Notes

1. The term "Clinical" denotes professors with significant industrial management experience and whose approach to teaching and research are oriented towards practice rather than theory.

Printed in the United States
21048LVS00004BC/1-45

9 780972 259101